TAKING BACK
THE WORKERS' LAW

IN Solidarity
Ellen Dannin

Taking Back the **Workers' Law**

HOW TO FIGHT THE ASSAULT ON LABOR RIGHTS

ELLEN DANNIN

ILR PRESS an imprint of
CORNELL UNIVERSITY PRESS
ITHACA AND LONDON

First published 2006 by Cornell University Press
First printing, Cornell Paperbacks, 2007

Printed in the United States of America

Library of Congress Cataloging-in-Publication Data

Dannin, Ellen J.
    Taking back the workers' law : how to fight the assault on labor rights / Ellen Dannin.
        p. cm.
    Includes bibliographical references and index.
    ISBN 978-0-8014-4438-8 (cloth : alk. paper)
    ISBN 978-0-8014-7446-0 (pbk. : alk. paper)
    1. Labor laws and legislation—United States.   2. Employee rights —United States.   3. United States. National Labor Relations Act. 4. Industrial relations—United States.   I. Title.
KF3369.D36   2006
344.7301—dc22   2005027433

Cornell University Press strives to use environmentally responsible suppliers and materials to the fullest extent possible in the publishing of its books. Such materials include vegetable-based, low-VOC inks and acid-free papers that are recycled, totally chlorine-free, or partly composed of nonwood fibers. For further information, visit our website at www.cornellpress.cornell.edu.

Cloth printing   10 9 8 7 6 5 4 3 2 1
Paperback printing   10 9 8 7 6 5 4 3 2 1

CONTENTS

Foreword by David E. Bonior — vii

Acknowledgments — xi

Introduction: Reviving the Labor Movement — 1

1 Why Judges Rewrite Labor Law — 16

2 Developing a Strategy to Take Back the NLRA — 36

3 NLRA Values, American Values — 51

4 Litigating the NLRA Values—What Are the Challenges? — 79

5 Litigation Themes — 99

6 NLRA Rights within Other Laws — 117

7 Trying Cases—The Rules — 128

8 Using the NLRB as a Resource — 144

9 An Invitation — 164

Notes — 169

General Index — 191

Index of Cases Discussed — 195

FOREWORD

David E. Bonior

This book addresses two concerns that have been at the heart of my work in public service for the past thirty years: the importance of citizenship and the meaningfulness of work. In many ways, citizenship and work are inextricable. When I conversed with new immigrants in the congressional district that I represented for nearly twenty-six years, I was consistently reminded of how much they wanted to be valued as contributing members of American society and saw their jobs as the primary medium for adding value to their new communities and homeland.

But when workers are prevented from exercising their democratic rights, it becomes nearly impossible to establish dignity in other critical spheres of their lives. As Ellen Dannin states, "The National Labor Relations Act says that the private workplace is not truly private because what happens at work does not remain there. It spills out into society, and society as a whole pays the price for inequality."

Verna Bader, for example, a 72-year-old grandmother and machinist from Taylor, Michigan, tried to form a union to address $5-per-hour pay and unsafe working conditions that included maneuvering around exposed live wires. In 1992, she and five other machinists in her department were fired after they stood up for themselves and voted to form a union at Taylor Machine Products.

When she fought the company for illegally firing her, the National Labor Relations Board ordered the company to pay her lost earnings. Adding insult to injury, however, the Board allowed this issue to drag out for over a decade. The Agency failed to fully implement the values that underlie the law and to recognize the importance of a timely payment, ensuring that the spirit of the Act and its underlying values were upheld. This book demonstrates that this is a common occurrence. More than twelve years after the order was issued, Verna Bader finally received the restitution she deserved. Her victory was bittersweet. In the end, she "won," but the wait almost destroyed her faith in American justice, and understandably so. As Dannin argues, "Our work lives become incorporated into our intimate physical and mental selves. Over time, the undemocratic workplace grinds away at the belief that we have a right to participate in the decisions that affect our lives and societies."

Today's labor law, signed by President Franklin D. Roosevelt seventy years ago, embodied the profound aspiration of providing "industrial democracy" to American workers such as Bader. The centerpiece of workplace democracy was and remains the ability of workers to form unions and collectively bargain with their employers.

The Wagner Act, known more prevalently today as the National Labor Relations Act, created the National Labor Relations Board to administer and enforce the law. The NLRB is charged with upholding the law's underlying values of democracy, fairness, and justice. These underlying values have the power to transform our workplaces, empowering workers with the necessary skills to be active citizens in democracy. By shining light on these tenets of the Act, Ellen Dannin's book examines how the potential value of the NLRA transcends the workplace by serving, more broadly, as a barometer of the health of our democracy.

Until we recognize the interplay between citizenship and work, we will compromise American democracy and undermine its advancement. It is well documented that union membership enhances people's ability to be better citizens of a democracy. As Dannin notes, we know that union members vote, volunteer, and participate in politics and civic life in percentages far higher than those for unorganized workers. And, as Dannin asks with prescience, "If workers are told that their participation, involvement, intelligence are not wanted, will they try to increase their participation, involvement, or intelligence? Can a democracy exist when this is its raw material?"

In his *Washington Post* column on September 9, 2004, David Broder drove home the reason why protecting workers' rights to form unions is so important. In it, he makes the link between "the decline of progressive politics, the near decline of liberal legislation, and the steady weakening of organized labor." He goes on to say that "when labor lobbied powerfully on Capitol Hill, it did not confine itself to bread-and-butter issues for its own members. It was at the forefront of battles for aid to education, civil rights, housing programs, and a host of other social causes important to the whole community. And because it was muscular, it was heard and heeded."

This is a critical time for American workers and the future of their unions. Tremendous resistance by employers, with help from the flourishing anti-union consultant industry, has inhibited workers' ability to form unions without fear of reprisal. A *New York Times* article exposed an anti-union campaign at a single factory in South Carolina where the employer allegedly paid $2.3 million to the law firm that ran the campaign. The use of illegal campaign tactics is now so widespread that every twenty-three minutes, a worker is fired or discriminated against for attempting to exercise his or her freedom of association.

As if this were not enough of a challenge to workers, trends in the economy have shifted employment away from the heavily union manufacturing sector to the largely nonunion service sector, contributing to declining union representation. As of 2004, only 12.5 percent of the American workforce belonged to a union. And in the private sector, which the Act covers, only 8 percent of employees were union members.

Given the challenges to workers' efforts to form and sustain unions, we would expect that the National Labor Relations Board would act to protect the freedom of association now more than ever. But under the presidency of George W. Bush, the Board has issued decisions that narrow the protections of the law and fail to make the Act more relevant for today's workers. The Board has limited protections for disabled workers, graduate teaching and research assistants, and temporary employees. Its decisions have weakened the rights of nonunion workers to join together for mutual aid and protection on the job. The Board has also taken steps that could undermine the ability of employers and unions to reach private agreements on the recognition process that could further industrial peace.

In the midst of this crisis in workplace democracy, Dannin advances a controversial argument: take back the Workers' Law. She calls on workers' rights advocates to reclaim the very words and enunciated values that form the basis of the Act and to insist that courts of law base decisions on the actual tenets of the Act. The controversy lies not in the crisis itself but in the solution Dannin offers to advance the rights of workers. Years of frustration on the part of those who have witnessed the transformation of the law from one that addresses the imbalance of power between employees and employers to one that exacerbates it has led to calls to scrap the Wagner Act altogether. Some suggest creating stronger labor laws at the state level.

Having firmly established the significance of workers' rights in American democracy, Dannin turns her attention to proposing concrete actions. She calls for workers' rights advocates to pressure the judiciary to make rulings consistent with the values laid out in the Act, such as the importance of modeling democratic citizenship at the workplace and allowing freedom of association to flourish regardless of whether it occurs in a community hall or at a workplace.

Some may agree with Dannin and follow her into the legal battle she proposes, and others will not. But none can doubt her resolve to address one of the most pressing issues of our time: the social inequity that results from the violation of workers' human rights. I welcome her ideas and the spirit with which she offers them to us. We need more scholars and practitioners to follow her lead and use their energy and skills to find solutions.

ACKNOWLEDGMENTS

The ideas that became this book were in my head for many years before the first word was written. For years I tried to put together a group of labor academics and practitioners to brainstorm ways to take back the Workers' Law. The expertise needed for a project of this breadth seemed too daunting to take on by myself. Fortunately Fran Benson of Cornell University Press told me I should—and could—write it myself. I decided that she had a point. If the work was ever going to get started, I would have to do it. I owe Fran an enormous debt. She balanced encouragement and demands to help me get out a book I could not have written otherwise.

In fact, I did not take on this project alone, nor did I write this book by myself. Many people read all or part of the manuscript. They gave me valuable comments and criticisms. All of them encouraged me to continue. There is no greater gift to a writer than this kind of support. So let me thank Robert Baillie, David Bonior, Fred Feinstein, George Gonos, Immanuel Ness, and Michael Yates for their comments and criticisms.

After Christopher David Ruiz Cameron read the first few chapters, he supported me in this project by making the book the centerpiece for the Labor and Employment Section panel at the Association of American Law Schools conference in January 2005. He and Martin Malin also arranged to have that session taped for publication in the *Employee Rights and Employment Policy Journal*.

I owe a very special debt to David Williams. He was a stranger to me when I asked if he would read my manuscript. To be useful to a wide audience, the book needed to include not only my perspective as a lawyer but also insights from a labor perspective. David supplied that. He was unfailingly helpful and as excited by the project as I was. He not only read every chapter, but he did so in record time, despite his own taxing schedule. David was what every writer needs. He understood what I was trying to do and made criticisms and suggestions that challenged me and helped me improve the book.

Finally, let me thank those in my personal life for their support and for suffering the neglect that is part of the price paid for work such as this. Bob, Emma, Sadie, and Sebastian, I promise there will now be more time for walks in the woods and to listen to your needs. "Two are better than one, because they have a good reward for their efforts. And if one falls, his friend will help him rise up" (Ecclesiastes 4:9–10, author's translation).

INTRODUCTION

Reviving the Labor Movement

A few months after graduating from law school, I decided to stop at Detroit's Eastern Market on the way to my new job. As I entered an intersection, I saw the largest Chevrolet Detroit ever made speeding toward me and my new compact car. Before I was hit, I had only enough time to think, "There's no getting out of this one."

When I regained consciousness, my new car was a crumpled mess. I was too. I had a concussion and bruises. But with paid sick leave, health insurance, and car insurance, my body was soon as good as new and my car was replaced. Life is better when you have enough money to live on.

Since then, I have gone on to live a middle-class life. My middle-class child has never suffered from want. Needing a new tire does not mean choosing between eating or getting to work. I do not live one paycheck away from homelessness. I can be confident that my child will have the education, parental guidance, self-confidence, and connections that will enable her to pass on her middle-class status.

But it was not always that way for me. That shopping trip to the Eastern Market was the first time I had money. I grew up in poverty that is hard for many to imagine. I was raised by a single parent after my father deserted us. We would have starved had my grandfather not given us food from his small farm, provided us with rabbits and squirrels he shot, and slipped money to my mother. We children worked on that farm and were paid in food, grew our own food, and foraged in the woods for berries, asparagus, and mushrooms. I never had new clothes, didn't see a dentist for checkups till I was in college, and remember only one visit to the doctor, to put in stitches after an accident at school. He took me as a charity case.

Today, many in this country live in this sort of poverty and worse. In the richest country on earth, many of us live on the edge, always having to tell the kids there is not enough money, never able to make ends meet, housed in ugly and dangerous buildings and neighborhoods, and with hope for the future beaten out of us.

The gap between rich and poor yawns wide in this country and continues to grow, because far too many are not paid enough to live above desperation. Why is this?

Apologists for this state of affairs claim the market pays people exactly what they are worth. They claim that the poor have only themselves to blame, and the rich deserve every penny they get.[1] I have to wonder about people who make these claims from the comfort of a class status inherited from their parents. Are they blind to the structures that support them but weigh down those at the bottom? Don't they see that hard work often goes unrewarded? Do they even try to imagine what it means to be paid too little to live in dignity? If they know, why do they accept this?

I contend that these conditions lie more in who has power and who does not. Money flows to power, and power flows to those with money. Over time, this cycle magnifies differences in wealth and power. Most people in this country—and in the world—have neither wealth nor power.

But it does not have to be this way. In this country—and in this world—the poor get power when they are organized. For workers, the best form of organization has always been unions. This is the only way workers can get a more equal division of power and money. The same workers doing the same work make from $4,000 to $10,000 more a year when they have a union.[2] They can be fired only for cause instead of at an employer's whim. They know they have an advocate to stand beside them when there are workplace problems. That's what power and organization can do.

But we are on the verge of losing this power and organization and, as a result, these benefits. As power and organization are lost, wages and working conditions spiral down. There has long been a wholesale attack on the key institutions that create, protect, and buttress power for those who would otherwise be powerless.

This book focuses on unions and on the National Labor Relations Board

(NLRB) and National Labor Relations Act (NLRA)—the agency and the law created to promote unionization and collective bargaining. This is not a story of mourning. Rather, this book advocates borrowing from and building on the methods the civil rights movement, and in particular, the NAACP Legal Defense Fund, used to recapture union power. They teach us that a litigation and activist strategy can overturn unjust judicial decisions, even those by the Supreme Court. More recently, the National Right to Work Legal Defense Foundation is proving that a targeted litigation strategy can still be used to "amend" the law. Of course, the NRTW-LDF has powerful friends who have funded and supported it, and it has faced fewer barriers than did the NAACP.

Both these groups provide models that can be used to target judicial decisions that created striker replacement, restricted the right to strike, undermined the right to bargain, denied the NLRA rights of worker freedom of association and speech, and weakened remedies. These and other decisions have perverted the plain language and express intent of the NLRA.

The NAACP experience provides inspiration and helpful guidance. In the 1940s, institutional and legal apartheid were the law of the land. An apartheid state was protected by state statutes and Supreme Court decisions. Brave and visionary individuals put together a multidecade strategy of both activism and targeted litigation to remake the racial landscape of this country.[3] While they have not yet achieved full success, the story is more one of success than of failure. And given the forces of law and power arrayed against them, it is a story of the power of the weak.

The problems unions face today are serious, but unions are not as powerless or as friendless as were those civil rights activists. Union power is rooted in the representation of a huge absolute number of American workers who are already organized. The basic law of the land is not anti-unionism. The law of the land on unions says:

> The inequality of bargaining power between employees who do not possess full freedom of association or actual liberty of contract, and employers who are organized in the corporate or other forms of ownership association substantially burdens and affects the flow of commerce, and tends to aggravate recurrent business depressions, by depressing wage rates and the purchasing power of wage earners in industry and by preventing the stabilization of competitive wage rates and working conditions within and between industries.

Experience has proved that protection by law of the right of employees to organize and bargain collectively safeguards commerce from injury, impairment, or interruption, and promotes the flow of commerce by removing certain recognized sources of industrial strife and unrest, by encouraging practices fundamental to the friendly adjustment of industrial disputes arising out of differences as to wages, hours, or other working conditions, and by restoring equality of bargaining power between employers and employees. . . .

It is hereby declared to be the policy of the United States to eliminate the causes of certain substantial obstructions to the free flow of commerce and to mitigate and eliminate these obstructions when they have occurred *by encouraging the practice and procedure of collective bargaining and by protecting the exercise by workers of full freedom of association, self-organization, and designation of representatives of their own choosing, for the purpose of negotiating the terms and conditions of their employment or other mutual aid or protection.*[4]

This declaration of worker rights is from Section 1 of the National Labor Relations Act. This is the Workers' Law. The NLRA's insights about work, conflict, justice, and the role of law are as valid today as they were when it was enacted in 1935. Moreover, if unionists were drafting a statute today, surely they would also include language about promoting freedom of association, self-organization, free choice of representatives, equality of bargaining power, improved wages and working conditions, and collective bargaining.

Why, then, do so many union leaders speak so negatively about the NLRA and NLRB? Union representative Wade Rathke accuses the NLRB of being "complicit with employers."[5] Larry Cohen, CWA president, advocates a national day of civil disobedience to shut down every NLRB office across the country. He says, "Labor needs to show the public that the NLRB is broken."[6] The AFL-CIO's Web site is full of condemnations of the NLRA and NLRB as worthless.

This anger is nothing new. Former AFL-CIO president Lane Kirkland repeatedly said he would prefer "no law" to current labor law and that

he prefers "the law of the jungle" over the current system because the law places too many restrictions on what unions can do to assist each other. "The law forces us, our unions, to work on products that are manufactured by law-breaking employers, employers that are in violation of the law in fact and in spirit . . . [It] forbids us to show solidarity and direct union support," he declared.[7]

Richard Trumka, while president of the United Mine Workers of America, described the NLRB as "clinically dead."[8] He told Congress:

> I say abolish the Act. Abolish the affirmative protections of labor that it promises but does not deliver as well as the secondary boycott provisions that hamstring labor at every turn. Deregulate. Labor lawyers will then go to juries and not to the gulag of section 7 rights—the Reagan NLRB. Unions will no longer foster the false expectations attendant to the use of the Board processes and will be compelled to make more fundamental appeals to workers. These appeals will inevitably have social and political dimensions beyond the workplace. That is the price we pay, as a society, for perverting the dream of the progressives and abandoning the rule of law in labor relations.
>
> I have a profound faith in the judiciary and jury system as it exists at common law. It has been the enduring bulwark against biased decision making by "experts."[9]

So if the NLRA still has strong, clear, inspiring language advocating core labor rights, including the rights to organize and bargain collectively, why is it today so detested by organized labor? The simple answer is that the way the NLRA has been interpreted and applied by judges has perverted the express language of the law.[10] Union critics are right to point to problems such as striker replacement, and remedies so weak as to be useless.[11] But they are wrong when they blame the NLRA and the NLRB for these problems.

The NLRA does not say strikers may be replaced. Section 8(a)(3) says that an employer who retaliates against employees for their union activities violates the NLRA. Section 13 says that the right to strike is not to be interfered with or impeded or diminished in any way. Despite this clear language, the Supreme Court invented the employer's ability to replace strikers out of whole cloth. This judicial amendment must and can be overturned.

Section 10(c) says that remedies must make the NLRA's purposes effective. Unfortunately, judges' interpretations have created a menu of remedies that fail to make the NLRA more effective. They do not promote NLRA policies, such as freedom of association, equality of bargaining power, employee mutual aid and protection, and collective bargaining. Therefore, these remedies violate the NLRA's clear language. Taken together, judicial "interpretations" have "amended" the law to put a heavy thumb on the employer's side of the scale.

It does not have to be this way. But as long as unionists attack the NLRA, as long as they go after the wrong target, they re letting the real perpetrators off the hook and they are complicit in their own demise. It is possible, instead, to go after the real problem and the real perpetrators and put an end to unions' slide. The campaign must enlist allies and develop multiple strategies. There is no single solution. Each strategy is important if workers are to take back their law.

Law must be one part of the campaign. Labor law has enormous potential when practiced by the creative and the courageous. It can be used to rock the boat, to push the envelope, and to push steadily forward.

This book maps out a strategy to take back the Workers' Law and the agency Congress created for unions and workers.

A Strategy for Taking Back the Workers' Law

The litigation strategy to take back the Workers' Law is not based on a trivial, esoteric quibble about how judges have interpreted the NLRA. These decisions are lawless actions by judges who have not interpreted the law but have rewritten it. They have created a law that is diametrically opposed to the language of the NLRA and to Congress's clear intent and purpose.[12] How and why this happened is the subject of the early chapters of this book. The later chapters lay out a detailed strategy to reverse these decisions and restore the original values and ideas of the NLRA.

To develop a successful strategy it is necessary, first, to analyze what makes judges rewrite the NLRA. This information is then used to develop ways to repeal the judicial amendments and to enforce the Workers' Law. Both trial and activist strategies must be rooted in the NLRA's policies. The law Congress enacted was supposed to radically remake the workplace and society. It was not some timid law with hidebound procedures and trivial rights. Sadly, most of us do not read the NLRA and are not aware of what it was enacted to do. We have come to believe that the law as amended by judges is in the NLRA. To repeal those judicial amendments, we need to know what the NLRA says. In this book, the core chapters lay out ways to use the NLRA's policies as the foundation on which to build a litigation strategy.

The book also looks for legal allies that can help restore the Workers'

Law. Some of these allies are our founding documents, the Declaration of Independence and the United States Constitution. The NLRA also has allies in international law. It cannot be said too strongly that the judicial amendments do not meet human rights standards.[13] All these documents create a law consistent with the NLRA as enacted by Congress.

The Attack on Unions

Just how badly have the courts distorted the law and set the United States at odds with international law and the NLRA? As an example, here is how collective bargaining is supposed to work under the NLRA. The employer and union are to meet as equals in terms of bargaining power, to codetermine the conditions of work. They are to negotiate, using their full powers of persuasion, including the right to strike. The right to strike is fully protected by Section 13, and it is illegal to interfere with that right, impede its exercise, or diminish it. Employers who fail to bargain in good faith violate the NLRA. They cannot fire or retaliate against workers who support unions, who join with other workers to improve each other's working conditions, or who strike in order to improve their own or other employees' working conditions.

When an employer does any of these things, Section 10(c) imposes whatever remedies are necessary to promote the NLRA's policies. These policies include "encouraging the practice and procedure of collective bargaining" and "protecting the exercise by workers of full freedom of association, self-organization, and designation of representatives of their own choosing, for the purpose of negotiating the terms and conditions of their employment or other mutual aid or protection." If an employer illegally discharges a worker, the backpay awarded must be substantial enough to ensure that workers feel free to associate with one another and to support their union and to encourage the employer to abide by the law.

But here's how "collective bargaining" works under the judicial amendments. If a union and employer reach an impasse in bargaining, the employer may implement any part of the terms it calls its final offer. Nothing requires, or even encourages, the employer to try to reach middle ground and an agreement. If the union strikes, the employer may hire new workers to permanently take the jobs of the strikers. Even though the strikers may never get their jobs back, this is not to be treated as firing strikers because of their union activities. If the employer bargains in bad faith, it is simply ordered to bargain in good faith and to post a notice telling employees it will bargain in good faith. If the union doesn't strike, the employer can lock out the workers and hire "temporary" replacements. The average lockout now lasts more than three years, so those temporary replacements will fill those jobs for years.[14]

In short, the courts rewrote the NLRA to permit employers to exit collective bargaining and dictate the terms of work. An employer can retaliate against workers by taking away their jobs through a lockout or through permanent replacement if they strike. Moreover, the courts say that Section 10(c) may give only the most limited of remedies.[15]

In doing so, judges have taken away the rights the law gave to workers and have given employers virtually irresistible incentives and opportunities to avoid unions and collective bargaining. What employer would bargain when the law says it can insist on what it wants even if it is unreasonable and that it can reach impasse, implement its final offer, lock out workers, replace strikers—and use all this as a tool to deunionize and to send a cautionary message to other workers about what happens to employees who vote for a union?

This is not the only attack on the NLRA and NLRB. Republican Congresses have weakened unions directly with actions such as denying employees of the Department of Homeland Security the right to join a union, and a Republican president destroyed the Professional Air Traffic Controllers Organization (PATCO). They have also weakened unions by boldly attacking the NLRA and NLRB. Congress has tried to restrain the NLRB from prosecuting employers for refusing to hire salts (workers who apply for jobs in order to organize an employer) and from expanding the use of Section 10(j) injunctions.[16] Congress has so severely restricted NLRB budgets that investigator and attorney staffing in regional offices fell from 930 in 1994 to 874 by 1999. This has led to a severe backlog of cases.[17]

These actions are part of a program that is returning unionization to its numerical levels and status before the NLRA was enacted. Those were not good times for unions. The NLRA replaced a system that saw unionization as an illegal conspiracy with one that said unionization was a legal right and a social necessity.[18] With this multipronged extremist attack on union rights, unions have not fared well. Unionization has plummeted,[19] and with it the working standards and prospects for so many of us and our families and neighbors.[20] As power has tilted ever more toward employers, workers have lost the ability to be heard and to negotiate their workplace conditions.

This shift in workplace power affects all of us. In the United States, virtually all social benefits come through the workplace and not from the state. As a result, anything that shifts the balance of power toward employers and away from employees has direct consequences for the welfare of individual workers and their families. Our children are robbed of a fair start in life. Lower wages mean less money to spend and fuel the economy. Children who are raised poor suffer from that deprivation all their lives. Some have no reason to buy into the society and may then fight back against it—through crime, for example.

The consequences, however, are even more serious than a decline in social welfare: our very democracy is at risk. Unions and union members play a powerful role in promoting democratic values and action. They are active in all phases of the electoral process, from registering new voters to getting out the vote to lobbying for new laws that benefit us all. Unions were instrumental in the enactment of Title VII, the Occupational Safety and Health Act (OSHA), the Family and Medical Leave Act (FMLA), the Americans with Disabilities Act (ADA), increased minimum wages, improved unemployment insurance, the Employee Retirement Income Security Act (ERISA), and many other laws.[21] These laws make all workplaces safer and provide greater equality of access to jobs and fair treatment.

Some argue that union decline means that unions are no longer useful. Some claim that unions are adversarial in an era when what is most needed in the workplace is cooperation.

Nothing supports these claims. Day after day, unions are actively involved in protecting workplace privacy, living wages, gender and racial equality, and workplace safety. Unions are the only ones that enter every fight for all these rights and more. Only unions give workers the information they need to protect themselves.

If there were no more unions, how long would these laws exist? Would new laws be enacted to meet new problems? Would they be updated as the need arises? How can a system of individuals come together to exercise the power and vision that make this happen? Who would do the lobbying and research? Who would get out the vote for sympathetic legislators? Without union support, eventually these laws and their protections would be lost.

The judicial rewriting of our fundamental collective bargaining law means that, in the international arena, the United States is a country that fails to abide by international laws declaring that freedom to join a union is a fundamental human right. Human Rights Watch's comprehensive report *Unfair Advantage*[22] details how U.S. labor law now betrays its promise.

It may be easy to shake off concern for the poor or for the opinion of the international community, but all of us are poorer in innumerable ways when workers are denied their rights under the NLRA to collectively assert power. It is, therefore, in the interest of our entire society to make effective the promise of the NLRA to protect workers' "right to self-organization, to form, join, or assist labor organizations, to bargain collectively through representatives of their own choosing, and to engage in other concerted activities for the purpose of collective bargaining or other mutual aid or protection."

What Can Unions Do?

Ultimately, union success or failure depends on attacking those who have led the campaign against unionization. Proposals to replace the NLRA or to avoid the NLRB fail to take on the fundamental problem unions face. The NLRB and NLRA are weak because they, just as much as unions, have been under assault. Attacking the NLRA and NLRB means that unions have failed to take action to protect the precious resource that the NLRA is. Furthermore, attacking the NLRA and NLRB is not cost-free.

Attacks distract unions from going after the real sources of their problems. It is curious that more union leaders have not considered why their allies in assaulting the NLRB are archconservatives. Why have unions not thought about whose interests they promote when they are on the same side as those who promote corporate interests?

These attacks actually make the NLRA and NLRB less effective. The public servants who work for the NLRB are themselves members of unions. They work for the NLRB because they believe in the Board's mission. Consider the impact on the morale and effectiveness of these workers—and union brothers and sisters—when they are under attack from both the right and the left. These attacks also hurt workers because they are so broad that workers may not go to the NLRB, even when it is their only recourse.

Unions need to be more active in filing Board charges and using the law. (Chapter 8 discusses strategies for using the Board to enhance union strength and the right to organize.) Because statistics on filed charges are used to measure the level of law violations, when unions let unfair labor practices go without filing charges, they send a message that we have achieved labor peace. Filing charges demonstrates to workers that employer actions are illegal. An increase in filing also supports the case that the NLRB needs more staff and more funding. Rather than calling for sit-ins at NLRB offices, union leaders should be sitting in at congressional offices. They should be even more vocal on judicial appointments, and they should demand money and respect to strengthen the NLRA. To take back the Workers' Law, unions must support the NLRB as an institution and attack those who have undermined it. They must develop a multipronged strategy to take back the NLRA so workers have the power to stand up against corporations. Staughton Lynd said, "From my point of view, the historical miscarriage of the NLRA makes it more and not less important to 'celebrate and seek to restore to its intended vigor the right to engage in concerted activity for mutual aid or protection.'"[23]

Unions need to wage a broad campaign that speaks to this country's workers in language about working-class and democratic values. Unions must challenge their political foes and support their allies. As part of this effort, unions must be in the forefront of developing a litigation strategy to reverse the judicial amendments and restore the NLRA to its original purpose. They must fight to make the NLRB a powerful institution that can uphold worker rights.

A litigation strategy can achieve these goals without the need to campaign for new legislation. These ideas are novel, and it is reasonable to be skeptical. They are based on the contention that, since judges' decisions have radically altered the plain language of the NLRA, it is judges themselves who must be called to account.

First, consider the legal protection of salting. Salts are workers who apply for jobs in order to organize nonunion employers. Once hired, they boldly assert their rights under the NLRA. Having someone in the workplace who is fearless in advocating unionization can be a powerful tool. If employers fire a salt for promoting unionization, unions lose an advocate but can file charges with the NLRB to prosecute the employer for violating the law.

Over the years, the NLRB has found it a violation of the law to fire a salt for union activity or to refuse to hire a salt. But the courts of appeals were hostile to salting. They reversed case after case. Despite this, the NLRB steadfastly supported the right to use salting as an organizing tactic. In 1995, the NLRB persuaded the Supreme Court that its interpretation was right.[24] As a result, an employer could not refuse to hire and could not discharge an employee for being a salt.

That is not the end of the story, however. Employers were outraged that they could not refuse to hire pro-union workers who were also fearless organizers. So the Republicans held congressional hearings at which they condemned the NLRB's decisions, attacked the NLRB for prosecuting employers who discriminated against salts, and tried to enact laws reversing the Supreme Court. They have so far been unsuccessful in amending the law or using the power of the budget to prevent the NLRB from enforcing the law and protecting organizing.[25]

But how long can the agency hold out, given the power of those against it and the lack of union voices in support of the NLRB? Unlike unions, the Republicans take the NLRB very seriously and have gone to the mat to prevent the appointment of NLRB members who would be sympathetic to labor and to the NLRA's policies and to ensure the appointment of pro-business, anti-NLRA members. How long will these NLRB cases stand in the face of this campaign to destroy the Workers' Law?

Or consider the Supreme Court's decision in the case of *Lechmere, Inc. v. NLRB*.[26] This case is widely seen as an anti-union decision that makes organizing more difficult. Lechmere's store was located in an open shopping plaza. When union organizers tried to place union literature on employees' cars in the far end of the parking lot, Lechmere threatened them with arrest for trespass. Those who refer to the NLRB as labor's enemy should recall that the Board decided that union organizers had the right to go onto Lechmere's property to organize workers. It was the Supreme Court that decided the employer's property rights trumped its employees' NLRA rights. The Court—not the NLRB—made it harder for unions to organize.

There is a second aspect of the *Lechmere* decision that is more subtle but potentially more damaging to employee rights to organize and engage in collective bargaining. In order to decide the case as it did, the Supreme

Court had to define the word "employee." It said "employees" meant only the employees of a specific employer. This is the common meaning of the word, but the NLRA says exactly the opposite. The NLRA says that the term employee "shall include *any employee*, and *shall not be limited to the employees of a particular employer.*"[27] This definition is intended to promote and protect worker solidarity across workplaces.[28]

Thus, under the NLRA, Lechmere's employees, the union organizers, and workers at other employers were all employees and had the right to make common cause with one another so that they could increase their bargaining power and improve their working conditions. But the Supreme Court majority made that very difficult when it wrote the *Lechmere* decision.

It is hard to believe that justices of the Supreme Court cannot read the plain words of a statute, but the only other explanation is that they decided to judicially "amend" the NLRA. In trying to understand what drove the Court to do this, it is not enough to attribute its decision solely to class bias. Doing so does nothing to change this sort of decision making. To make effective change it is necessary to explore what affects judges so that they engage in judicial amendment. In *Lechmere*, this was a force that was powerful enough that the justices decided the case that overturned the plain language of the law. Understanding the processes that lead to judicial amendments makes it possible to develop effective strategies to counter them.

Making the NLRB Part of the Solution

Not only is the NLRB not the enemy, but unions can make it part of the solution. True, the NLRB cannot do everything for unions, but the union movement would benefit enormously by thinking creatively about how to make the best use of the NLRB and the NLRA, rather than throwing them away because they are not perfect.

Of course, the truth is that unions have not avoided the Board. Labor's infantry knows it needs the NLRB. They know that the NLRB is the only place to go for some remedies. No law other than the NLRA makes it illegal to fire workers discharged for union activities. True, the current remedy is not adequate, but it does provide reinstatement and backpay. While it would be better to have a larger remedy, these are certainly better than no remedy at all. There is a price to be paid for union rhetoric against the NLRB. For example, I have seen workers who heard this message fall prey to charlatans who told them that they should not go to the Board. They offered to represent the workers in court and promised huge awards. Of course, those cases were quickly dismissed because the only remedy is through the Board.[29]

Union leaders also need to consider how their anti-NLRB rhetoric affects the public servants who work for the NLRB, who care about its mission, and who put in long hours trying to enforce the law. These are potential allies labor should not alienate. Union leaders need a steady stream of young people who are eager to go to work for the NLRB because they want to promote justice and enforce the Workers' Law. Union leaders need to ask how attacking the NLRB affects who applies for a job with the Board. They should work to make these jobs attractive to graduates from labor studies, industrial relations, or other labor-friendly programs. Unions need to make working for the NLRB a legitimate career goal for these students.

NLRB employees know the remedies are too weak, but they also know what it means to help people who are in desperate circumstances. From my years with the NLRB, I carry the memory of people in trouble who were profoundly grateful that their government had provided them an attorney at no charge who would fight for their rights. Even years after I left I occasionally received thanks from people who said I had made a difference in their lives.

The NLRB is staffed with many dedicated workers—who themselves are unionized—who work hard to further the NLRA's goals of promoting equality of bargaining power, collective bargaining, and freedom of association. The NLRB has supporters who have good reasons to feel the way they do.

What I propose is building on what exists to make it more effective. I contend that the NLRB can be used even more strategically by unions to increase union power and improve the lives of workers. Even now, some unions use NLRB filings, decisions, and settlements for propaganda value. They send out messages to the workers and call press conferences to announce that the government has decided that an employer is a lawbreaker. Even in this antigovernment age this is a powerful statement. But when unions vilify the NLRB and NLRA, they risk hurting labor's image. Union leaders need to ask why any worker would risk becoming a member of a movement that says its worst enemy is a small government agency.

Of course, and as our labor leaders know, U.S. common law was and is uniformly hostile to unions and the rights of workers. Thus Congress had to pass law after law before it could outlaw the common law labor injunction and overrule court decisions that said labor unions were criminal conspiracies. Even now, the common law says that an employer can fire a worker for no reason or a bad reason. If the NLRA were repealed, all workers would be covered by that law.

Workers in unorganized workplaces—that is to say, most workers in the United States—are especially vulnerable. They may not be aware that the NLRA applies to them. Employers who retaliate against them for taking the first fledgling steps toward collective action violate the law. Recent NLRA cases have protected employees who spoke out against a wide range of employer policies, who challenged rules telling them they could not discuss their working conditions, and who blew the whistle on their employer's illegal conduct.[30] Without the NLRA, they would have no protections at this critical stage.

This is not to say that the NLRA and NLRB don't have flaws. Their critics have made valid charges about the NLRA, the NLRB, and problems unions face in relation to them. Taft-Hartley outlawed important union economic weapons and organizing tools. Election processes can too easily be subverted by anti-union employers,[31] the appeal process means waiting years for a remedy, and remedies are so late and so weak that it may pay to violate the law. Add to this that NLRB regional offices are perennially understaffed, and some Board personnel are bureaucratic and unsympathetic.

In short, the problem is not criticisms; it is that the criticisms have been so extreme that they encourage discarding rights and what can be a useful tool for unions. As long as unions still have these tools and these rights, they need to take a course that is realistic and strategic. This book does not argue that the NLRA is a panacea or that it can solve all labor's problems. No one thing—not even if unions devoted 100 percent of their budgets and time to organizing—can alone make the difference in union success or failure. This book attempts to open a discussion on strategies to make better use of the NLRA and the NLRB now, even without statutory reform.

1

WHY JUDGES REWRITE LABOR LAW

Some will naturally be skeptical of a legal strategy to promote unionization. They will argue that law is irrelevant to union success or is a crutch that inevitably will weaken unions. Or they may argue that the only way to union success is through a social movement. These discussions tend to break down into debates over which is the one correct strategy.

I do not advocate a legal strategy as the only approach. Success depends on a campaign that uses many kinds of tactics and that draws on a wide range of skills and talents. It needs activists, organizers, those who serve the needs of members, strategists, and good lawyers.

The legal issues I discuss here provide useful information to anyone interested in union success. I urge taking a realistic view of the NLRA as one among many resources unions can use. The NLRA embodies rights that our forebears worked and struggled for over many decades. In recognition of their struggle, we have an obligation to protect, preserve, and strengthen them.

We need to apply the lessons our forebears did when they faced the Great Depression and fought valiantly against evil and oppression in World War II. Those who lived through those hard times learned that you make the best of what you have. And generals do not refuse to engage the enemy because the battlefield's conditions are not perfect or there might be losses. To wait for and plan only for the perfect battlefield is to concede the war to the enemy. Nor is there only one appropriate strategy for fighting a war. A war must be fought on many fronts using approaches from land, sea, and air. Each situation calls for using the tool appropriate to the resources, time, and conditions.

What I urge is to identify all potential resources and to use them wisely and effectively and certainly to squander no resource. Law is one of these resources. This book advocates using law as part of a campaign to increase worker and union power in order to better all our lives.

What Judges Do to Labor Law Matters

Workers quite rightly deserve effective labor law, but this is not a problem that new legislation can fix. First, any new law will be subjected to the same judicial processes that have affected the NLRA. The tendency of judges to rewrite workplace law is not unique to the NLRA. Judicial interpretations have weakened or undermined federal antidiscrimination laws, such as Title VII, the Family and Medical Leave Act, the Americans with Disabilities Act, and the Occupational Safety and Health Act. In some cases, these interpretations have completely undermined the statutes' purposes.

In the case of the NLRA, within five years of its enactment, the courts had given employers the right to permanently replace strikers. This permits what the NLRA forbids and undermines the statute's intent. In other words, since at least 1935, the courts have been judicially amending workplace statutes, and they continue to do so.

Given this conclusion, it is fair to say that if the NLRA were replaced— even if it were replaced by a law that had the blessing of all unions—judicial interpretations would soon "rewrite" those laws. This means that enormous resources could be put into enacting a new law that judges would quickly undermine. In short, there is no choice but to grapple with this issue of judicial amendments.

Second, there is little likelihood that unions will be able to enact new labor law anytime soon. While easy to propose, even small changes to labor and employment statutes have proved impossible for political reasons.[1] Third, there is also no guarantee that a new statute would be favorable to unions or would be an improvement on the NLRA. A proposed new statute would create an attractive target for anti-union groups.[2]

This means that a litigation strategy is at least a viable method for "enacting" law that supports collective bargaining. A litigation strategy can start now rather than waiting for both a Congress and a president who make labor issues a priority. Our common-law system means that judges have the right to make law.[3] This power can be used to create new rights and to overturn doctrines such as striker replacement. During the 1970s and 1980s, for example, judges created new employee rights based on tort and contract.[4] Just because judges are now taking more conservative positions does not mean they always will. Under the right circumstances, they can be persuaded that justice demands that they enforce the Workers' Law.

The question is how to encourage judges to interpret laws to support worker rights, not whether it can be done. We know that, at one time, separate but equal was the law of the land, embedded in statute and court decisions. Now, even though there is still much work to be done, legalized racial discrimination does not exist. Labor law, too, can be changed. William Corbett observes that

> the difficulty of effecting change is no excuse to stop advocating for change. All that is needed is time and pressure. The evolution of the common law is often slow, but it does evolve to address new challenges and reflect society's evolving values. . . . Because of the limitations of legislation and the value of a common law approach to these problems, it is no answer to dismiss the common law because of the difficulty and pace.[5]

Thus, if the labor law we have and will have is the NLRA, then restoring it to its original purpose must come through the courts. A fair reading of the NLRA shorn of judicial amendments reveals a law that unions would support. It was enacted to replace totalitarian workplaces with ones based on democratic principles of workers' empowerment, equality, and justice. The law was intended to promote social and economic goals of fair working conditions and a just society. To say we must restore the law by using the courts is not to deny how extreme the courts' remake of the NLRA has been. Judges have literally replaced the NLRA's plain language and purpose with that of the prior common law, a regime that was implacably hostile to unions.

It is also not to suggest that developing and using a litigation strategy is an easy task. We must identify the mechanisms that will push the courts to interpret and apply the law as written. We must also develop strategies that take into account which doctrines are most amenable to being overturned. This depends on many factors, such as whether the doctrine has been decided only by the court of appeals and not by the Supreme Court. It also depends on how firmly embedded the doctrine is. For example, it should be easier to eliminate the doctrine that allows employers to implement their final offers at impasse because the Supreme Court has never directly ruled on the issue.[6] This does not mean that striker replacement, which was created by the Supreme Court in 1938[7] and since endorsed by the Court many times and justified by the idea that it is an essential part of collective bargaining, is untouchable. It means developing a strategy that persuades the Supreme Court it must reverse itself.

NLRA remedies have been ruled on by both the Supreme Court and courts of appeals, but so far there are no decisions mandating specific remedies for specific violations.[8] Remedies are also specific to the unfair labor practice, and the courts have not made them part of a comprehensive theory. As a result, inadequate remedies should be amenable to immediate improvement through a litigation strategy. Even Taft-Hartley may be susceptible to interpretations that are less harmful to unions by using a comprehensive litigation strategy.

Litigation that gives the NLRB teeth with regard to unfair labor practices will have positive results for organizing as well. Organizing can never be successful when unions are hemorrhaging members as a result of striker replacement and collective bargaining that is weakened by the employer's ability to implement its final offer upon reaching impasse. Judicial amendments such as these mean union numbers decline through lost members, and they give employers a powerful argument against organizing.

Fourth, there is evidence from recent court cases that courts will respond to thoughtfully developed records. To give two recent examples, the D.C. Circuit Court of Appeals said that academic research and arguments made to it by the Board had led it to conclude that it might be appropriate to give the implementation-upon-impasse doctrine a second look.[9] In other words, the D.C. Circuit said it was willing to reconsider a judicial amendment whose origins go back to the 1940s. The Ninth Circuit recently relied on expert testimony and research in issuing a decision about union dues that was favorable to unions.[10] These and other cases suggest that using research and testimony to support outcomes can persuade a court to redress doctrines that have undermined the purposes of the NLRA.

In sum, the problem lies not so much with the NLRA's language as with those who interpret and apply the law.[11] Missing this point means wasting energy trying to replace a law whose fundamentals are sound. It risks ending up with a new statute that is far inferior to the one we have. It also fails to address the futility of amending the law when any statute can suffer from judicial amendment. Thus, new legislation may be of no more than temporary help. In both the long and short run, the only thing that can restore collective bargaining rights is persuading judges to reverse course and enforce the NLRA's language and policies.

Developing a litigation strategy is no easy thing. The first step is to identify the forces that have caused judges to amend the NLRA and then use that information to create a strategy for taking back the Workers' Law.

Why Judges Do What They Do to Labor Law

A recent study found that there was a major shift in Supreme Court NLRA decisions after 1970. Before 1970, over 80 percent of decisions were favorable to unions. After 1970, only 50 percent were.[12] In other words, something has changed that affects the way judges decide NLRA cases. Another study examined court of appeals decisions in NLRA cases involving employer violations. Among other things, it found that the courts of appeals were especially likely to reverse NLRB decisions to negatively affect the survival of the collective bargaining relationship.[13]

It would be easy to write off judges as conservatives who simply make decisions based on their class interests. While there may be some evidence of this,[14] it alone is insufficient to explain the processes that have led to judicial amendments of the NLRA and other workplace laws. It is also an answer that can lead to only one solution—ensure that no judges with a class bias are on the bench. But this is no solution in the real world. Decades of Republican administrations and Congresses have left us with a bench full of lifetime appointees who are deeply conservative. These are the judges who will be deciding cases for at least the next quarter century. They cannot be avoided, so attempts must be made to argue cases that can speak to such a judiciary. The processes that lead judges to amend labor law may be subtle and nearly invisible, but they can be analyzed, understood, and addressed.

The NLRA was intended to fundamentally alter the roles of employers and the employed. However, all workplace litigation takes place under the influence of the pre-NLRA worldview as expressed in the common law. Judges'—and all lawyers'—common-law training leaves judges ill-equipped to understand labor law,[15] because it cultivates a worldview that is wholly at odds with labor law. The parts of the common law that most affect interpretations of the NLRA are property law, at-will employment, and concepts of master and servant. These construct the idea that employers have "reserved rights" that give them ultimate power over the workplace.[16]

In addition, common-law reasoning is based on incremental decision making. This is a slow but inexorable process that has a power, like that of glaciers, to grind even the tallest mountains into valleys. Incremental reasoning inevitably leads to results in all areas of law that sooner or later need to be corrected. Labor law is at that point now.

Finally, it is the court's role to fill in legislation. The NLRA's drafters left gaps in crucial areas of the law, and the courts have naturally stepped in to fill them.

History and Its Hold on Today's Law

The worldview that existed when the NLRA was enacted still influences how we all think about the roles of employers and workers. It is a powerful force that shapes the way lawyers and judges understand the legal rights of the workplace. As a result, though the language of the NLRA remains, historical understandings have radically rewritten the way it is read and applied.[17]

In 1935, when the NLRA was enacted, most workplace relations were governed by the common law doctrine of employment at will. Unfortunately, they still are. In an at-will relationship, an employer can fire a worker for a good, a bad, or no reason. Employees are legally free to quit for the same reasons. As Professor Clyde Summers describes it:

> The premises of the doctrine are quite clear; the employer has sovereignty except to the extent it has expressly granted its employees rights. The doctrine thus expresses and implements the subordination of workers to those

who control the enterprise. . . . Their terms and conditions of employment can be changed in any way at any time and they can be dismissed without reason and without notice. . . . Perpetuation of employment at will, with its toleration of injustice, signals the continued presence of a deep current in American labor law.[18]

At-will employment is still the default rule for all employment relationships. Because most workers do not realize they are at will,[19] they are unlikely to ask for a just-cause relationship. Even if they were aware of their legal status, most employees lack the bargaining power to persuade an employer to agree to just cause. Union representation is the simplest way to move from an at-will relationship to a just-cause relationship, but the decline in private-sector union membership means that most workers remain at will.

At-will employment does more than let employers unilaterally set the terms of employment and control the right to terminate; it also embodies and perpetuates a worldview of employer–employee relationships that judges are likely to bring with them whenever they decide a case involving workplace issues.

The at-will worldview means accepting a logic that is not true. For example, it assumes that employees like at-will employment and are comfortable with employers' having the right to fire them at will.[20] The law assumes that employment is a contractual relationship and that its terms are agreed to by the parties. This assumes that workers and employers agree to an at-will relationship, unless they specifically agree to other terms.

However, these assumptions are not correct. Studies by Pauline Kim have found that 80–90 percent of employees thought they worked under a legal system that required fair and just treatment in the workplace. Most thought that they could be fired only if the employer had cause.[21]

Judges say that at-will employment is based on contract law, but the at-will doctrine makes no sense when contract law is applied. First, contracts are supposed to be based on the parties' intent, but Kim's research shows employees think they are agreeing to just-cause and not at-will employment. Judges, however, will overturn even written statements of intent that employment is to be based on just cause. Judges have not only made at-will employment the default, but they have imposed requirements that make it almost impossible to agree to any other term.[22]

Second, courts say at-will employment is based on the contractual concept of mutuality of obligation. They say this means that if one party is free to end the relationship at will, the other must have that same freedom. Nowhere outside at-will employment does any doctrine of contract law require that the obligations of one must be the same as the obligations of the other.[23] Outside the employment relationship, mutuality of obligation only means that both parties are bound to perform the contract's terms. Furthermore, those obligations usually are reciprocal but not identical. For example, there would be no point in a contract to purchase something if both the buyer and seller had to sell.

In fact, this is the case even in employment, except when it comes to firing or quitting. Employment relationships are based on hierarchy and not on matching or symmetrical rights. If one person has told another: "Jump," and the second person has asked, "How high?" we know who is the employer and who the employee. A worker who ordered the employer to jump would be told, "You're fired." Another example is the duty of loyalty. If an employee solicits her employer's customers and her fellow employees—while that employee still works for the employer—to join her new business, she violates the duty of loyalty. But an employer who prepares to move work to a new plant and to replace its workforce with workers paid lower wages is a smart entrepreneur.

Third, employees' right to quit is protected by the Thirteenth Amendment of the U.S. Constitution, which prohibits slavery and involuntary servitude. An employer's right to fire a worker has no basis in the Constitution. At-will employment did not even exist until American judges created it in the late nineteenth century.[24] Workers at that time in England—and in other common-law countries—had rights to notice and severance pay.

At-will employment says that employers should be able to fire workers for a good reason, a bad reason, or no reason because workers can quit work for a good reason, a bad reason, or no reason. But is it likely that most workers quit jobs for any but a good reason? Workers are most likely to quit because they are unhappy with the conditions or pay or they have found a job that provides better working conditions or pay. Workers may also quit because of family obligations or to go to school. While an employer may be unhappy that a worker has quit, this does not mean that any of these are bad reasons to quit, and they certainly are not "no" reasons to quit. In fact, each of these reasons to quit is just cause for leaving a job. If this is correct, then for the employment relationship to be symmetrical, employers would not be allowed to fire a worker for any reason other than just cause.

Despite all this, judges enforce at-will employment as the default law. They say employment is a contractual relationship, but they make it virtually impossible to contract out of at-will. Even showing that the parties agreed to a just-cause relationship or putting the terms of a relationship in writing has not been enough. The at-will system was created and enforced by judges, not by statute. It has a logic that does not reflect real-world experience and is even contrary to common-law contract doctrine. It is fair to conclude that this system—a system of hierarchy, lack of protections for workers, and support for employer hegemony—provides a window into how judges think about the workplace and the roles of employer and employee.

When the NLRA was enacted, this worldview governed the workplace. In the pre-NLRA world, as now, law, power, economics, and social ordering could affect the employment relationship. Put most simply, when employees have enough power to extract "more" from the employer, the employer has less, and when employees lack bargaining power, the employer has more. "More" for employees means more money, health and safety, industrial due process, equal protection, democratic engagement, empowerment, and self-actualization.

The NLRA was enacted to change the balance of power created and enforced by the courts and by laws, such as corporation law. U.S. corporation law exists to allow and encourage employers to become collective and immortal, and to limit their liability for wrongs they commit. All this is illegal without corporation law, and it meant that corporation law changed the balance of power that existed before it was enacted. The NLRA was enacted to rebalance the power that corporation law had unbalanced.

In 1937, employers argued that the NLRA should be held unconstitutional because it radically weakened employer rights. They said that it was "an unlawful interference with the right of the respondent to manage its own business."[25] They were correct that the NLRA was intended to change the way businesses operated. Congress enacted the NLRA because it had concluded that allowing large imbalances of power between employers and employees created harms that were not confined to the single workplace. They injured the foundations of our society. As Congress put it in the NLRA's Policies and Findings in Section 1:

> The inequality of bargaining power between employees who do not possess full freedom of association or actual liberty of contract and employers who are organized in the corporate or other forms of ownership association substantially burdens and affects the flow of commerce, and tends to aggravate recurrent business depressions, by depressing wage rates and the purchasing power of wage earners in industry and by preventing the stabilization of competitive wage rates and working conditions within and between industries.

Congress intended the NLRA to establish a relationship between employers and employees different from that of the common law and different from how most people, even more than seventy years after its enactment, think about employer and employee rights and obligations. It was created to restore more equal employer and employee bargaining power in order to promote improved working conditions and create labor and social peace.

Rather than interfering with the free market, the NLRA was intended to correct the harms created by corporation law. Given its findings, Congress's only alternative would have been to outlaw corporation law or severely limit it in order to restore market freedom and prevent the damage these laws had caused.

Enforcing NLRA rights is difficult because the pre-NLRA worldview shapes our thinking about the workplace and the proper rights and roles of workers and employers. These ideas affect judges' decision making and has led them to gradually restore the preexisting system in the guise of interpreting and enforcing the NLRA.

The Influence of Common-Law Thinking

Students come to law school thinking that law means statutes. However, they spend virtually the whole first year reading judges' decisions. The purpose is not just to learn the law by reading those decisions; it is also to learn the process of judicial reasoning so law students can learn to think like lawyers. The common law is also powerful and important. In the case of labor law, it is judge-made law, common law, and judicial interpretations of the NLRA that have shaped what we now know as labor law.

Judges come to the bench with minds shaped by and imbued with the common law as a body of law and as an analytical process.[26] As a result, they are less able to understand and sympathize with legal regimes that operate on other principles.[27] For example, the common-law concepts of property law and master and servant law make it difficult for judges to sympathize with the goals and methods of collective bargaining.

Jobs as Property

Legal decisions often speak of an employer as "he" rather than "it" even when the employer is a corporation. This personification of employers suggests that judges may decide cases based on a vision of an employer as a human being. It means that judges are more likely to think of a job as an employer's personal possession. Judges assume an employer will be a good steward of this property because the employer will not want to risk its loss.[28] Society as a whole benefits from protecting private property because we expect an owner to be motivated to be a good steward. On the other hand, if one is careless with his personal property and damages or loses it, that is his right, as the one who must bear the loss.[29]

Of course, most employers involved in NLRA cases are more likely to be corporations than sole proprietorships. Ownership of corporations is generally not personal. The true owners are the shareholders. They will have no idea how the property is treated and no ability to manage it.[30] Furthermore, company actions will be decided by directors, managers, and officers whose tenure with the company is likely to be short as they further their careers by moving from one position to another. They are unlikely to suffer any losses from damaging the property, and their pay and benefits may bear no relationship to the way they have treated the corporation.[31] This means that assumptions that grow out of concepts of personal property and the relationship of ownership and property rights should not automatically apply to all employers.

The common law has trouble finding a place for employees in this structure. Even if employees have long tenure and have invested resources in their jobs, the common law tends not to give them any rights to those jobs, even though employees are dependent on them and know they will suffer the consequences if the company is harmed. Thus, the human beings in this scheme—the employees—have fewer protections than the abstract or fictional corporate person.

The NLRA was intended to create a different structure, one based on equality of bargaining power between employer and employee. This differs from the common-law ideas that the workplace is solely the employer's property, and that only the employer should have the right to control workplace terms.[32] Yet the "courts continue to rely on common law notions of property rights to dilute the strength of employees' statutory rights."[33] In the court's view, any other system would take the employer's property without due process of law.

There are other ways of looking at this issue of property rights. For example, do workers acquire ownership interests as a result of their "sweat equity"? Or can they acquire something akin to a limited easement that gives them certain rights to the job and a say in the conditions under which they work? In addition to employees' contributions to create and maintain jobs, generous subsidies are provided to employers by the public at large. These include building and maintaining roads, sewers, utilities, and mail service; educating those who will become workers; creating and making available police protection, laws (especially corporation law), the court system, tax benefits, and incentives; and sometimes offering outright handouts. Is a society that provides these generous benefits to employers barred from having some degree of control over whether that employer runs a business in a way that promotes or undermines the public interest?

Seeing a job as the employer's property leaves judges in a quandary. They need to fit employees into this scheme. Obviously employees are not exactly trespassers; they have the employer's permission to be there. But just how far does that right extend? Could employees who believe in good faith they are working in unsafe conditions not only inform OSHA but also give the OSHA inspector permission to enter to inspect and enforce the law if the employer refuses entry? And if they do not have that right, what exactly is their status?

The common law has the capacity to find in property law some status that more accurately describes the role of employees and employers and the importance of a job in the lives of those who do the work. But it has failed to do this. The NLRA, however, provides a structure that makes that possible. Although it does not speak in these terms, the NLRA embodies a recognition that employees have an emotional and physical investment in their jobs and that the law must recognize, protect, and support their investments.

Master and Servant

The term "master and servant" law comes from an era in which the employment relationship was one between a literal master and his servants.[34] In the founding years of this country, virtually all workers were in bonded servitude, and the workplace was also likely to be the employer's home. In that day, the father was also the employer, and the employee was likely to be a blood child or a child apprentice living in the home. Thus, the law of master and servant developed in a context of intermixed personal and business relations where adults needed to educate and control the children in their care.[35] That sort of workplace has been gone for over a century now, and the master-and-servant concept does not comfortably apply to a world in which almost no remunerative work is done in the home and employment relations are likely to be the impersonal contacts of a distant transnational corporation with its employees.

The NLRA rejected master-and-servant law seventy years ago. Senator Robert Wagner wanted to convert the relation of master and servant into an equal and cooperative partnership that planted a sense of power, individuality, freedom, and security in the hearts of men and made them the people they were meant to be.[36] Judges, however, are still influenced by concepts of master and servant when they interpret labor law. Thus the employer (as father) has a legal right to protect *his* property and control *his* workplace and *his* employees. In this workplace the workers are children who have no legal stake in their jobs and no right and capacity to act for their own benefit in dealings with their employer. The employer is justified in fighting a union, who is an interloper who stands between the employer and *his* employees. If a union wins an election, the employer can still set *his* terms, except those the law forbids. And if the employees strike and leave *his* workplace, the employer has every right to give *his* jobs to those who will treat *his* property with greater care.

Clashes between common-law tradition and legal and social change can, in some cases, be "integral—and usefully vital—to the evolution of the common law." But this is not the case when judges are not candid about hidden biases that affect their reasoning.[37] Unfortunately, too often, this has been the case when judges interpret the NLRB.

Incrementalism

Labor historian David Brody says:

> The striking feature about the law's evolution is its sheer inexorability. . . . With virtually no further legislation [since Taft-Hartley], the work of interpreting labor's rights out of existence has steadily proceeded. The incremental dismantling of the duty to bargain . . . can be replicated many times over in the case law governing interrogations, captive audience meetings, union access, coercive speech, you name it. . . . This suggests that, beyond politics, deep-seated ideo-legal biases are built into the law's development.[38]

The judicial amendment of the NLRA has been affected both by the ideas of the common law and by its decision-making processes—in particular, incrementalism. The common law depends on slow, case-by-case development and reliance on analogies. Often this is a positive way to develop law.[39] In each case the judge applies the appropriate law to a particular set of facts. The judge must first decide which version of the facts is most credible. This depends on a witness's demeanor and evidence about whether the witness is biased and an accurate observer and reporter. Judges use their own experiences as human beings. They also rely on tools such as the rules of evidence. The rules of evidence guide a judge in thinking about the value of types of evidence.

Even when all parties work to provide the most credible evidence and the judge is fair and intelligent, determining what happened can be difficult. This is more likely to be the case when a judge must make a decision about law and events outside her experience. Cases involving labor law and especially those involving working-class people present events with which most federal appellate judges will have little personal experience. They will be more likely to have relationships with those who are in management and therefore to understand their point of view.

Appellate judges decide NLRB cases only on appeal, so they never see or hear the witnesses and cannot ask them questions to fill in gaps in their knowledge. Rather, they make judgments only from the transcripts of hearings. For these reasons appellate judges are not supposed to substitute their credibility judgments for those of the judge who held the hearing. They are also not supposed to substitute their judgment for that of an agency like the NLRB with expertise appellate judges do not have.[40] However, judges often fail to defer and regularly substitute their judgment for the NLRB's.[41] When they explain why they have done so, they often express bewilderment that the NLRB has made a different assessment of fact and law. That befuddlement is genuine: they truly do not understand.

A study of court of appeals judges found that few had labor law experience and that having labor law experience affected decision making. What was most surprising and encouraging is that judges who had practiced labor law, even on the management side, were more likely to find for unions and against employers in Section 8(a)(5) bargaining violation cases. "Judges who supported the union under other sections of the statute appeared less likely to register that support under section 8(a)(5), while judges with the most experience interpreting and litigating under the statute showed a special propensity to protect union interests."[42]

The impact of a lack of judicial understanding can be seen in a case such as *NLRB v. Adkins Transfer Co., Inc.*[43] The court of appeals in Adkins decided that the employer did not violate the NLRA when it terminated employees who had joined a union. The court reasoned that the employees would want a raise and firing workers who want a raise was not anti-union discrimination. In *Textile Workers Union v. Darlington*,[44] the Supreme Court found that the employer committed no violation when it closed a plant where the employees had voted for a union. The Board had agreed that the employer had a right to close its business if it wanted to but still had to pay a price for violating its employees' NLRA right to join a union. The NLRB ordered the employer to give the workers backpay and a right to work in nearby plants the employer owned. The Supreme Court was unable to see that NLRA rights mattered in the face of an employer's traditional right to choose to be in business or not.

This is not a problem of class bias or of a judge's conscious intent to destroy union rights; rather, the limited backgrounds of judges mean they do not understand the law and facts. The remedy for this is to educate judges.[45]

Once the facts are determined, the judge must settle on which law should apply. This is easiest when the facts in the case before the judge are very similar to those in prior cases. The more cases differ, the more difficult it is for judges to decide which law most closely fits the facts before them. Over time, as more cases are decided, this process incrementally extends the law. The positive side of this is that it allows gradual change in the law to fit new situations.[46]

Unfortunately, the process of incremental change can be myopic. When this happens, courts become so focused on technical issues that they pay no attention to a law's purpose and, as a result, subvert it. This happens in areas outside labor law,[47] but this process has been especially pernicious in labor law. *International Paper Co. v. NLRB*[48] is a good example of how incrementalism can lead to radical results. International Paper gave the union its "best and final" offer and said it would lock out the employees if the union did not accept it. When the union rejected the offer, IP unilaterally implemented its proposal. It hired temporary replacement workers through BE&K and then locked out its Mobile, Alabama, employees. During the lockout, IP gave the union a proposal stating that the company could, "at its option, contract out any or all mill maintenance work on a temporary or permanent basis."

The union said it was willing to bargain about the subcontracting proposal, but it was in a powerless position. The union could offer the employer nothing because the employer had implemented its proposal so nothing was on the table except the subcontracting proposal. The union also knew that if the parties reached an impasse on the subcontracting offer, IP had the right to implement it. If the union opposed the proposal the parties would be at an impasse. The union could not strike because it was locked out. Finally International Paper declared an impasse and implemented the proposal. It then permanently subcontracted the maintenance work. With no apparent irony, the court of appeals summed this up as "fulfilling [IP's] bargaining obligations on the issue."[49] But what the NLRA requires is good faith bargaining to codetermine working conditions by parties of relatively equal bargaining power.

What made it possible for the court to reach a conclusion that was contrary to the clear language and policy of the NLRA?[50] First, the court applied each legal doctrine in isolation to each employer act and never looked at the whole. This allowed the court to conclude that, since each step was sanctioned by prior judicial decisions, all the employer's actions must be legal. Second, each doctrine the court relied on was one that judicial decisions had incrementally moved to a point at which it did not promote the NLRA's policies but, rather, undermined them. Third, most federal judges do not know labor law, and this court was no exception. The court was unfamiliar with the complex requirements that had been developed for applying each of these doctrines. As a result, it found acts to be legal that should have been violations.

More specifically, the court said that the lockout was legal because judicial decisions allowed employers to lock out employees. This conclusion was probably wrong because International Paper had already unilaterally implemented its final offer; thus it had no offer on the table and no reason to exert economic pressure. It also could not suffer from a threat of the union whipsawing it—that is, striking while its competitors took its business—because all its "competitors" were other International Paper plants.

The outcome was based on individual decisions that did not take into account how they were connected. Judicial amendments now allow employers to hire temporary replacements for locked-out workers. The implementation-upon-impasse doctrine gave IP the right to propose subcontracting bargaining unit work permanently and solely at its discretion. The employer knew that the union could never agree to this term and that there would be an impasse. This allowed IP to declare a bargaining impasse, implement the subcontracting proposal, and permanently subcontract the work. This is how the court looked at the case.

When put together, the facts look completely different. IP had no incentive to reach agreement and every incentive to reach an impasse. Impasse would let it implement its terms. Implementing its offers, locking out its employees, and hiring replacements meant that IP had de facto discharged the unit employees because they did not agree to the employer's offer, destroyed the bargaining unit, and ended the union's status as the employees' representative. These are acts that violate Sections 8(a)(3) and (5) of the NLRA. Even had the court failed to consider the express language of the statute, it might have asked how permitting an employer to do this furthers the Act's goals of promoting equality of bargaining power and collective bargaining.

It ought to be possible to limit incrementalism, a problem not confined to labor law, by drafting laws that make it clear when a legal doctrine has gone too far. Judges are supposed to use a statute's stated goals to guide them and prevent them from making a decision that undermines the law's purpose. It would seem that stating a law's goals or policies should guide judges as they decide cases. Obviously, however, this does not always work. The NLRA has a clear statement of its policies, but in case after case, judges fail to consider those policies. Instead, they import common-law concepts into the NLRA and decide cases without paying attention to the purposes of the Act. Once they have started on this path, incrementalism leads them to veer ever farther from enforcing the law. Incrementalism blinds them to just how great a detour has been taken, because it gives a sense of tradition and almost scientific precision. These processes have undermined and radically reshaped the way the NLRA is applied, even though the statute's language has been untouched.

Gaps as Minefields

It is common for a statute to be ambiguous or have gaps.[51] Gaps may result when Congress fails to predict problems that will arise in enforcing the law. Legislatures may also purposely leave gaps: they may decide not to speak clearly on a controversial issue but to return to it later when they see how the new law works, or they may leave a gap for reasons of political expedience or in the hope that the issue left unaddressed will never arise.

The effect of leaving gaps is to delegate to the courts the job of deciding how to handle a controversial, difficult, or novel problem. Examples of gaps that have led to enforcement problems include OSHA's failure to spell out benchmarks for issuing health and safety standards and the Americans with Disability Act's failure to be more specific about what disabilities are covered.

In some areas of the law, gaps do not create as many problems as in others. Civil procedure, the law that sets out rules for filing and trying cases, is an example. It is not possible to predict who will be a plaintiff or a defendant. When it is impossible to predict whom a particular procedural statute or rule will help or hurt, no party has a vested interest in drafting a law that tilts the balance of power one way or another. Workplace law is different. It is almost always clear who will be strengthened or weakened by any rule. As a result, statutory reform in labor law has been and will always be highly contested. One purpose—and often the only purpose—of labor law reform is to change the balance of power.[52] This makes it difficult for the legislature to avoid leaving gaps.

The NLRA suffers from all these problems. It has gaps in areas where serious problems are likely to arise. Some arose because of a failure of imagination. This was new law, so it was impossible to predict all the problems that might arise. Other gaps exist because though the problem was recognized, it was too contentious for the legislators to resolve. As a result, they compromised on ambiguous language or were silent, leaving it to the NLRB—and, as it turns out, the courts—to resolve the problem.[53]

The judicial amendments that permit an employer to implement its final offer upon impasse and striker replacement are good examples. Congress failed to include anything in the new law about events it had to know were likely to arise: how to deal with impasses, strikes, and an employer's desire or need to keep its business going. It seems unlikely that Congress would have opted for permanent replacement of strikers or the employers' right to implement its final offer upon impasse, since they so distort the rest of the law. However, the NLRA's drafters left the door open for courts to make these choices when they decided to leave to the parties the responsibility for resolving bargaining impasses. In retrospect this was a bad decision. They left a gap despite knowing that there is nothing so likely as that people will not agree. This is even more true in the case of the NLRA because it was radical legislation that overturned traditional concepts of property and master and servant law, as well as ideas about the natural relationship of employers and employees.

A draft of the NLRA provided for conciliation, mediation, and arbitration to resolve impasses. During hearings on the bill, it was argued that the legislation must remedy "the matter of bringing collective bargaining negotiations to a conclusion."[54] But this did not pass.[55] Instead, the NLRA opted to give "the reality of *opportunity* . . . to labor to bargain collectively."[56] Given the NLRA's goal of promoting collective bargaining, it seems surprising that its drafters decided to leave bargaining almost unregulated and not even to state that the Act's goals as to collective bargaining be promoted, but this is exactly what they did.

Leaving gaps at such crucial points meant that Congress, by default, turned the decision over to the courts. Congress should have known better. It had been forced to enact a series of statues to keep courts from applying antitrust laws and injunctions to unions.[57] The courts had shown they were likely to rely on the tools of the common law and incrementalism to aid them in interpreting the NLRA, even though the Act was intended to overturn the concepts of master and servant, property law, and workplace control. "The [NLRA] undertook to effectuate revolutionary policies and to foster a new institution: collective bargaining. The fear that common-law courts would be unable fully to carry out these policies because of the lack of appropriate analogies—and the presence of so many inappropriate ones—may well have been justified."[58] Judicial amendments have filled the gaps Congress left by handing down decisions that have limited the remedy for bad faith bargaining to a bargaining order when they could—and still can—impose monetary sanctions, require interest arbitration, impose terms, or require other effective sanctions that "effectuate the policies of this Act."[59]

The enactment of the NLRA provided a basis to force all of us—lawyers and judges included—to rethink what was, and still is, assumed about a relationship fundamental to social ordering and to the economic prospects of each member of this society. However, as with all workplace law, the NLRA exists at cross-purposes with the power of the common law. Must this be the case?

The answer is no. In the next chapter I begin to lay out the elements of a litigation strategy that can be used to repeal the judicial amendments.

2

DEVELOPING A STRATEGY TO
TAKE BACK THE NLRA

To succeed, a litigation strategy must demonstrate to judges that they must reverse or alter precedent because that precedent is indisputably contrary to law. Ironclad cases must be constructed to show judges that there is no alternative but to overturn these doctrines. Merely arguing that striker replacement or weak remedies conflict with the NLRA's plain language and policies is not enough. Cases must be tried by taking into account the way judges view and decide cases.

In chapter 1, we discussed some of the forces that affect the way judges decide labor cases. This chapter focuses on the methods—not the content—of a litigation strategy. Later chapters will focus on the content of the litigation strategy I advocate. A litigation strategy cannot be a simple cure-all. It cannot be done by one or a few people. To succeed, it needs critical thinking and analysis, talented lawyering, rigorous and creative social science research, and a campaign to change the way our society sees unions and communal action. The ideas here are intended to provoke thought, discussion, and collaboration. They are an invitation to others to join a collaborative effort to take back the Workers' Law.

The core litigation strategies I describe in this and later chapters are carefully constructing cases to

1. Bring the purposes and policies of the NLRA front and center
2. Demonstrate to judges that the NLRA's policies must be a yardstick against which to measure their decisions

3. Spell out to common-law judges the consequences of their decisions, giving them a better understanding of labor law and the NLRA.

Sensitizing Judges to NLRA Goals

Along with unions, institutions that once supported unionization and labor values are declining. Few newspapers cover labor stories or assign a reporter to a labor beat. Stories that are most likely to appear are about labor corruption. There are almost no stories comparable to those that analyze or describe companies, their leaders, or their policies. On those rare occasions when newspapers carry stories related to the role of unions, they are written by business reporters or rank beginners.

The study of industrial relations has been transformed into human resources management and moved into business schools, where it is a stepchild subject. Law schools are less likely to teach labor law, and if they do, they are more likely to use adjuncts when full-time labor law professors retire. The excuse is that labor law does not raise the big issues that merit the attention of a regular faculty member. It is supposed to be, at best, a technical, practitioner's subject. As a result, most law school graduates will not have taken a labor law class, and those who become judges will continue to be uneducated about labor law, the role of unions, and collective bargaining. Not teaching labor law as a core course has a direct, negative impact on how unions fare in labor law cases and how labor law develops. The evidence is that judges who know labor law—including judges who have practiced management-side labor law—are far more likely to protect union interests.[1]

All these losses add up. They suggest that labor issues are marginal and unexciting and that the only way to understand workplace issues is from a business point of view. As a result, when NLRB cases come before a court of appeals, the labor attorney must reach across a huge gulf of ignorance and antipathy. This is even worse when no effort was made at trial to present the testimony and exhibits were not tailored to communicate with and educate judges who know nothing of labor law.

A trial attorney must see the world through the eyes of the people who will decide the case. If it were easy to understand how someone else thinks, there would be far fewer relationship counselors and books on dealing with those we are closest to. It is far more difficult to construct the reality of those we disagree with and whose worlds we do not inhabit.

There is no point in demanding that judges bridge this gap or in writing them off as hopeless. These are the people with the power to decide cases. In fact, they are far more in sync with our society's values than are labor unions. The fact is that the NLRA was intended to create a new sort of workplace and society, ones that radically violate our culture's norms and assumptions. We are still far from that worldview today.

A few years ago, I was called by the producer of a public radio talk show about being a guest to discuss a local strike. These shows have two formats. One is to have representatives with opposing views—one from a union and one from management. The second is to have a nonpartisan guest, such as a labor law professor. Some shows combine these.

The producer was trying to feel me out as a guest by asking me questions about collective bargaining and strikes. I gave him standard labor law that could be found in any text on the subject. I said that employers have a legal duty to bargain with a union, that the law protects strikes, and that it is illegal to fire workers who strike to pressure the employer to give them higher wages. I could tell he was shocked by my answers, so I was not surprised when the producer did not call back. I was stunned, though, when I listened to the show. Since there was only one guest, it should have been someone to give an impartial explanation of the strike. That guest, though, was the struck company's human resources director. Apparently we have reached the point where any business representative is regarded as a neutral source about workplace issues, and anyone else is partisan and unreliable.

We have to accept that enforcing the rights written into workplace law means communicating across a huge chasm. Those familiar with labor law often forget just how uncomfortable is the fit between our common-law legal tradition and the NLRA. The judicial amendments that led to striker replacement and weak remedies are only a symptom of this gulf that divides the legal and practical understanding between the NLRB and appellate judges. This division cannot be ignored if we are to reverse the judicial amendments. Cases must be tried that demonstrate to judges how fundamentally the NLRA "violates" common-law principles. Cases must show judges why, nonetheless, NLRA rights must be enforced. This gulf of understanding means that to enforce the NLRA and other workplace laws at odds with the common law and cultural norms, we must use different strategies than we would if labor law were based on the spirit of the common law.

The NAACP Legal Defense Fund's fight for racial equality and equity teaches us important lessons about developing a legal strategy. First, success depends on being ready for a long struggle. *Brown v. Board of Education*[2] was decided in 1954 after more than two decades of litigation that strategically attacked winnable targets. Each victory incrementally moved the cause forward. In other words, the NAACP LDF used the common law's tendency to incrementalism as one of their weapons.

Second, the NAACP LDF chose its targets wisely. The NAACP LDF lawyers filed cases that had the greatest potential to be understood by judges and thus to gain judges' synmpathy. Had they filed a *Brown v. Board of Education*–type case in 1930 in order to desegregate public schools, they would have lost. Desegregating public school education from kindergarten through undergraduate was a sensitive issue that involved mixing of races and genders and could have touched off fears of miscegenation. Graduate and professional education, on the other hand, was a more promising target. Most of the students at those levels were male, so there was less concern for interracial dating and marriage. By the time *Brown* was filed, NAACP efforts to change society's views about racial injustice and NAACP LDF legal victories had created a climate in which success was more likely.

Third, when the NAACP Legal Defense Fund began its attack on segregated education in the early 1930s, it chose as its earliest cases those that involved race-based admission to law school. Choosing a law school over other professional or graduate schools meant trying cases in which judges needed less education to understand the consequences of their decisions. Judges "know a great deal about law schools and how to compare them. They are law school graduates and they spend their professional lives working with law school graduates. They have an expertise in the subject matter far beyond that which they have in other kinds of cases." The court opinion in *Pearson v. Murray* (1936)[3] noted that if a student were barred from attending the state's law school, "he would miss the benefits of a state law school education, specifically gaining a familiarity with the courts of the state in which he intended to practice law."[4]

In contrast, not only do judges not have this familiarity with labor law, but labor law actually undercuts the legal concepts with which judges are familiar. In addition, they do not come from backgrounds where they have personal experience with collective bargaining, at least not on the union side. This means that every aspect of NLRA cases must be presented with a consciousness that the very purpose of the Act was to supplant fundamental laws that controlled the workplace and that are still the default mode for controlling workplace relations. Just as law students must learn to think like lawyers before they can be successful in practice, so, too, must non-labor lawyers—and especially judges—be helped to learn to think like labor lawyers as they decide NLRA cases.

The NAACP LDF lawyers faced similar problems: how to make visible to the judges what was not visible to them. The most well-known example of this evidence was the use of research by Kenneth B. Clark and Mamie Clark to demonstrate the ways racism harmed children. The Clarks testified about the reaction of children, even as young as three, when they were asked to choose which doll they preferred to play with, which doll they liked best, which doll was the nice doll, which doll looked bad, and which doll had a nice color. The choice was between brown-skinned and white-skinned dolls.[5]

Unfortunately, all too often, this is not done when NLRB cases are tried. As a result, the record lacks fundamental information judges need to understand the issues, the facts, and the impact of their decisions. Even more baffling, nothing is done to help judges even in briefs to and arguments before the courts of appeals. When I was a judicial law clerk—and already knew I wanted a career in labor law—I saw several cases argued on appeal by NLRB lawyers. Their arguments were rote, full of specialized jargon, and based on assumptions and knowledge the judges did not have. I watched the judges puzzled as their questions went unanswered. Richard Michael Fischl, a former NLRB attorney, describes how NLRB cases on Section 7 rights are litigated:

> At the most banal level, of course, there are influences that arise from the institutional context. . . . The presence of a repeat player with a powerful institutional memory can have a dramatic—and quite conservative—impact on the way cases are pitched to the judiciary. (I can almost hear one of the deputy assistant general counsels I worked with now: "Defending a sympathy striker? No problem. Look up that Hand opinion in *Peter Cailler*; and you might want to take a peek at our brief in *Eastex*.")[6]

Professor Michael Hayes observes:

> The National Labor Relations Board is a specialized agency that is focused exclusively on the National Labor Relations Act. Every day, day af-

ter day, the five members of the Board, their staff lawyers, and the administrative law judges and regional directors whose decisions the Board reviews, devote their time and attention entirely to the National Labor Relations Act. These Board decision makers review thousands of cases each year, they rule on the same relatively narrow band of issues again and again, and, consequently, they become thoroughly familiar with these issues and all their ramifications. By contrast, for federal appellate judges, labor law is but one small part of an entire body of federal law (and even state law, in diversity cases) that they must administer. Empirical studies of federal circuit courts' workloads have found that NLRB appeals constitute only about 1% of the courts' dockets. And of this relatively small pool of cases, a substantial number are settled, so that an even lower percentage of labor cases are actually decided by appellate judges. Professor Daniel Meador has contended that when an appellate court does not decide a "critical mass" of cases in a subject area, the court will perform inadequately in ruling on such cases, and he cited NLRB cases as one type in which courts were likely to be deficient.

Even if one does not accept Professor Meador's "critical mass" theory, the fact remains that the odds are against an appellate judge's being able to build up an expertise in labor law and policy.[7]

NLRA cases do not have to be tried or argued this way, but they are. I saw only one case in which the NLRB attorney spoke directly to the judges about the difficult parts of the case. She understood Judge Robert Vance's caution that NLRB cases, though argued by professionals, are decided by amateurs.[8] She gracefully and respectfully gave the judges clear explanations as to why the facts showed that the law had been broken and what the judges need to do to enforce it. She gave clear, respectful answers that spoke to judges' level of understanding. The judges peppered her with questions, even about labor questions not directly part of her case. It seemed to me that they were relieved at last to get answers for questions that had long puzzled them. When the NLRB attorney finished her argument, it was easy to see she had carried the day.

Trying an NLRA case means being prepared to educate and explain. It means being conscious that few judges have been labor lawyers, and few will have law clerks who have taken even a single labor law class. Law clerks are drawn almost exclusively from the most elite law schools in the country and therefore are unlikely to have experience with the lives of working-class people—white or blue collar. Judges with no training in labor law before coming onto the bench have little opportunity to improve their understanding once on the bench. Chances are they will find NLRA cases to be baffling and not exciting or inspiring. Their natural instincts will be that troublemakers who are fired because they betrayed their employers by trying to unionize their workplaces deserve what they get.[9]

But it must not be forgotten that judges and law clerks are trained—and sworn—to enforce the law and see justice done. In the case of labor law, if judges are to enforce the law, someone must help them understand how to do this. Someone must explain the significance of the facts and connect them to NLRA law and policies. The NLRB and union attorney must anticipate the unique difficulties at every stage of each case and be proactive about meeting them. It is too late to do this by filing an amicus brief before the Board or waiting until oral argument before the court of appeals.

The most fundamental education needs to be about the very existence of the NLRA's policies and goals. Few cases even refer to specific goals listed in Section 1 or Section 7's methods for achieving those goals. When they do, the goals most often mentioned are promoting labor peace or interstate commerce. These are easy goals for common-law judges to understand. Unfortunately, they are likely to have a narrow view of what these mean, so they will see them met when there is short-term labor peace achieved by an employer's imposing its will and suppressing disagreement. Such a result might be attractive to a common-law judge because it fits with a preexisting understanding that the employer has the right to control the workplace. However, the NLRA's drafters did not intend a type of peace bought at the price of retaining the hierarchy of master and servant law.[10]

This sort of labor peace ignores fundamental NLRA policies, such as those of "restoring equality of bargaining power between employers and employees," "encouraging the practice and procedure of collective bargaining," and "protecting the exercise by workers of full freedom of association, self-organization, and designation of representatives of their own choosing, for the purpose of negotiating the terms and conditions of their employment or other mutual aid or protection."

It has to be acknowledged and accepted that not all NLRA policies have widespread support among the public, let alone among federal judges and their law clerks. The NLRA's policies oppose acts that depress wage rates and purchasing power. They also promote "the stabilization of competitive wage rates and working conditions within and between industries." This does not fit with a view that it is normal and just for employers to move work to countries with the lowest wages and least regulation. If NLRA cases were interpreted to promote the goals of preventing depressed wage rates and cutthroat competition, employers could not defend against violations by claiming their actions were based on seeking lower labor costs, as they now can.

The judges who sit on this country's courts of appeals set labor policy and determine labor's fate as they decide each case. If unions are to improve their lot, every NLRA case must be tried in a way that makes it impossible for courts to consciously or unconsciously evade the NLRA's commands. Even though not every case goes to the court of appeals, every case must be analyzed and tried as if it were headed there. This means creating a new way of trying NLRB cases by committing more resources of thought, time, and money in framing issues, trial preparation, trial, and posttrial briefing. It also means a commitment to building the infrastructure that supports these efforts.

Helping Common-Law Judges Decide Cases

To reverse years of judicial amendments and take back the Workers' Law NLRB cases must be litigated in a wholly new way. The judges who review NLRB cases are intelligent, experienced lawyers, but, as pointed out previously, few have studied labor law. Therefore, cases need to be litigated in a way that respects judges' strengths and offers them information and assistance where necessary.[11]

Judges are not legally allowed merely to substitute their judgment for the NLRB's. If the NLRB has done its job properly, the law requires judges to uphold its decisions. The Board's findings of fact are supposed to be conclusive when they are supported by "substantial evidence in the record."[12] However, we know that other factors affect how judges view evidence and how they understand the NLRA. Given this, it makes no sense not to try cases in a way that makes it easy for judges to enforce the NLRA—and difficult not to.

Cases must be tried with a conscious focus on illuminating the violation, the NLRA's policies, the remedy, and how these fit together. To try a winning case means more than merely putting the facts of a violation in evidence or mentioning NLRA policies in a posthearing brief or completely ignoring them. The labor lawyer cannot assume that merely proving a violation will result in the appropriate remedy. It is the lawyer's—not the judges'—job to connect the dots.

In other words, the evidence must do more than demonstrate that certain acts have taken place; it must show how those actions violate the Act's language and purposes and why a particular remedy is appropriate in promoting those purposes. For many years to come, NLRB cases must include detailed and persuasive evidence as to why the current interpretations must be reversed.

This strategy has already been proven to be effective. For example, consider a recent case on union dues and dues dissenters handed down by the Ninth Circuit Court of Appeals. In *United Food & Commercial Workers Union, Local 1036 v. NLRB*,[13] the dissenters argued that their dues should not include money to be used to organize those who worked for other employers. The legal standard the court had to apply was whether organizing those other workers affected working conditions in the dissenters' bargaining units. The NLRB had already decided that the dissenters' dues should include the cost of organizing new members. This case was not tried in the traditional way. It did not merely put in the bare facts of nonpayment and argue on the basis of legal precedent that the court should defer to the agency's expertise in labor matters. This sort of trial approach makes it easy for courts of appeals to reverse the Board's decisions because there is nothing in the record evidence to support its findings.

In this case, however, the record included testimony about research on the effect that levels of unionization in a community have on bargaining results. The decision states:

> The NLRB's conclusion in this case that extra-bargaining unit organizing is germane to collective bargaining and a proper use of nonmembers' dues was supported by extensive economic research and data on organizing and collective bargaining in general, as well as with respect to the retail food industry. Expert testimony by several witnesses established that generally economists have found "a positive relationship between the extent of unionization of employees in an industry or locality and negotiated wage rates." Numerous studies by economists and labor scholars also documented a significant positive relationship between the rate of unionization and the negotiated wage rates in several union shop industries in the retail food area. Case studies of specific retail food geographic markets also confirmed the results of the statistical studies. The NLRB's findings reveal that

management is far more willing to negotiate higher wage rates when its competitors are subject to the same union costs. Conversely, management is comparatively unwilling to yield to union demands when its competitors are not subject to similar obligations and costs.[14]

The NLRB and UFCW were able to persuade these judges because they did more than just present compelling evidence in support of a particular outcome, although that certainly was important. Every competent lawyer tries to do this, and competent lawyering is certainly an essential part of what I advocate. Competent lawyers present the best witnesses they can find to testify about what the witness saw and heard. Competent lawyers write well-researched briefs that argue for the credibility of their witnesses and for the applicability of specific cases to the facts. Competent judges can read statutes and cases and make decisions about what law applies to the facts.

However, the litigation strategy I advocate requires far more than this and something far more difficult. It requires trying to anticipate each detail and nuance that judges will not understand and then figuring out how to help them understand. The NLRB and UFCW did exactly this. They presented economic studies and expert witnesses on the connection between level of unionization and the terms of collective bargaining agreements, rather than presuming or simply arguing that such a relationship existed.

In retrospect it is obvious that this evidence was critical to their success. However, before they tried the case, someone had to understand that proving—not just assuming—that a connection between level of unionization and collective bargaining mattered. Sadly, in most NLRB trials, no one realizes that winning depends on including exactly this sort of evidence. This is not to fault attorneys. It has been traditional to try NLRB cases based on expert knowledge and assumptions, and this worked well for decades. But the time has come to break with that tradition.

Even though it should be obvious that the NLRA cannot be enforced by trying cases using expert knowledge and assumptions, many barriers stand in the way of taking a new path. These cases will be longer, more complex, and thus more expensive in a time when budgets are tight. NLRB administrative law judges are likely to balk at permitting evidence on issues that are obvious to them because of their training. This will often put attorneys at odds with what judges assume should be included as evidence, and attorneys try not to annoy judges.

The greatest barrier is not time or money, however; it is changing minds and thinking about the nature of NLRB trials. It means focusing trial preparation and strategy beyond the administrative law judge to the court of appeals judges, even though the case will not reach the appellate level for a few years, if ever. Labor attorneys need to put aside their expertise, erase years of experience applying the law, remember the puzzlement a student has when first learning labor law, and figure out how to answer those questions and respond to that puzzlement. It means predicting what judges' gaps in knowledge and experience will be and consciously trying a case in a way that encourages judges to use new knowledge and rethink assumptions. It also means being conscious of one's own assumptions about the law of a case and its facts; actively challenging them; and then using the knowledge produced by that process to generate evidence and construct the case.

The process of making the invisible visible may seem obvious when outlined this way, but it is difficult to put into practice. Simply making arguments in briefs is not sufficient. Compare the outcome in *United Food and Commercial Workers* with the NLRB's effort to create a new remedy in *Cherokee Marine Terminal*.[15] Former General Counsel Rosemary Collyer wanted all Board orders to include a "visitatorial" clause that would give a Board agent access to an employer's facility to ensure it was complying with the terms of a court order.[12] Because courts tend to see the employer as having a special interest in "his" property, this was not a change they would take lightly. Collyer, however, did nothing to meet this concern. She simply had each brief include a boilerplate argument that a visitatorial clause should be an automatic remedy in every case.

It should come as no surprise that this strategy was doomed. Neither the courts nor the Board was willing to accept such a clause when there was no evidence in the record to support the change.[16] The Board in *Cherokee Marine Terminal* said:

> Such a clause would permit the Board to examine the books and records of a respondent and to take statements from its officers and employees and others for the purpose of determining or securing compliance with a court-enforced order. Counsel for the General Counsel first requested this clause in the posthearing brief to the judge pursuant to instructions from the General Counsel as part of an effort to persuade the Board to include visitatorial clauses in all remedial orders. Thus, the specific request was based not

on the facts of this case but on more general arguments regarding the Board's enforcement powers and recurring compliance problems in prior unrelated cases.[17]

After losing a number of cases as a result of pursuing an argument-only strategy and producing no trial record to support the request, the General Counsel simply gave up. Unfortunately, this is the way that most NLRB cases are tried, rather than using the methods that led to success in the *United Food and Commercial Workers Union* case.

Creating the Record

If a litigation strategy best succeeds when it applies the lessons from *United Food and Commercial Workers Union, Local 1036 v. NLRB*—creating a clear trial record that speaks to and demonstrates to the courts of appeals how to enforce the NLRA's policies—where is this evidence to come from?

One source is to present expert witnesses to testify about social science research relevant to the issues being litigated in a case. In the cases that were consolidated and argued as *Brown v. Board of Education*,[18] expert witnesses were used to demonstrate the psychological injuries caused by segregation, to expose the purposes of segregation, and to refute widely held beliefs. The result was that, if judges were intellectually honest, the extensive trial record made it impossible to uphold segregated education, despite the influence of long-standing traditions and legal precedent.[19] In fact, social science evidence was submitted by the NLRA in support of the 1937 Supreme Court decision that held the NLRA constitutional.[20] The Court there took the employer to task for failing to respond to the evidence presented and for relying only on its "constitutional" rights.[21]

Using an expert to explain research and its significance is a critical part of developing a record that non-social scientists can understand. It also makes the most effective use of their research. Judge Strine observes:

> The adjudicative process obviously hampers the judge's ability to put her hands on an unbiased, and sufficiently thorough, sample of the literature, much less to understand it fully. The joyous and, at times, maddening complexity of the human experience confounds the ability of social science to describe the way things are with the certainty that is often achievable in

some aspects of the natural sciences. Judges reviewing a skewed and incomplete body of difficult-to-understand social science articles whose composition is shaped largely by time-pressured personal research and citations by self-interested litigating adversaries must proceed with some hesitance. When possible, empirical evidence should be presented through live, expert testimony so that the judge can go beyond the cold page to an active dialogue with the social scientists on both sides of the question, aided by adversarial examinations.[22]

Unfortunately, labor attorneys are like these befuddled judges. Few labor lawyers have the expertise themselves to use experts. Few are familiar with social science research. This means that those trying cases before the NLRB need to develop new skills so they can be comfortable and effective in their use.

It is also possible that the necessary research has yet to be done. Research on labor issues has languished in recent years. For a labor law reform litigation strategy to succeed, it is critical to develop empirical evidence that shows whether and what change is appropriate and necessary to promote the NLRA's policies. Unfortunately, our knowledge of how many of the judicial amendments operate and whether they promote or undermine NLRA policies is unsystematic and based primarily on theory. We need reliable and relevant data, developed through case studies, surveys, simulations, and other experimental methods. This research can be used as part of a litigation strategy to change the NLRA. It could also be presented in support of statutory reform, should there be an opportunity to improve existing labor law.

Experts other than social scientists can be used to develop other sorts of evidence. Expert testimony can come from union representatives, mediators, lawyers, and employees whose experience qualifies them as experts on certain issues. For example, union officials can testify about their observations of the impact of standard remedies and how they are insufficient to promote the purposes and policies of the NLRA. The point is that a whole new group of witnesses addressing an entirely new set of issues must be brought into NLRB trials. Some may hesitate to use practitioners. While they have valuable experience, their testimony can be impeached as coming from biased witnesses. This does not mean it has no value. It means care must be taken in finding appropriate witnesses and being prepared to present them in ways that support their credibility.

Trial attorneys need to consider ways to make the greatest use of each witness. An example comes from my days as a judicial law clerk. A large part of the law clerks' caseload was Social Security disability appeals. Just as is the case with court of appeals judges, we saw only the transcript and parties' briefs. The cases were all short, and the transcripts and exhibits all followed a formula and, as a result, were similar to the way NLRB cases are tried. The applicant was briefly examined about the disability; a vocational expert was called about jobs the applicant could perform; and a few documents were put into evidence.

In one case, however, the attorney veered off this path dramatically. Rather than merely asking his client whether she was in pain and to describe the pain, he periodically would ask her, "I notice you are moving around in your seat constantly. Is there a reason for that?" "Yes." "What is the reason?" "If I sit still for more than a few minutes, the pain in my back gets so bad I can't bear it." "Would it help if you stood up?" "Yes." After a few minutes of standing, the process repeated itself. The witness's testimony and the medical records had stated—as did those of many other applicants—that she was unable to sit or stand or lie down for more than a few minutes without being in such pain she had to move to a different position. In all those other cases, the witness had said nothing during the time she was examined. Yet in this case the problem was not only stated; it was illustrated.

More cases need to be tried so they illustrate what is at stake. Nothing less will restore the NLRA to its original purpose. This method requires that the lawyer who tries the case think about more than proving the facts of what was said when and meeting the opposing side's evidence. It means providing evidence as to the goals of the NLRA and demonstrating and explaining how the issues in the case being tried connect with those goals.

The discussion so far assumes that the NLRB attorney, the Counsel for the General Counsel, is willing to use the litigation strategy. But what if the General Counsel is unwilling or unable to do so?[23] In that case, and perhaps in all cases, unions must be prepared to take the lead in developing and presenting this evidence and in identifying areas of law to target. Unions are the only ones who have been so negatively affected by the judicial amendments, and they have the greatest interest in taking the steps necessary to change this law.

This new way of trying cases provides a useful—and perhaps the only—

way to "amend" the NLRA in order to make it effective in the way its drafters intended. It may not seem as straightforward as new legislation and starting from a clean slate. But new legislation does not guarantee success, nor is it less expensive. To enact a new statute, there must be agreement on its contents. This must be accompanied by intense and expensive lobbying for the new law, and a majority of Congress and the president must support the new law. The reality is that the NLRA is already the law, and we need to work to improve what exists. This means support for targeted litigation, the encouragement of useful research, the development of expertise in areas relevant to litigation, and the employment of creative litigation techniques.

While litigation is the focus of this book, litigation, no matter how well done, cannot succeed alone. It must be supported by efforts to reach the wider society so it understands and appreciates the value of unionism and of the NLRA. There must be a parallel campaign of education. The rest of this book provides a foundation for creating both a litigation strategy and these parallel strategies.

3

NLRA VALUES, AMERICAN VALUES

The NLRA's policies are far more than a list of goals. They embody values that were intended to, and still can, transform our workplaces and our society. NLRA policies are supposed to empower workers, promote worker solidarity, and support workplaces governed by collective bargaining between parties with equal bargaining power. These policies, in turn, are supposed to lead to the NLRA policies of improved wages and working conditions throughout society—not just in individual workplaces. The result will be to promote the NLRA's policies of industrial and social peace and the free flow of commerce. For far too long, the NLRA's policies have been forgotten, to the harm of our society. No strategy to take back the Workers' Law can succeed unless built on the bedrock of the NLRA's policies and the values they embody.

Why NLRA Values and Policies Matter

NLRA policies matter in two ways. First, they say that work and the way workers are treated are central to the sort of country this is. The NLRA's values are emphatically pro-democracy. Its policies set out steps to give us workplaces consistent with a democracy and to empower workers by giving them the skills needed to be citizens of a democracy.[1] They say that the welfare of our country depends on what happens within the workplace between employer and employee.

The NLRA's vision of what leads to a just and democratic society is what unions need if they are to survive and thrive. It supports the fundamental mission of unions: to improve wages and other working conditions, to promote workplace justice, to support employee bargaining power, and to help workers stand together and advocate for one another. My experience is that workers seek union representation out of a deep sense of unfairness. A noble vision of the role unions can play in promoting fairness is one that will appeal to American workers.[2]

Second, NLRA polices and values play a practical role in enforcing the law. They are the standard against which every labor case must be decided.[3] These policies include promoting collective bargaining; safeguarding workers' full freedom of association, self-organization, and choice of representatives; acting in solidarity for mutual aid and protection; achieving equality of bargaining power; protecting the right to strike; preventing business depressions; improving wage rates; increasing the purchasing power of wage earners; and stabilizing competitive wage rates and working conditions within and between industries. In other words, we can and must assess each decision in NLRA cases by asking whether and how it promotes one or more of these policies. Any decision that does not promote NLRA values is not a legal interpretation of the NLRA.

Unfortunately, NLRA values and policies have too often been forgotten, their power untapped. We see the result in the decline of unions and increasing inequality and worker disempowerment. But these policies are still the law, and the time has come to use and promote them if the NLRA is to be effective.

How can they make a difference? Suppose we wanted to improve NLRA remedies. The NLRA does not have a rigid scheme of remedies. Rather, what we tend to think of as NLRA remedies have been created by NLRB and judicial interpretations.

> Congress deliberately drafted section 10(c) to include all reasonable remedies consistent with the Act's purposes. The final version of section 10(c), authorizing "such affirmative actions . . . as will effectuate the policies of [the NLRA]" replaced earlier provisions that had enumerated specific types of remedies available to the Board. The broader language was intended to "delegate to the Board the primary responsibility for making remedial decisions that best effectuate the policies of the [NLRA]." The Board's choice of remedy "should stand unless it can be shown that the order is a patent

attempt to achieve ends other than those which can fairly be said to effectuate the policies of the Act." And, "[the court is] obliged to defer heavily to the Board's remedial decisions."[4]

In other words, the NLRA says that remedies for unfair labor practices must make the Act's policies effective. The NLRB is an expert agency whose job it is to ensure its decisions accomplish this goal.[5] If a remedy does not make NLRA policies effective then, by law, the NLRB must find a remedy that will.

This means that remedies can be strengthened without having to enact a new statute. Litigation can be used to persuade the NLRB and judges to impose remedies that promote NLRA policies by (1) identifying the policies that apply to the violation and the injury it has caused, (2) identifying in detail how current remedies for the violation do or do not promote specific NLRA values, (3) identifying remedies that can undo the harm and promote those policies, and (4) developing a plan for proving at trial why the standard remedy does not promote NLRA policies and why the proposed remedies will promote those values. There is a fifth issue created by a judicial amendment. The Supreme Court's 1938 decision in *Consolidated Edison Co. v. NLRB*[6] holds that NLRB remedies may be only remedial, not punitive. As long *Consolidated Edison* is the law, it is necessary to demonstrate why a proposed remedy is not imposed in order to punish the violator.

Consider how the strategy would be used to improve backpay remedies for workers who have been illegally discharged during an election campaign. Instead of appealing to policy or NLRB expertise, lawyers would put evidence in the record that demonstrates exactly how such a discharge undermines NLRA policies that promote self-organization, mutual aid and protection, equality of bargaining power and collective bargaining. The evidence must demonstrate why the current standard for calculating backpay does not promote those policies. The proofs must also show what level of backpay will ensure that workers feel free to exercise their right to organize a union.

It is not sufficient, however, to focus only on the injured workers. The Act cannot be effective unless its remedies encourage the employer who committed the unfair labor practice—and other employers—to abide by the law and respect workers' legal right to organize. Meeting the concerns of *Consolidated Edison* is difficult because of the case's logic. The Court said remedies are punitive when they are imposed to deter violations. This suggests that effective remedies cannot be imposed, but it is not necessary to go that far. The proofs should demonstrate that the remedy is imposed not to punish but to remove the consequences of the violation, which would otherwise thwart the Act's purposes. It may be that this remedy does deter future violations, but any remedy has some deterrent effect. The Supreme Court did not say that there can be no remedies for NLRA violations. Remedies that pass muster seem to be ones that do not have deterrence as their main purpose. Clearly, *Consolidated Edison* undercuts Section 10(c) and, as a result, makes the NLRA less effective than it should be. Therefore, any litigation strategy must have overturning *Consolidated Edison* as a long-term goal.

Critics of the NLRA argue that its basic remedy for bad faith bargaining—an order to bargain in good faith—is worthless. They say it does nothing to keep an employer who has been found to have violated the law from going back to the same illegal bargaining practices it has already used to deprive employees of their NLRA rights to bargain collectively.

What, then, would be an effective remedy for bad faith bargaining? Ordering a party who has bargained in bad faith to agree to a specific term might be effective. It would restore to the injured party what it had lost and take away any advantages gained from bad faith bargaining. It might encourage good faith bargaining in the future. But it is not an option. The Supreme Court has held that the NLRB may not order an employer or union to agree to any contractual provision.[7] On the other hand, an order to go to interest arbitration on the parties' proposals could have many of these desirable effects while not running afoul of the Supreme Court's ruling.

Interest arbitration is used widely in the public sector by law and can be used in the private sector to set the terms of a bargaining agreement through arbitration rather than negotiation. Interest arbitration is similar to grievance or dispute arbitration in that each party presents evidence to the arbitrator in support of its proposed terms. Depending on the type of interest arbitration, the arbitrator then picks either one complete proposal or assembles a contract by picking terms from each proposal.

Interest arbitration would better promote equality of bargaining power after unfair labor practices had been committed than would a bargaining order. It would make it impossible to use bad faith bargaining to delay agreement because parties do not have unsupervised license to drag out negotiations. It might also make good faith bargaining more attractive than delaying tactics, because the price of bad faith bargaining is losing the ability to have a say in the contract's terms. In addition, each party must provide evidence in support of its proposals. This means that the employer would have to open its books and demonstrate that its records support its proposals. The union could also be given discovery of the employer's records so it could present the case for its proposals. Neither of these is likely to be attractive to an employer and might persuade this and other employers that bargaining is to be preferred.

Interest arbitration is just one example of a remedy for bad faith bargaining, but others are possible and might be more appropriate, depending on the situation. In every case, careful thought should be given to what would be an appropriate remedy, and to the evidence that would demonstrate this. The same basic strategy should be used to overturn even well-entrenched doctrines that do not promote NLRA policies, such as striker replacement. The idea that the NLRA's policies should matter in deciding cases is not new. In NLRB v. *Curtin Matheson Scientific, Inc.*,[8] the Supreme Court said that the Board "may adopt rules restricting conduct that threatens to destroy the collective-bargaining relationship or that may impair employees' right to engage in concerted activity." In *Trans World Airlines, Inc. v. Independent Federation of Flight Attendants*,[9] Justice Blackmun reminded his fellow justices that they should not issue decisions whose logic undermines the basic purpose of a statute. He argued that an employer "cannot be permitted to reap rewards from a strike so much in excess of the rewards of negotiation that it will 'have a strong reason to prolong the strike and even break the union.'" Blackmun criticized the majority's interpretation because it encouraged "employers to test the limits" of the law. By doing this, the Court "needlessly creates incentives to undermine long-term labor stability and to expand labor conflicts beyond their natural bounds."[10]

Judges are not the only ones who have forgotten about the NLRA's policies. Even people who regularly handle NLRA cases need to learn about its policies and the opportunities they present to remake and strengthen the Workers' Law. The rest of this chapter explores NLRA polices as the foundation to taking back the law.

The NLRA Workplace and Society

In Section 1 the NLRA begins by painting two pictures of society and work, employers and employees. In the first, it shows the dangers to society when there is a power imbalance in the workplace. It then explores how this unequal power between employers and employees came about. Finally, the NLRA presents its vision for curing the imbalance and laying the foundation for a very different sort of society.

The NLRA's first picture portrays a society with a power imbalance that is similar to ours today. Wage rates and the purchasing power of wage earners were depressed because employers had so much power they could compete by lowering working conditions. With wages depressed, workers were able to buy little. This led to a society plagued with recurring business depressions. Eventually, workers reached their limits and struck back. Society itself was being destroyed.

Today both corporation law and free trade agreements have given corporations greater power by removing trade barriers on goods and money and thus made it easier to outsource work, both nationally and globally. Globalization is a complex phenomenon, so it should be no surprise that there are conflicting studies on its causes and impact. Changes in technology, in particular computers and the internet, have made it possible and easier to outsource work. It will be several years before we can accurately assess its effects.

Whether caused by globalization or not, we see signs of increasing corporate power[11] and decreasing employee power. The effects of these trends have led to worsening working conditions for workers, especially low-waged workers.[12] Since January 2001, the nation has lost 2.7 million manufacturing jobs.[13] Bureau of Labor Statistics data show that the rate of job creation has been anemic in recent years. In June 2001, unemployment began increasing, hitting levels over 6 percent. Although it has declined to about 5 percent in 2005, there are other disturbing workforce trends that suggest this is not a sign of an improving economy. In particular, the percentage of labor force participation has continued to decline since 2000. This suggests that unemployment may have declined because of factors such as discouraged workers dropping out of the search for work and large numbers of people deployed in Iraq and Afghanistan. The unemployment rate does not measure all people who have no work. Rather, the government classifies as unemployed only people have been actively looking for work in the prior four weeks and are currently available for work. As a result, discouraged job seekers who have given up looking for work, prisoners, and active duty and injured soldiers are not counted as unemployed. Indeed, a recent report by the Federal Reserve Bank of Boston found that current unemployment rates are not presenting an accurate picture of the economy for many of these reasons. It also concluded that there appears to be a high level of slack in the economy.[14] This report concludes that the true unemployment rate may be from 1 to 3 percentage points higher than the official figure.

Persistently high unemployment rates may explain why one-fourth of the U.S. workforce earns poverty wages[15] and why wages have been declining. The official poverty rate in 2004 was 12.7 percent, up from 12.5 percent in 2003, and in 2004, 37.0 million people were in poverty, up 1.1 million from 2003.[16] In eleven of the thirteen months from May 2004 through May 2005, real wages have declined.[17] In other words, wages are not keeping up with inflation. We see a very different picture for top executives. Executives at the 50 largest outsourcers of service jobs made an average of $10.4 million in 2003, 46 percent more than they as a group received the previous year and 28 percent more than the average large-company CEO. The gap between CEO pay and worker pay is growing. In 2004, executive pay was up 45 percent. The ratio between CEO pay and worker pay is now 431:1, up from 282:1 in 2002. If the minimum wage had increased at the same rate as CEO pay has since 1990, the minimum wage would today be $23.03 per hour, rather than $5.15 per hour.[18] Put another way, we are seeing increasing income inequality in this country. The share of national income going to the bottom 80 percent of wage earners is lower than it was in 1980, while the share for the top 20 percent is higher.[19]

One explanation for the failure of wages to increase could be low productivity, but that is not the case. Compensation has grown only 37 percent as fast as productivity. Since 2001, most of the income growth from higher productivity has gone to corporate profits, in contrast with other business cycles where most of the income growth has gone to workers' pay.[20]

Statistics are useful in seeing our current economic situation. However, to understand them it is also helpful to have information about the individual effects of these trends. David Shipler's recent book, *The Working Poor: Invisible in America*[21] puts a human face on the poor and explores the forces that have put them in this condition.

The cause of the problems described in Section 1 of the NLRA was that law, especially corporation law, helped one side—employers—to become collective and immortal. Employers were able to gain power far in excess of that of individual employees, who lacked not only equal bargaining power but also freedom of association. This left employees unable to contract as equals with employers.

The NLRA also says that the private workplace is not truly private because what happens at work does not remain there. It spills out into society, and society as a whole pays the price for inequality. The NLRA also creates a process to remedy workplace inequality and thus to repair societies, such as ours today, where we see unparalleled levels of corporate power and workers whose wages and benefits have stagnated for years.

The NLRA's most basic policies are Sections 1 and 7. They give employees the right to give one another mutual aid and protection, to seek union representation, and to bargain for better working conditions. Both protect employee voice and collective power.[22] Section 13 protects the right to strike. Finally, Section 2(3) says that employees have the legal right to aid one another, even if they work for different employers.[23]

NLRA rights are built on the value of employee solidarity. Staughton Lynd says that NLRA rights are communal rights and that unions are built on collective values:

> I suggest that the right of workers "to engage in concerted activities for . . . mutual aid or protection" now guaranteed by federal labor law is an example of a communal right. More than any other institution in capitalist society, the labor movement is based on communal values. Its central historical experience is solidarity, the banding together of individual workers who are alone too weak to protect themselves. Thus, there has arisen the value expressed by the phrase, "an injury to one is an injury to all." To be sure, at times particular labor organizations, and to some extent trade unionism in general, fall short of this communal aspiration. Yet it is significant that trade union members still address one another as "Brother" and "Sister" and sign their correspondence "Fraternally yours."[24]

The NLRA's policies protect fundamental values and provide processes to enforce them and create a good society for all. Some polices promote personal values, while others promote commercial values. The NLRA's personal processes and values include the following:

promoting equality of bargaining power between employees and employers creating actual liberty of contract

protecting the right of employees to organize and protecting employees' exercise of self-organization

protecting employees' exercise of full freedom of association

protecting employees' right to mutual aid or protection

ensuring employees' right to self-organize and to form, join, or assist labor organizations

protecting employees' exercise of choosing their own representatives

protecting the right of employees to bargain collectively and encouraging the practice and procedure of collective bargaining

encouraging practices that lead to the friendly adjustment of disputes about wages, hours, or other working conditions

protecting employees' right to negotiate the terms and conditions of their employment

safeguarding the right to strike

The NLRA's commercial values include the following goals designed to promote the interests of individual workers, employers, and society as a whole:

improving wage rates

increasing the purchasing power of wage earners

stabilizing competitive wage rates and working conditions within and between industries

promoting the free flow of commerce

preventing business depressions

In 1947, the Labor-Management Relations Act (Taft-Hartley) added additional policy goals. These coexist with the original NLRA values:

eliminating practices by some labor organizations that burden or obstruct the free flow of goods in commerce and that impede the rights guaranteed by the Act

protecting individual employees' freedom to refrain from joining unions, engaging in collective activities, and engaging in collective bargaining

It is a great loss that, for nearly seventy years, most of the NLRA's values have remained unexplored and virtually unused. Even though the courts and the NLRB itself should be guided by these policies when they decide whether some action violates the law and what remedies are necessary to promote the NLRA's purpose, they are not. It is a rare case that even touches on any NLRA policy.[25] At best they are given mere lip service. The core personal rights of equality of bargaining power, actual freedom of contract, freedom to choose a representative, and collective bargaining are rarely cited by courts. Instead, the personal rights the courts most often cite are the right to refrain from engaging in NLRA rights and encouraging the friendly adjustment of disputes.

This is a highly selective and truncated list of NLRA rights. "Encouraging the friendly adjustment of disputes" is an edited version of encouraging *"practices that lead to* the friendly adjustment of disputes about wages, hours, or other working conditions." The truncated version radically alters a key underpinning of the NLRA.

Indeed, Robert Wagner, the author of the NLRA, saw "the important legislative goals of industrial peace and macro-economic growth and stabilization" as

> always secondary to the achievement of social justice through democratic consent in the workplace. As to industrial peace, Wagner often advanced the proposition that tranquil labor relationships were not the sole consideration: "It all depends upon the basis of tranquility. The slave system of the old South was as tranquil as a summer's day, but that is no reason for perpetuating in modern industry any of the aspects of a master-servant relationship."[26]

The commercial values that the courts most frequently name are also highly selective, limited to promoting the free flow of commerce. It is hard to find a mention of the importance of improving wage rates, increasing the purchasing power of wage earners, or stabilizing competitive wage rates and working conditions within and between industries.

In short, the NLRA policies and rights cited by the courts suggest they see the NLRA as a narrow statute whose purpose is to promote resolving disputes, even when the resolution means trampling on the rights to freedom of association and collective bargaining. Judges elevate individual rights over collective rights, even when the individual rights undercut the rights of the majority. Courts also reflect what has become the popular view today that we must value commerce even when it undermines wages and working conditions. Unions need to be clear that these interpretations are wrong and that, as the NLRA predicted, they are destroying this society. Robert Wagner rejected this narrow view:

> Although Wagner was one of the earliest advocates of counter-cyclical public spending and redistribution to sustain mass purchasing power, he often said unequivocally that "the moral injustice of gross inequality . . . is more important than its economic unsoundness. . . . Economic stabilization is desirable; social justice is imperative." Wagner further insisted, in an exchange of letters with John Dewey, that even if distributive justice could be achieved by tax-and-transfer policies, the latter would not remedy the injustice of authoritarianism within workplace relations. Only collective empowerment would implement "the new freedom"—"a freedom for self-direction, self-control, cooperation."[27]

If the NLRA is to be restored to what it was intended to be and what it can be, that restoration must be built on a foundation of NLRA rights and values. If there is a short list of the most important rights, it must be those that the statute itself gives primacy to. The NLRA says that it is not enough to have a goal of promoting the free flow of commerce. Rather, if that goal is ever to be reached, the focus must be on the process that leads to it. The process is based on "encouraging the practice and procedure of collective bargaining and by protecting the exercise by workers of full freedom of association, self-organization, and designation of representatives of their own choosing, for the purpose of negotiating the terms and conditions of their employment or other mutual aid or protection." Justice Marshall observed: "These are, for the most part, collective rights, rights to act in concert with one's fellow employees; they are protected not for their own sake but as an instrument of the national labor policy of minimizing industrial strife 'by encouraging the practice and procedure of collective bargaining.'"[28] Skipping the process means the ultimate goal cannot be achieved. In 1937, the Supreme Court observed: "Experience has abundantly demonstrated that the recognition of the right of employees to self-organization and to have representatives of their own choosing for the purpose of collective bargaining is often an essential condition of industrial peace. Refusal to confer and negotiate has been one of the most prolific causes of strife."[29]

Restoring these values to a central position is critical to a robust NLRA. Its values and policies have been so long ignored that, now, nearly seventy years after the law was enacted, we need to learn what they mean.

Exploring NLRA Policies and Values

In 1941, the Supreme Court said:

> A statute expressive of such large public policy as that on which the National Labor Relations Board is based must be broadly phrased and necessarily carries with it the task of administrative application. . . . In the nature of things Congress could not catalogue all the devices and stratagems for circumventing the policies of the Act. Nor could it define the whole gamut of remedies to effectuate these policies in an infinite variety of specific situations. Congress met these difficulties by leaving the adaptation of means to end to the empiric process of administration. The exercise of the process was committed to the Board, subject to limited judicial review.[30]

In other words, helping the NLRB and the courts enforce the NLRA includes the challenge of exploring and expanding the meaning of its policies, values, and vision.[31]

This large—and crucial—task needs wide participation if it is to succeed. What follows is but a piece of what must be an inclusive conversation about NLRA policies and values. That conversation is begun here with a discussion of issues that concern work and citizenship; NLRA dispute resolution, including the procedure of friendly adjustment of disputes; freedom of association; mutual aid or protection; and improving and stabilizing wages and working conditions.

Work and Citizenship

The NLRA's portrait of work and its place in our society differs from that which existed when it was enacted in 1935. It is certainly different from the ideas most of us have of the connections between work and society today. In the NLRA world, work and the workplace were to be infused with the values of a democratic society. NLRA rights were to help workers master the skills needed by citizens of a democracy. In our world, we surrender our status as citizens of a democracy when we work.

The NLRA's ideas about work and its role in society are not new. They existed at the founding of our country. The preamble to the United States Constitution sounds like NLRA values. It says that if we are to have "a more perfect union," we must "establish justice, insure domestic tranquility, provide for the common defense, promote the general welfare, and secure the blessings of liberty to ourselves and our posterity."

History shows that democracy is gained and retained only at great cost. Democracy faces the ever-present danger of being lost to simpler forms of governance. The philosophy and practice of democracy—the desire, right, and ability to participate in governing ourselves—must be learned and must have institutions that support them. But in what school is the grammar of democracy learned?

In our society there are only three places in which the practice of self-governance might be learned. The first possibility is the family. But differences in age and experience among family members mean the family is innately hierarchical. As a result the family is fundamentally not a democratic institution.

The second potential school for democracy is, of course, school. Primary and secondary school are filled with patriotic symbols. We recite the Pledge of Allegiance, learn American history and civics, and run for office in student clubs. But at the same time, students, teachers, and the administration are bound up in maintaining control, being controlled, or scheming to subvert control. Little time is spent actually practicing inclusive and effective participation in shaping one's environment.

This leaves only the workplace among the major institutions that socialize us.[32] True, the modern workplace takes many forms, but the reality is that most U.S. workplaces are deeply antidemocratic. In any workplace, a few have the right to control what others do. That hierarchy is both broadly and deeply imbedded. One group can curse the other out in foul and humiliating terms, while, if others did the same, they would lose their jobs. The law gives employers some right to control what workers do off the job. This unequal power is supported by laws, judicial decisions undermining unionization, and the economic realities of the roles of employer and employee. A single employee is helpless in dealing with an employer because most employees are dependent on their wages. This means that even if an employer refuses to pay a living wage, many employees do not dare to quit or resist arbitrary and unfair treatment.[33]

Whether we look at the family, schools, or work, we see the same thing: a few control, but most are controlled. This is true for both traditional workplaces and those that tout new managerial philosophies or practices. Even their terminology exposes the reality: "management techniques" is not the language of inclusion, responsibility, citizenship, or democracy. Worse, when corporations offer only the illusion of democratic involvement, "corporations may poison workers' views of democracy."[34] These systems remain at heart ways to maintain control and prevent workers' subverting control, something that is a nuisance to an employer who is trying to get work done.

Today we and unions operate in a society in which work takes place in nondemocratic institutions. Management defines and decides. Despite years of quality circles and employee involvement, most of us would find the idea of truly running a workplace as a democracy to be ludicrous.

What is the impact on society when most of us spend our waking hours living under undemocratic conditions based on a hierarchy of rights and duties and do so not out of free choice but out of economic necessity? We come to see this as the way things must be. We accept hierarchy. We believe that managers are responsible and sober and must maintain control over workers who are irresponsible and will only work under compulsion. In Robert Wagner's view,

> The relation between employer and employee in modern industry—"the most important relationship" in the worker's life—had taken on the character of the authority relationship between sovereign and subject or citizen. In his introduction of the NLRA in the Senate, Wagner quoted Brandeis's charge that employers who sought legal sanction for their obstruction of worker organization were "seeking sovereign power"—seeking "to endow property with active, militant power which would make it dominant over men." The analogy between political and managerial power had lodged firmly in the progressive mind at the height of political appeals for industrial democracy during and after the First World War. Many corporate leaders, too, had come to justify their exercise of political influence by the sovereign-like authority they already wielded as "industrial statesmen" controlling the "vital institutions" of social life.[35]

Not only we but also our legal structures assume managers deserve their positions because they plan for the long-term well-being of the company.

Workers need to be controlled because they think and act only in the short term. Therefore, since society depends on corporations, we must give employers freedom to act as they see fit while preventing workers from undermining those efforts. Of course, experience shows that none of these stereotypes is necessarily true. We have seen repeated experience with corporate misfeasance in recent years, and this undermines assumptions about managers and hierarchy.

My experience working with the NLRB showed me long ago that these assumptions are not accurate. NLRB work provides a rare opportunity to move among many worlds of work and to meet a wide range of people. My years as an NLRB attorney taught me that this society does not always sort us out by merit.

When I met with workers who had been discharged for their union activities, I was often impressed by how thoughtful and observant they were. I had fewer opportunities to meet with company owners and management representatives, other than at trial. Many were also thoughtful. However, I also found managers and owners who were destroying their businesses through their bad judgment. I also met company owners who had nothing but contempt for their workforces. I recall one employer who referred to his workers as trash and lowlife. I had already met many of these workers. They were poor, uneducated, powerless, and beaten down by hard work, but they were also the people whose work kept that company in business, and they were keen observers of life in this company.

The NLRA says that the nondemocratic, totalitarian workplace endangers us all. Workers may shake the dust of the workplace off their boots, they may shower the grease of a fast-food restaurant off, they may try to talk away their angst with friends and family, but the reality is that our work lives become incorporated into our intimate physical and mental selves. Over time, the undemocratic workplace grinds away at the belief that we have a right to participate in the decisions that affect our lives and societies. The NLRA's vision of the fundamental importance of democratic principles is accurate. We are increasingly a society more of subjects than citizens. This must change if we are to remain a democracy.

Sadly, with only about 10 percent of workers unionized, we have an enormous citizenship deficit. It is not the case that only union members are or can be good citizens, but we know that something about union membership creates citizens of a democracy. Union members vote, volunteer, and participate in politics and civic life in percentages far higher than unorganized workers.[36] Collective bargaining creates citizens by pushing workers to gain skills that matter as they face issues that matter, such as wages, working conditions, workplace injury, and discharge, while getting work done. Bargaining collectively means giving workers the power to say no and the ability to choose to say yes to what an employer wants. With collective power, workers can ask the employer to consider other ideas, goals, or methods. Unions can put on the brakes if more time and reflection are needed to solve a problem. Collective bargaining teaches the citizenship skills of assessing needs and goals and creating realistic strategies to achieve them. It teaches workers how to communicate, advocate, make decisions, listen, persuade, and compromise. Most important, it develops a sense of empowerment and right to participate.

NLRA values prompt us to rethink our stereotypes about the rightness of a hierarchy of work. They force us to question the concepts of employment as a master-servant relationship and of a job as the employer's property. Instead of the stereotype of employer as an entrepreneur who controls by right and ability, we may take on a more realistic assessment of the stake employers and employees have. Some managers and owners may act greedily, shortsightedly, or even criminally, and their work ethic may be based more on careerism than on the best interests of the business, while workers may be more tied to the company and more concerned about its long-term welfare.[37]

Workers suffer a real loss when their companies fail. Yet without collective bargaining, they have no way to affect the conditions that can lead to that loss. A worker who has dedicated herself to the company's needs may be left with skills no longer in demand. The worker who has been injured on the job has been used up by the job. With no golden parachutes, the unemployed worker may move to the ranks of the even less well paid or drop into joblessness and homelessness. At that point, society has lost the person's productive labor, taxes, and other contributions.

Are laws that treat workers as no more than a tool in human form wise? What sort of society discourages workers from having a sense of responsibility to work? If workers are told that their participation, involvement, intelligence are not wanted, will they try to increase their participation, involvement, or intelligence? Can a democracy exist when this is its raw material? The NLRA says the lack of workplace democracy is a serious problem. It pushes us to rethink the structure of the workplace and gives us processes that can change our acceptance of the status quo, moving us toward a more democratic society that invites all members of the society to have a seat at the table.[38]

NLRA Dispute Resolution—The Procedure of Friendly Adjustment of Disputes

Mark Barenberg claims that events since the enactment of the NLRA have led to "a more adversarial mode of unionization, even if workers achieved a substantial degree of de facto 'mutualism' in shop-floor decision-making."[39] Barenberg says that several factors have transformed a regime intended to promote the procedure of the friendly adjustment of disputes into an antagonistic one. These include labor policy put in place during the Second World War, the 1947 Taft-Hartley amendments, and post-World War II administrative and judicial interpretations. The task is to identify the power that can exist in the NLRA workplace despite the impact of these forces.

First, collective bargaining and workplace grievance resolution are not the same as commercial contract negotiations and breach-of-contract lawsuits. In contract bargaining, the contract creates and governs the relationship. The seller can choose which buyer to negotiate with and whether to negotiate at all. Both can walk away when there is a bargaining impasse. But walking away, other than for a brief time, is not a real option in employment or collective bargaining. Employment and collective bargaining contracts fit within a relationship that continues to exist regardless of the outcome of bargaining. That relationship is based on status, custom, and layers of informal and formal understandings that are constantly reshaped to meet new conditions. Employment is more long-term, complex, and personal than the typical commercial contract.

Furthermore, the nature of employment makes employee exit difficult. Workers accrue equity in their jobs that makes leaving increasingly difficult and costly as the years pass. Benefits, seniority entitlements, firm-specific skills, social ties, fear of the unknown, the emotional and practical difficulties of searching for a new job, and the cost and disruption of moving to a new job often tie a worker to a job, even when the worker is unhappy there.

Employers, too, bear risks from disputes. Unresolved disputes mean losing productivity as time and energy are absorbed in battling. Even simmering disputes that do not result in outright conflict may lead to low employee commitment to the job, lost loyalty, and even conscious or unconscious sabotage.

For both employer and employee, if workplace disputes are not held in bounds, they may destroy the job. Both employers and employees feel they have ownership rights in the job. As a result, workplace conflicts are emotional, and this makes dispute resolution difficult. Employment problems are deeply felt and thus spill over the boundaries of the workplace and affect communities. Add to this that employees may have different views about how a specific problem should be handled or even whether there is a problem. All this means that resolving workplace disputes is far from easy.

Robert Wagner created a system based on group worker interests that encouraged decision making by parties with equal power. Its focus is not on driving toward quick solutions. Wagner

> stressed that norms of fairness, shared interests, and mutual trust could be nurtured by institutional structures cleansed of excessive power disparities. Wagner and his circle recognized that even if hierarchical organization solves certain strategic problems, it also produces cultural and psychic conflict over legitimacy, trust, and resistance—conflict that may significantly influence institutional performance.[40]

Wagner stressed processes rather than achieving a fixed goal. Focusing on process made room for employers and employees to "engage in a creative constructive function." Mark Barenberg observes that "Wagner's almost utopian optimism about social plasticity extended, significantly, to the malleability of the very consciousness that pragmatist thought identified as a dynamic element in social experience."[41]

Indeed, collective bargaining should properly be considered to be a form of alternative dispute resolution. Collective bargaining also resembles legislation because it can resolve disputes on a broader, more forward-looking basis than individual litigation. It takes a collective, social, and long-term view recognizing that disputes need to be resolved in a way that does not imperil the employment relationship. Collective bargaining provides flexibility that lets employees and employers legislate the legal regime that best fits the workplace, rather than depending on state or federal laws whose standards may not be a good fit because they must apply to a wide range of workplaces.[42]

Collective bargaining, including contract negotiations and informal dispute resolution, can prevent workplace problems from ever reaching the stage of a formal filing. We can see the value of collective bargaining by looking at the consequences of the decline of unions. Having collective bargaining as a way disputes are resolved for only 10 percent of our workforce has brought a greater legalization of the employment relationship. The more adversarial and individualistic form of workplace dispute resolution is based on a confusing array of tort and contract doctrines, whistleblower and antiretaliation statutes, and antidiscrimination laws. Litigating rights under these laws is expensive and slow. Employers are unhappy with these rights, so they cut off employee access to them by demanding predispute arbitration agreements as a condition of employment. As the courts have experienced an explosion of employment cases, they have tried to siphon cases off into other dispute resolution processes.

None of these does what negotiations and the presence of a workplace steward can do. These laws are not tailored for each workplace's needs. Instead, they are standards imposed on employers and employees. Their remedies are expensive, slow, and therefore less available to those who are aggrieved. They do not encourage quick intervention. They cannot provide low-level resolution of problems by parties who have equal bargaining power and who care about fostering the long-term relationship. These laws are merely ways of cleaning up after the divorce.

Freedom of Association

We have two sets of laws that allow employers and employees to take advantage of freedom of association.[43] Employers are encouraged to become collective through corporation law, which allows them to have immortality, limited liability, and tax benefits. The NLRA encourages freedom of association as a necessary counterbalance to employer collectivity. Employees do not receive the same advantages from becoming collective as employers do from corporation law. Employees who unionize face employer retaliation, but employees have no power to retaliate against employers who choose to incorporate. Government offers employers who incorporate direct benefits, but employees who join together receive no comparable benefits and support. Finally, employers have often banded together in industry associations as well as a wide variety of political and advocacy groupings. Except for the AFL-CIO, employees have nothing comparable.

Employers do not tend to see employee freedom of association as on a par with the employer's and as its quid pro quo. The Supreme Court said that an employer who claimed it had a right to operate free from union-ization—or as the employer put it, free from "arbitrary restraints"—failed to understand that employees have a correlative right to organize.[44] "Em-ployees have as clear a right to organize and select their representatives for lawful purposes as the [employer] has to organize its business and select its own officers and agents. Discrimination and coercion to prevent the free exercise of the right of employees to self-organization and representation is a proper subject for condemnation by competent legislative authority."[45]

Even today, some believe employers have a right to interfere with em-ployee freedom of association while also believing that employees and unions have no comparable right. An employer is free to invite other em-ployers to join the Chamber of Commerce or send money to the National Right to Work Foundation. But employers feel that employees do not have a right to ask one another to join a union. As Daniel Yager of the Labor Pol-icy Association testified before Congress, a worker who asks a fellow worker to sign a union authorization card becomes "an interested party" whose actions are suspect, and such a card signing is illegitimate unless there is "governmental supervision" of it.[46] Yager is saying that a worker who exercises the right to organize is behaving in an illegitimate way. He must know that the law says otherwise, yet he thinks it is appropriate to make such an argument before Congress. Labor scholar David Brody says that property rights, employer free speech, and liberty of contract are val-ues imprinted "on the case law governing free choice."[47]

These misguided views of worker rights need to be fixed. Employee free-dom of association depends on making it clear that employers have no le-gitimate right or interest in intervening against workers who organize. To do this, courts must be persuaded to support the right to freedom of asso-ciation given in the NLRA. They need to protect NLRA freedom of associ-ation, not as an isolated individual freedom of choice to associate or not. Rather, it needs to be protected for the role it plays in promoting collective bargaining. NLRA freedom of association makes it possible for employees to bargain as equals with the employer—that is, to bargain collectively; to engage in mutual aid and protection; and to have an active part in improving and stabilizing their working conditions. The right of freedom of association is a right that is recognized in the First Amendment of the U.S. Constitution and in international law.

In 1947 Taft-Hartley amended Section 7 of the NLRA to add as a goal that an employee would also have the right to refrain from concerted activities.[48] This makes a consistent interpretation of freedom of association more complicated. It grafted the goal of individual freedom of choice onto the NLRA's basic vision of transforming the power relationship of employer and employee. This divided purpose affects the interpretation and application of the law and the ability to achieve the other NLRA goals just listed above. Judges with widely divergent philosophies can find support in the law for outcomes at direct odds with one another.

It should be remembered, however, that the Taft-Hartley amendments are limited. They added to, but did not replace, the language that was enacted in 1935, the core of the NLRA. That language and those values are still there. In addition, the Taft-Harley amendments must be interpreted as just one part of the statute. It is important not to lose sight of the fact that nearly the entire subject of labor law is helping employees become collective in order to increase their bargaining power. The NLRA outlaws employer actions to curb this power, actions that would be legal without the Act. The rights of the majority can be fitted together with those of dissenters and those who hold minority opinions. In fact, unionization is made stronger when it is democratic and makes room for many viewpoints. In other words, unions can benefit by taking on the complexity that Taft-Hartley's concern for minority rights represents.

The decline of union membership has left unions obsessed with numbers, but while numbers matter they do not by themselves necessarily make unions stronger. New Zealand's recent experience is a good example. Before 1991 it had union membership above 40 percent. Union membership was required by law, as was dues payment. As a result, at least some union representatives neglected members. The result was a thin unionism in which most workers were members only because the law required them to be. When a new law was passed in 1991 that eliminated compulsory membership and dues payment, the results of that neglect were revealed: membership plummeted to below 20 percent in less than five years.[49] The point is that American unions need numbers, but they also need members who are enthusiastic about the value of freedom of association.

But individual choice also creates problems. Some things can be bargained for on an individual basis, while others cannot. Achieving agreement on goals and material support for goals is no easy thing. Michael Gottesman describes the problem of negotiating a new benefit:

> Indeed, there would seem to be two ingredients essential to negotiating for the benefit: (1) the employees (or at least a large number of them) must get together and agree that they all wish to spend an agreed-upon sum to purchase this benefit; and (2) there must be some means to impose the fair share of the costs of the benefit upon those employees who would not be willing to spend the necessary sum (or who would attempt to "free ride") but who would inevitably enjoy the benefit were it purchased.[50]

In other words, even though the ideal is voluntary support—that is, association that is truly free—human nature often makes some degree of compulsion necessary.

Economic experiments have found that free riding can undermine collective behavior. It can lead others to become free riders, even though all would be better off with collective negotiations. Most people are reciprocators, not committed free riders. But most will only cooperate if others will. This means that a few free riders can destroy cooperation. Reciprocation is a socially useful but finely balanced quality. So if society's needs are to be protected, reciprocation needs to be supported with incentives and penalties, including through penalties for free riders.[51] Research such as this can be helpful in developing a conception of freedom of association that moves courts away from theory to more functional interpretations of freedom of association.

When courts are struggling with issues such as membership and dues, one way to help them is to try these cases so they focus on the role of freedom of association. In other words, courts need to be educated so that they do not see freedom of association as something that has no effect on other rights. The record needs to show the courts that too great an emphasis on the right not to associate fails to promote, and actually undermines, other NLRA policies, such as collective bargaining and improving wages and working conditions. This result judicially amends the NLRA so that Taft-Hartley's right not to associate repeals all other rights. Had Congress meant this repeal, it would have done so itself. As discussed earlier, when social science evidence demonstrated a relationship between dues and the ability of unions to bargain, the court easily found in favor of enforcing dues payment over a claim of freedom not to associate.[52]

Mutual Aid or Protection

Most people are not aware that the NLRA protects far more than just the right to organize a union to bargain with an employer. The NLRA goal of stabilizing wages and working conditions within and between industries can only come about if employee rights extend beyond the four walls of one employer.[53] This can happen only if workers have the legal right to make common cause with one another. When workers at a competitor are not organized, this affects employee/union bargaining power at an organized employer. When an industry or an area is completely organized, wages can be taken out of competition so that employers can compete elsewhere—for example, on product or service quality.[54]

To achieve this goal, the NLRA gives employees broad rights—as a class—to make common cause with one another. The breadth of these rights is affirmed in the definition of "employee" in Section 2(3): Employee includes any employee, and is not to be limited to the employees of a particular employer.[55] The NLRA's definition of employee includes employees of a particular employer as well as employees of other employers, former employees, and applicants for employment. This inclusive definition gives employees the right to define their own interests, to define them broadly, and to make common cause with one another to advance their collective interests.

A second reason for the NLRA's broad definition of employee is to promote and protect employee solidarity. The broad definition protects well-paid employees who distribute union newsletters at work that call for support for minimum wage workers who are employed elsewhere.[56] Mutual aid or protection is part of the whole NLRA structure. It is closely related to freedom of association and is a halfway house to self-organization and full collective bargaining. Employee solidarity has little value if it is limited to employees of a single employer. The NLRA protects steps toward collective action because those steps move employees toward collective bargaining. The single actor may be protected under the NLRA but only because of its ultimate aim to promote collective action and mutual aid or protection. If the individual is not protected, the collective can never occur.[57]

Congress made group—collective—action the central process that would be used to attain all its other ends. Thus, "the Act reduced certain individual values to secondary status."[58] As a result, the NLRA is at odds with American traditions of individualism. We feel this conflict in every union organizing campaign. It is no surprise, then, that judges tend to opt for individualism and self-interest over solidarity and fellow feeling.

It is ironic at the same time that some courts have rejected solidarity and selflessness in interpreting the NLRA—a statute that clearly supports these values—many state court judges have created protections to safeguard workers discharged in violation of public policy.[59] These judges are protecting people who commit selfless acts of solidarity with the faceless public.

The fact that judges have created this sort of doctrine suggests that they are not implacably hostile to supporting NLRA mutualism. Solidarity is a value that we all can understand.

> In a family, when I as son, husband, or father, express love toward you, I do not do so in order to assure myself of love in return. I do not help my son in order to be able to claim assistance from him when I am old; I do it because he and I are in the world together; we are one flesh. Similarly in a workplace, persons who work together form families-at-work. When you and I are working together, and the foreman suddenly discharges you, and I find myself putting down my tools or stopping my machine before I have had time to think—why do I do this? Is it not because, as I actually experience the event, your discharge does not happen only to you but also happens to us?[60]

Evidence based on new experiments in behavioral economics can be used to flesh out the meaning of mutuality. Scientists have systematically found that people tend to have a natural inclination to altruism coupled with a demand for just treatment.[61] This evidence can be presented to help judges understand the meaning and operation of mutual aid and protection as NLRA values.

Improving and Stabilizing Wages and Working Conditions

The NLRA promotes both improving wages and stabilizing wages and working conditions across industries in order to sustain the economy and society. At the time the NLRA was enacted, during the Great Depression, it was easy to see why this was important to the economy and society. Higher wages would promote consumption and improve motivation to work. Society as a whole would benefit. The alternative was chaos.

But today employers are constantly seeking lower wages, and governments actively assist them through policy, trade agreements, privatization, and globalization. The change in values seems complete. Few seem concerned that today many jobs do not pay living wages. Moral, social, and economic arguments for improving wages and working conditions now seem embarrassingly out of touch with reality.

Consider these arguments, for example:

1. Supply-side economic policy argues that overall social wealth is greater if tax cuts are given to ensure the richest have greater income. Examples would include cutting taxes on profits from stocks and eliminating the estate tax. But could it be argued that income should be distributed among workers, because we are better off, as a society, with a more equitable allocation of income?

2. The investments workers make to the welfare of their companies, by doing their jobs, are real but are harder to see than are dollar investments. Therefore, increasing wages is a way to make up for decades of short-sighted decisions that valued monetary investments while undervaluing the contribution employees make.

3. Society is better off when workers receive a living wage, rather than depending on welfare or other subsidies, because work should engender self-respect.

4. Employees who receive good wages feel more self-esteem and more commitment to their jobs and society. This means we are all better off economically and as a society when all workers receive living wages.[62]

Robert Wagner supported these ways of thinking about work, wages, and the good of society, and these ideas are embodied in the NLRA. He linked the idea that high wages lead to increased consumption and higher work motivation "to aggressive support for collective bargaining as the means to permanent economic redistribution and growth."[63]

It is to unions' advantage to make these connections clear. A good example of how this can be done involved a California Carpenters Local that was bannering and handbilling an employer. In addition to standard language about area wages and "rat" (i.e., nonunion or anti-union) employers, its handbills said:

> Shame on Cadillac SAAB for contributing to erosion of area standards for carpenter craft workers. M&M Interiors is a sub contractor for Carignan Construction on Cadillac SAAB's dealership project located in the city of Thousand Oaks. M&M Interiors does not meet area labor standards for all its carpenter craft workers, including fully paying for family health benefits and pension.
>
> Carpenters Local 209 objects to substandard wage employers like M&M Interiors working in the community. In our opinion the community ends up paying the tab for employee health care and low wages tend to lower general community standards, thereby encouraging crime and other social ills.
>
> Carpenters Local 209 believes that Cadillac SAAB has an obligation to the community to see that area labor standards are met for construction work at all their projects, including any future work. They should not be allowed to insulate themselves behind "independent" contractors. For this reason Local 209 has a labor dispute with all the companies named here.[64]

All too often these sorts of banners talk of demands for improved wages and working conditions only for the union members. This makes them look greedy and self-interested. The employer will react by warning that higher wages mean higher prices and will hurt the community, especially the poor. The Carpenters' banner connected low pay with harm to the community. It showed that the employer was being selfish and greedy and that the union members were protecting the wider society. All of these actions were consistent with the NLRA's language, values, and intent.

Using NLRA values sends a powerful and appealing message. Promoting stability of wages within and among industries takes wages out of competition and also stabilizes union representation and bargaining power. If all an employer's competitors are providing the same wages and benefits, then an employer has less incentive to resist or escape union representation. The alternative is that union representation and working conditions can be maintained only by the strike threat, which becomes weak when an employer's competitors are not organized.

Employers resist unions for many reasons, but certainly employer worries that paying higher wages will give competitors an advantage is an important reason. Management hostility and opposition may also be based on fears that efficiency and profits will be lowered and that management will lose prerogatives of freedom of action and flexibility.[65] However, recent economic experiments support the NLRA view. They show that when employers pay higher wages, their workers reciprocate by voluntarily working harder.[66]

Other NLRA Rights

This is not a comprehensive discussion of NLRA policies and values, and many more than those touched on here matter. Far more remains to be said and done. In addition, this discussion is far too theoretical. While theory matters, it must be put to work with the data and strategy in order to win real cases. For that to happen many more people must join in a group effort to think through how to use each of these rights to take back the Workers' Law. There must be a long-term strategy that can be applied as each charge is filed, and as each case is tried that guides the plan for handling each case. We must place NLRA rights and values at the center of that strategy and each case.

In many ways, it is fortunate that the courts have paid so little attention to NLRA policies. This leaves them more open to interpretation than if prior case law had to be overturned. That said, giving meaning to these values is no simple matter. The biggest hurdle is that NLRA policies and values do not stand alone. Their boundaries are defined by this society's views of the proper legal roles and power relationships of employees and employers. These tend to be hierarchical, with the employer's property rights in the job paramount. These views are essentially unchanged from the time the NLRA was enacted.

So two tasks face us if we want to fulfill the promise of the Workers' Law. One is to give content to NLRA policies and values. The other is to develop a strategy that makes full use of them—in litigation, in activism, and in the message these deliver. Thomas Kohler observes that

> the diffused and locally-focused American scheme predominantly rested on a series of habits. A habit constitutes a way of being. Two distinctive

characteristics about the American way of being seem to have played a crucial part in supporting the employment-ordering scheme Congress had adopted. The first shows itself in the historically remarkable propensity of Americans to form associations. The second is the pervasive, if often indirect, influence that religiously conditioned understandings have exercised over the imagination, feelings, and motives of Americans. Both points typically are overlooked, especially the second. However, the diminution of our associational habits and related changes in religious conceptions and practices have had a far greater impact on our labor law schemes—and on nearly every other aspect of common life—than has commonly been realized.[67]

We need to break these habits and remake them using NLRA values.

4

LITIGATING THE NLRA
VALUES—WHAT ARE THE
CHALLENGES?

So far, we have discussed three of the components we need to construct a litigation strategy to invigorate the Workers' Law. First, we examined why judges have rewritten the NLRA. Second, we looked at ways to try cases that will help judges restore the NLRA. Finally, in chapter 3, we explored NLRA policies and values and the workplace and society they were intended to create—policies that would make democratic workplaces an integral part of a democratic society.

It is obvious that the NLRA's vision of what our workplaces and society could be differs radically from what now exists. Few today see collective bargaining as important for a good society. It seems unlikely that the NLRA and its vision could be enacted today and that many in the United States would endorse them. If a society and its institutions need to be in sync with one another, this may explain why unions and collective bargaining have had such a hard time in the United States. It may be that collective bargaining can only thrive or survive in the type of society envisioned by the NLRA but can only fail in a society too greatly at odds with the NLRA's vision. Research shows that a society's values affect how a law is interpreted and whether it is successful.[1] In other words, a litigation strategy alone can never succeed. It must be part of a comprehensive campaign to replace our society's values with those of the NLRA.

Given that the NLRA vision is so different from our society's values, it is only natural that there are fundamental clashes between the two. The clashes between the NLRA and the values of our society appeared in litigation the moment the NLRA was enacted, before its vision had a chance to take hold. There are recurring issues that appear over and over in NLRA cases. These grow out of the fundamental collision between employer rights and NLRA rights and between the NLRA vision of the workplace and the common view of workplace rights. Knowing that we should expect specific conflicts makes it possible to go into litigation prepared to deal with them. A litigation strategy to amend the NLRA must identify the conflicts of rights in each case and plan how to grapple with them in order to persuade judges to apply NLRA values. This chapter focuses on identifying fundamental conflicts that are most likely to arise in trying NLRA cases.

The Clash of Rights—Which Right Trumps?

Although unfair labor practice cases appear to be about whether the law was violated, in fact, they are actually a struggle between employer rights and NLRA rights. These are not small battles. Both employer rights and NLRA rights are concerned with the impact that actions within the workplace have on those outside the workplace, on society as a whole. It is therefore a mistake to try these cases as merely technical questions of whether the evidence shows certain actions took place. The judges who ultimately decide these cases will consciously or unconsciously see them through the larger lens of rights.

Employer rights include property rights in the job, the right to manage a workplace, and the right to make business decisions. NLRA rights include all the NLRA's policies. It would be easier to understand what is happening in the cases if conflicts were identified, discussed, and resolved. But most often, the rights and even the existence of a conflict remain in the background. However, if cases are read carefully, the clash of rights becomes obvious. Much of the time, judges see cases through the employer's point of view. When only the employer's rights are visible, they alone become the basis for the decision and make the outcome seem inevitable.

As discussed earlier, most judges will have a natural sympathy with and understanding of ideas such as master and servant law or property rights. As a result, these values can remain in the background but still influence decisions. As a result, NLRA policies, values, and rights must be consciously raised and litigated in order to overcome judges' reflexive understanding and acceptance of employer rights.

The cases below are used as an exercise in identifying how this clash of rights plays out. I have chosen cases that reflect a variety of common situations. These cases have been chosen for several reasons. First, although they are mostly older cases, they continue to be good law and to play a powerful role in shaping the interpretation of the NLRA. In other words, these are key cases that must be overturned. Second, their facts are well known, because most are studied in labor law classes. This makes it possible to focus on the decision-making process more efficiently here. Third, the nature of these cases and the fact that they are known to all labor practitioners provides a powerful way to refocus attention from the way these cases are traditionally studied and understood to the underlying decision-making process. Fourth, these cases are frequently taught because they have "good" facts. They present paradigms that frequently recur. Therefore, recognizing the patterns in these cases is training to recognize them in later cases.

The Employer's Right to Go out of Business

In *Textile Workers Union v. Darlington Manufacturing Co.,*[2] the employer closed one of its mills because the workers voted for union representation. The NLRB held that the employer had the right to close its mill but must remedy the harm it caused the employees. The Supreme Court agreed that an employer is free to close its business. However, the Court also held there was no violation, and consequently no remedy, even if the closing was done to retaliate against the employees for their union activities.

The NLRA says nothing about whether an employer can commit industrial suicide because it hates unions. It does say employees have a right to choose to be represented by a union. The NLRA is clear that an employer violates Section 8(a)(3) if it fires or lays off a worker in retaliation for joining a union. It also violates Section 8(a)(1) if it interferes with employees' rights to select a representative. In short, in *Darlington,* the violation was clear or would have been clear had the employer simply fired the workers.

An employer who can get away with retaliating against its workers for joining a union undermines important NLRA policies with effects far beyond its workplace. Employees and their families and friends are unlikely to even try unionizing. Since Darlington closed just one of the many plants it owned, word would spread to its other plants and throughout the community, making those employees fearful of joining a union and sending a message to other employers that they were free to take bold action to destroy unions.

The employer left a large number of workers suddenly without jobs in Darlington, South Carolina, a small town. It is not hard to imagine that this would ultimately lead to the decline of the town. There would be an explosion of unemployment. People would buy less. Some would move away. Businesses would collapse. Taxes would decline. The Supreme Court's decision is one that makes those losses more, not less likely. Of course, all this could flow from the loss of a major business. But in *Darlington,* the employer did not have to go out of business. It did so to deprive people of their legal rights. The Supreme Court's decision is one that destroys any hope these and other employees since then would have for collective bargaining, freedom of association, equality of bargaining power, and improved wages and working conditions. The loss of those rights inside the workplace would spread throughout the community and destroy trust in democratic values and commerce. Those losses would spread as employers and lawyers heard about the case and learned its lessons.

Yet, none of this mattered to the Supreme Court because it saw only the employer's rights. It held that an employer was allowed to go out of business without penalty for retaliating against its workers' right to union representation. To the Supreme Court, it was a simple matter. The employer had property and managerial rights. These allow it to manage its property, even to mistreat it, as it saw fit. Therefore, there was no room in the Court's analysis to consider that the NLRA said the employer's rights must make room for the rights of others who are affected by what happens in the workplace. The Supreme Court said, "A proposition that a single businessman cannot choose to go out of business if he wants to would represent such a startling innovation that it should not be entertained without the clearest manifestation of legislative intent."[3] It refused to see that intent in the statute.

> The Court thus held that an employer, with the meanest motive, with
> maximum pain to its employees, and with the most vivid object lesson to
> workers generally, could discharge all its employees, liquidate the assets,

and carry away the cash to invest elsewhere. The Court reached this result by reading into the statute a strong presumption of employer unilateral control and absence of any employee stake in the enterprise. The assumption undergirding employment at will overrode the explicit statutory protection.[4]

The Court saw this as a zero-sum game. Either the employer could close the business or the employer would be forced to reopen and operate a business. The employees were not in its focus at all. Of course, the employer had not destroyed itself. The work done at the closed plant would migrate to its other plants; the money from the sale of the plant and its fixtures would be invested; and the workers at those plants would never dare to unionize.

The Court, of course, could have promoted and accommodated both employer and NLRA rights. For example, it could have let the employer close its business in Darlington, South Carolina, but pay the employees until they found new jobs or for a reasonable period of time. Or it could have been ordered to hire them at its other plants and to pay their moving expenses.

Remedies like these would have let the employer run its business as it saw fit and also promoted NLRA rights. The employees would have had money and time to start anew, knowing that there was a law that would protect them the next time they tried to form a union. Their town would have had time to create new employment.

This remedy might have encouraged even more positive results. The employer might have decided that it would be the laughingstock of the community if it paid its employees to do nothing. The order might have helped the employer decide that it was better to stay in business and get work for the pay. Other employers might have decided it was better to respect the law than to follow Darlington's model and play hardball.

Over time, employees at many plants might have unionized, and competition based on wages and working conditions would have been ended. Mills would have been safer, and the taxes of well- paid millworkers would have built up the South's infrastructure. Workers of all races who learned the skills of negotiation and democracy on the job would have felt empowered to use those skills in their communities and in politics.

But the Supreme Court decided otherwise.

Anti-Union Discrimination

Ten years before *Darlington,* Adkins Transfer Company in Nashville, Tennessee, decided to fire its two truck mechanics after they joined the Teamsters and to have its trucks repaired by local truck and automobile dealerships.[5] Firing an employee for joining a union violates Section 8(a)(3) and undermines NLRA policies of promoting collective bargaining and protecting employee rights to join unions and bargain collectively.

Adkins explained that it fired the workers because it had been paying the employees 30–40 percent less than other trucking firms in Nashville paid their mechanics. Adkins said that union representation would mean paying each employee about fifty cents more an hour, the going rate of pay for other truck mechanics in the Nashville area.

The court of appeals said there was no violation because the employer had no anti-union motive; it just wanted to pay lower wages than the other employers. The employer never claimed it could not afford to pay the raises but that, if it did so, it would not make a profit in that department.

Not making a profit in a single department is an odd concern. This is especially true for one that needs to keep the trucks running and should have that as its highest concern. How would it even know if it was making a profit there? If the other Nashville trucking companies could operate profitably paying these wages, what was wrong with Adkins that it couldn't compete except by driving its workers' wages down?

The employer also claimed that it could do the work more cheaply elsewhere. It offered no evidence to prove this, even though it should have had the burden of proof on this affirmative defense. In fact, the defense would have been difficult to prove. The employer would have had to do more than show that the hourly wages at repair shops were cheaper. It would have had to take into account the cost of ferrying the trucks to the truck dealer and back, the increased time the trucks would be out of operation because of time lost in transporting them and waiting for them to be returned to service, the relative quality of maintenance and repair, the greater likelihood that the trucks would be better maintained by mechanics on-site who could more easily do preventive maintenance, the advantages of having a mechanic who was familiar with the history of each vehicle, and the cost of having to replace trucks prematurely as a result of poorer maintenance.

Even if Adkins had had a labor-cost advantage over its other competitors, why should it have been allowed to violate the NLRA to keep it? Why should it have gotten this cost advantage when this undermined the NLRA policy of stabilizing competitive wage rates and working conditions? If Adkins could fire workers to get a cost advantage, then should all Nashville employers have been allowed to fire all employees who didn't agree to lower wages than Adkins paid? But if all employers could do this, then the NLRA policies against depressed wage rates and for greater worker purchasing power would be undermined. If an employer can fire employees who join a union or seek better working conditions, won't that discourage union membership among all employees in the area?

As with *Darlington,* the court could have accommodated both legitimate employer and NLRA rights. It could have required the employer to bargain to try to reach an accommodation instead of assuming that bargaining would fail. Why was the Court so willing to absolve Adkins of an unfair labor practice violation on no more evidence than its claim of anticipated costs? If costs mattered to the existence of a violation, why not wait to see if they materialized?

The employer said that firing the workers was "purely and simply a question of costs." In other words, firing employees who want better wages is not anti-union discrimination. But, if this is not anti-union discrimination, what is? In fact, isn't the desire to pay employees less just one of the reasons employers oppose unions? Aren't the components of anti-union animus usually costs, profits, power, ideology, or is the issue managerial power and employer discretion? Are employer desires to pay lower wages and to have unfettered power different now than when the NLRA was passed? If not, then Congress intended to outlaw firings and other discrimination based on dislike of paying higher wages and of decreased employer power.

If unions have the power to negotiate higher wages for unionized employees than for unorganized workers, but all unionized employers can shut down parts of their businesses and pay no penalty, as did Darlington, or close the entire business, as did Adkins, then what is the fate of unions?

What is particularly interesting about *Adkins* is that the NLRA rights at stake were not limited to the rights to bargain collectively and to join a union. The employer's argument made clear that its motives were to pay lower wages so it could make more money than its competitors, actions that would pressure competitors to lower wages. In other words, Adkins succeeded by persuading the court of appeals that it had a right to take actions, even firing, to prevent an employee from receiving better wages. In addition, it had a right to engage in wage competition and to prevent the stabilization of wages and working conditions between and among industries. It even claimed a right to stymie employees who wanted to engage in mutual aid or protection.

If an employer has a license to fire employees because of the mere possibility it will have higher labor costs, even if the firing discourages or destroys unionization, then what are the limits? *Adkins* and *Darlington* together ask: Is the purpose of the NLRA to protect employee rights or to let employers destroy NLRA rights whenever they can profit by doing so? Had the court of appeals told Adkins it had to recognize the union and bargain, just how bad would that have been for the employer? What horrible things would have happened to it by obeying the law? And what was the fate of the two workers it fired? What happened when they told their story to family, friends, and folks they happened to pass time with? What are the thoughts of workers and others who know the law says they have rights, but courts read the law otherwise?

Striker Replacement

Decades earlier than *Darlington* and *Adkins,* and just three years after the NLRA was enacted, the Supreme Court decided *NLRB v. Mackay Radio & Telegraph Co.*[6] *Mackay* has come to stand for the employer's right to permanently replace strikers. This means that an employer may hire workers to keep production going during the strike, keep them on after the strike ends, and refuse to reinstate the strikers.

First, and least important, permanent striker replacement was not an issue in *Mackay*. The issue was whether an employer could discriminate among striking workers based on how active they had been in their union. No one recalls this part because the Supreme Court decision included some observations on an issue no one had asked it to address. This is "dictum," and dictum is not supposed to have any legal importance. Nevertheless, the Supreme Court's offhand musings have expanded to allow an employer to hire replacement workers, not just temporarily, to keep the business running during the strike, but permanently.

The Supreme Court said that the rights that controlled the decision were the employer's property rights in the job and managerial right to protect its business and run it as it saw fit. The Court said it did not accept the employer's argument that workers who strike have abandoned their jobs and assume the risk that they will lose those jobs. What the Courts did say was that the NLRA right to strike in Section 13 did not alter the employer's rights.

The NLRA itself says nothing about whether an employer can keep its business running during a strike. This is a serious gap in the law. We know that just as strikers try to cut production or sales, employers will try to keep the business going. Congress could have allowed an employer to hire replacement workers or forbidden it, or it could have created some other rule.

Perhaps, however, Congress thought it had spoken clearly on the importance of the right to strike. The NLRA said: "Nothing in this Act shall be construed so as to interfere with or impede or diminish in any way the right to strike."[7] In addition to Section 13, Sections 1 and 7 say it is NLRA policy to protect and promote collective bargaining and equality of bargaining power and to improve wages and working conditions In addition, an employer violates Section 8(a)(3) if it fires an employee for union activity and Section 8(a)(1) if it interferes with the rights to assist labor organizations, bargain collectively, or engage in acts of mutual aid or protection.

Hiring permanent replacements certainly interferes with, impedes, and diminishes the right to strike.[8] Who will strike if it means losing a job? If workers fear striking because they will be fired (as opposed to losing income), then they lose an important and traditional weapon, while employers have a highly potent weapon; thus inequality of bargaining power is increased.[9] Without the strike weapon, wages cannot be improved. We have seen this play out over recent decades as wages have stagnated even when the economy is strong. Some may argue that permanent replacement is not the same as being fired because the strikers have a chance to be recalled to work. But for most workers it is a distinction without a difference. Section 8(a)(3) is violated when an employer discriminates in regard to tenure of employment or any term or condition of employment because of union activity, and a worker who has been permanently replaced for striking in support of a union proposal has had his conditions of employment affected for the worse.

So the NLRA rights involved in MacKay and subsequent cases are clear and strong. Yet the courts do not see them as relevant to permanent striker replacement. Professor Summers contends:

> It would fit more comfortably into the statutory scheme to say that when the employer and the elected representative of its employees come to an impasse, operations should cease. This, of course, would assume that employees are members of the enterprise essential to its operation. The Court's assumption is the opposite. The decision to continue operations is legally vested in the employer; the employees have no legally protected interest and are disposable by replacement workers.[10]

Again, the courts have chosen to see and enforce only one right—the employer's—and, as a result, have destroyed the other. No effort is made to accommodate both, even though this is possible and more desirable for all parties than the conditions that striker replacement create. Studies of the employer's ability to permanently replace economic strikers demonstrate that it affects collective bargaining.[11] Unions have responded by developing alternate strategies, such as corporate campaigns, to assert pressure on the employer.[12] However, these are far more expensive and generally far less effective than the strike weapon.

None of the harm permanent striker replacement does to workers, the economy, or the effectiveness of the NLRA matters, however, as long as courts believe that employers have property rights in the job. This ignores the fact that employees also have ownership rights and that they have no more desire than the company to prolong a strike. Blaming workers for a strike also misses the fact that it takes two parties to create an impasse. Why is only one punished for that failure to agree? And why is that punishment so extreme?

In fact, it is possible to accommodate both the employer's need to keep the business functioning and the union and employees' needs to preserve jobs and bargain collectively to codetermine terms and conditions of employment. The dissent in *Trans World Airlines, Inc. v. Independent Federation of Flight Attendants*[13] listed a number of options that do a far better job of accommodating rights than does giving employers a blanket right to hire permanent replacements. Options could include allowing an employer to hire temporary replacements at its discretion, to hire permanent replacements based on need and a lack of harm to NLRA rights, or to have a waiting period before it could hire replacements of any kind. While each of these may have features that would be objectionable to unions or employers, any would remove the harm that permanent replacements do to the structure and policies of the NLRA and to the lives of workers. These and other options deserve to be given serious study.

Mutual Aid and Support

In *Lechmere, Inc. v. NLRB*[14] the Supreme Court majority opted for the employer's property right to exclude union organizers from entering its parking lot to place handbills on employee cars at the far end of the parking lot over any employee rights. This was a parking lot that all the rest of the public not only could enter but was invited to enter.[15] The Court's discussion of employer property rights is theoretical and never deals with the facts. The abstract discussion makes it easier to ignore the reality that the employer's property rights were quite weak. The majority also stated bluntly that the employer's property right to exclude is virtually inviolate, yet that position was not required by legal precedent.[16]

It would have been helpful had the Court discussed why the organizers were excluded, beyond the claim that a property owner has the right to exclude whomever it wants. The absolute nature of that right is made clear by the triviality of the employer's concerns. The only issue the Supreme Court raised was that Lechmere was concerned about litter from the union organizers' handbills and it had a long-standing rule barring solicitors. Certainly, it made sense for an employer to want to keep its premises attractive for customers. Shoppers will also have a more pleasant experience if they are not accosted by solicitors. The case tells us nothing about how vigilantly Lechmere defended its concerns. For example, how often did it eject customers who littered?

More important is the doubt that Lechmere really fought this case to the Supreme Court over litter, or even to vindicate an absolutist view of its property rights. It seems far more likely that Lechmere wanted to prevent its employees from organizing a union and gaining the power to demand "more"—two rights protected by the NLRA. Perhaps the real property right here was Lechmere's "property" interest in its employees—a right to exclude those who would give these employees access to their legal rights.

If the law grants the employer's desire to exclude the organizers so its employees will not organize a union, what happens to the employees' NLRA rights? What happens when the wages of the unorganized employees tempt or force employers at organized stores to demand wage cuts? The NLRA policies of preventing depressed wages and promoting the stabilization of wages and working conditions within and between industries had no weight in the Lechmere decision. Is the decision based on an unstated view that the employer had what amounts to a property interest in its employees that gave it the right to withhold information and assistance from them?

If all the employees in the area who worked in Lechmere's industry had been organized, then Lechmere would have had to compete for customers on the basis of the quality of its service—not by undercutting employee wages. This is what the NLRA vision promotes. The community would have benefited from having workers paid wages that let them contribute taxes to maintain and improve public services. The employees could have better supported their families and would have needed less public support.[17] The quality of service and goods that the public received would have been improved because that is where Lechmere and its competitors would have been forced to compete.

But instead of the NLRA vision of what makes the good workplace and job and how those promote the good of society, we have the *Lechmere* vision that a corporation's property is its castle. The NLRA intended to remove wages and terms of employment from competition. The labor laws of other countries support systems that achieve this goal. In Europe, this is done through industry-wide agreements. In New Zealand, until 1991, the law supported a system of agreements that set conditions for workers in certain occupations or industries throughout a region or the country. These systems act to narrow the areas on which employers compete to quality of service or product, the areas that matter most to their customers. Those employers who do not offer good service or products may not survive. It may seem harsh, but why should they? Furthermore, employers who offer very low wages and no benefits shift their costs to the communities where the workers live. The social services that are provided to the employees are subsidies to the employer. At the same time, that community suffers because these workers cannot contribute as much through taxes as their better paid counterparts.

Implementation upon Impasse

The cases discussed so far have not focused on collective bargaining, but in each of them, collective bargaining was the real concern. Collective bargaining is the point of unionization. To the employer it means the potential of higher labor costs and less autonomy. For employees joining a union is meant to change their lives, to get them respect, just treatment, and more control over their working conditions.

Each court decision tilts the balance of bargaining power. The strike is a critical weapon for achieving bargaining power, and one that has been weakened by narrowing the right to strike. As discussed above, courts permitted permanent striker replacement. The courts have also made certain kinds of strikes illegal, such as the sit-down strike, slowdowns, and partial strikes. In addition, courts have defined secondary boycotts broadly.[18]

All these problems have received a great deal of attention. Less attention has been paid to court decisions that have given employers the right to implement their final offers when they reach an impasse. Indeed, the courts have never seemed to notice that it is an odd thing to give one party to bargaining the right to pick the terms of the contract. This is not the case in nonlabor contract bargaining, where the parties either keep their current terms until they agree to new terms, look for a new bargaining partner, or seek mediation to help reach an agreement. In contract bargaining, when one party imposes terms on the other, this is referred to as a contract of adhesion, and the contract may be struck down.

Yet when a union and employer fail to agree to new terms, the employer has the right to implement any or all of its proposals. Certainly, collective bargaining differs from commercial contract bargaining: neither employer nor employees can easily look for a new bargaining partner. The workers will not want to quit just because they are having trouble negotiating new terms, and the employer will not want to hire a new workforce. The available options are to use a mediator or interest arbitration to settle terms or to keep the current terms until the parties agree to a change.

Congress failed to choose any way to resolve collective bargaining impasses, a serious gap that ensured the courts would have to step in. As the Supreme Court put it, "Without spelling out the details, the Act provided that it was an unfair labor practice for an employer to refuse to bargain."[19] When the courts filled in that detail by creating the employer right to implement its final offer at impasse, the courts tilted the balance of power and affected the process of bargaining. Both parties realize that an impasse in collective bargaining does not merely mean that the parties are stuck and need to work out the conflict. Reaching an impasse is actually a desirable goal for the employer but to be avoided at all costs by the union. It means that the more strongly a union feels about an issue, the less it can insist on it. Insisting on a proposal creates an impasse that lets the employer implement its entire proposal. If a union cannot push an issue, what is the point of collective bargaining? If collective bargaining is no more than avoiding impasse, then what is the point of unionization?

The following are some options for how collective bargaining works in a world with implementation upon impasse and striker replacement.

1. The parties reach an agreement.
2. The parties reach an impasse, the employer implements its final offer, the parties then fail to reach an agreement, and the union becomes moribund, leading to deunionization—either by its walking away or through decertification.
3. The parties reach an impasse, the workers strike, the employer replaces the strikers, the parties reach an agreement on workplace terms and on striker reinstatement, and many or all strikers are recalled to work.
4. The parties reach an impasse, the workers strike, the employer replaces the strikers (permanently or temporarily), the parties reach an agreement on workplace terms and on striker reinstatement, few or no strikers are recalled to work, and the union eventually becomes moribund and is decertified.[20]

Other outcomes are possible, some of which lead to agreement, some of which lead to disempowering the union, and some of which lead to the end of collective bargaining. Judges talk about this as nothing more than the *free* play of economic forces. Whether that is correct or not, the point is that this is not how NLRA bargaining is supposed to work. The judicial impasse amendments create a system that is nothing more than collective bargaining in effigy.

A good collective bargaining law should make reaching a negotiated settlement desirable for all parties and should discourage any path away from bargaining. While not all employers will use implementation upon impasse or striker replacement to the fullest, they tempt all employers not to bargain because the reward is gaining unilateral employer control. For the many employers who harbor anti-union attitudes,[21] impasse becomes a goal rather than a glitch on the way to a negotiated agreement.[22] In short, the judicial impasse amendments undercut NLRA values of worker self-representation by destroying equality of bargaining power.

The decisions suggest that the courts have done this because they assume that what the employer wants is what is good for the workplace and the union is in the wrong for not agreeing. In addition, some courts are more influenced by the employer's property and managerial rights and less concerned with whether employer offers are wise. The courts have had other options for dealing with bargaining impasses, including options that accommodated both employer and NLRA rights. They could have left the parties in status quo to resolve the dispute themselves. They could have sent them to mediation or interest arbitration. They could even have left the decisions as to whose offer would be implemented to be decided by a neutral third party through interest arbitration or even by chance after impasse was declared. Any of these dispute mechanisms would better support collective bargaining by helping the parties get past their disagreement or would make alternatives to bargaining unattractive.

In addition to unbalancing collective bargaining processes, the court decisions have taken issues that matter to the parties off the table. The most important of these concern whether jobs will exist. The courts have held that employers have no obligation to bargain about managerial decisions and that decisions that lead to job loss are likely to be purely managerial decisions.[23] Whether a decision is solely managerial or must be bargained is complicated, highly subjective, and hard to litigate. The Court in *First National Maintenance Corp. v. NLRB*,[24] stated:

> Congress did not explicitly state what issues of mutual concern to union and management it intended to exclude from mandatory bargaining. Nonetheless, in view of an employer's need for unencumbered decision-making, bargaining over management decisions that have a substantial impact on the continued availability of employment should be required only if the benefit, for labor-management relations and the collective-bargaining process, outweighs the burden placed on the conduct of the business.

In other words, the Court held that the default position is that an employer has no obligation to bargain about "entrpreneurial" decisions: decisions are entrepreneurial unless the union can prove that the benefits for collective bargaining outweigh any burden such bargaining causes for the business. This is a difficult burden for a union to overcome. First, the employer has most of the information needed to satisfy this burden in its possession, while the union has very little. This differs from the norm of placing the burden of proof on the party with greatest access to information. Second, the decision as to what is a benefit or a burden is highly subjective. For example, slowing down decision making may be seen as a burden, because it impedes making quick changes. On the other hand, being forced to take time to gather more information and to reflect may be a benefit—both to the process of bargaining and to the business. The test does not ask whether bargaining could benefit the business; it assumes it is a burden. Third, there is no way to accurately weigh or compare the sort of evidence that would be provided. Fourth, courts are reluctant to second guess employer decisions, and for good reasons, so they normally will tend to defer to employer choices. Finally, a study of cases shows that the courts demand little of the employer to prove that bargaining is a burden.[25]

Implementation upon impasse lets an employer propose subcontracting out work, agree to bargain about the decision, quickly reach an impasse, and implement the subcontracting proposal, as in *International Paper Co. v. NLRB*.[26] Implementation upon impasse can be especially attractive in long-term bargaining relationships. In a study of NLRB decisions involving implementation of final offers, nearly one-fourth of the cases involved relationships of over twenty-five years. Long-term relationships are likely to mean work is performed in older facilities by an older workforce, which increases the employer's costs. This makes relocation and subcontracting as a way of deunionizing attractive,[27] but these acts are devastating to the workers.

Each year the labor movement loses about 250,000 members, many through business decisions to move work. This is a huge loss that organizing new members is hard put to make up for. Professor Clyde Summers says:

> Despite the statutory obligation to bargain with the employees' representative, management retained the prerogative to make this decision which

vitally affected the working lives of its employees by depriving them of their jobs without even listening to the employees' representative. This is a virulent expression of the presumption which underlies employment at will—the sovereignty of the employer to dispose of its subjects' jobs, with no duty to listen or explain.[28]

The language of the NLRA seems clear that refusing to bargain about whether jobs continue to exist violates Section 8(a)(5). Section 8(d) says that employers and unions have an obligation to bargain in good faith about "wages, hours, and other terms and conditions of employment." The existence of a job seems to fall into these categories. NLRA policies promoting collective bargaining and equality of bargaining power and preventing depressed wage rates lend support to this conclusion. The courts, however, say the employer's entrepreneurial rights should normally trump NLRA rights and policies. An employer has a duty to bargain about such a decision only if the benefits for labor relations *outweigh* the burden on management's conduct of the business.[29] If the benefits to both are equal, there is no requirement to accommodate both interests. Instead, the employer need not bargain.

Much is lost by taking such a crucial issue off the table. It undermines fundamental NLRA policies and deprives employers of critical information and support they could use to build their business. It assumes that employers going it alone make better decisions than they would by cooperating with a union and their employees in seeking a solution. In short, these decisions completely overlook the NLRA value of collective bargaining and the role it is supposed to play in strengthening our economy.

Take the saga of *Dorsey Trailers, Inc. v. NLRB*.[30] The court of appeals decided that Dorsey Trailers had no duty to bargain over the company's decision to relocate work from its Northumberland, Pennsylvania, plant, which had been unionized since 1967, to a new—and unorganized—plant in Cartersville, Georgia. The union had a history of working with the company during hard economic times. It had given concessions in the early 1990s that helped the plant become profitable. In the first six months of 1995, the plant made a profit of $1,500,000.

In the 1995 contract negotiations, the union hoped to reap the rewards of its cooperation. It wanted to regain some of the benefits it had conceded in the last contract and asked for wage increases. But the company wanted to give the union less. It demanded the ability to subcontract work and impose mandatory overtime. It imposed a new attendance policy that let the employer fire workers for fewer absences and refused to bargain about it. Company president Marilyn Marks said she would shut down the plant if the union did not agree to subcontracting and mandatory overtime. Management told employees that if they struck, the plant would close. One supervisor told a union member that the company had "no time to waste" on negotiations.

The workers struck, and management began planning the move to Cartersville, Georgia, a site it said had many advantages. These included a more modern assembly line, lower shipping costs for customers located in the Southeast, and state subsidies.

When the employer told the union it planned to move, the union immediately called off its strike. The company did not reinstate all the strikers immediately and told the union it wanted thirty-one concessions to keep the plant open. These included a 20 percent wage cut followed by a wage freeze for the duration of a five-year wage contract. The union made a counterproposal, but after a couple of weeks, the company announced it was closing the plant. All Northumberland employees were terminated.

This is the sort of "bargaining" the judicial impasse amendments promote in the name of supporting employer rights to manage. But the rest of the story suggests that the courts are not making a wise decision when they make it so easy to avoid bargaining. We can assume the workers' lives have been difficult since the closing, but no one has followed their story.[31]

We do know what happened to Dorsey. The move to the Cartersville plant was a disaster. It had a total net loss of $1,500,000 in 1996. By December 2000, it had declared bankruptcy.[32] In March 2001, it liquidated most of its assets and terminated president Marilyn Marks.[33]

This story does not prove that bargaining would have saved the company or the jobs, but it does show that giving management unfettered power to behave unilaterally and not to bargain collectively—and seriously—with the union does not guarantee that it will make wise decisions. What it certainly shows is that giving the employer that power allowed it to leave workers in Pennsylvania jobless and to wreak havoc on communities that had supported the company and depended on it for over thirty years. Georgia made a bad bet in subsidizing the company, and its taxpayers have had to pay for that mistake.

Finding a Way to Balance Rights

The *Dorsey* case affirms the NLRA's insights that what happens within the workplace affects society—for good or ill. The cases discussed here tell stories of losses that could have been avoided had the courts not ignored NLRA rights and policies in favor of unilateral employer rights. In each of those cases, the courts could have reached more satisfactory outcomes had they at least sought to balance and accommodate rights and had they asked what impact their decisions had on the NLRA's policies. Judges' decisions have repeatedly overwritten NLRA rights and policies with employer rights. As a result, judges have created a labor law riddled with inconsistencies that have weakened the NLRA.

Congress is at least partly to blame because it failed to say anything about how employer and employee rights were to be accommodated. Perhaps it expected that the NLRB would find the proper balance as it decided each case and gained expertise. However, it failed to foresee that the NLRB would not be given the final word on interpreting the NLRA. Congress also failed to deal with the problem that courts would not understand or sympathize with NLRA rights while they would tend to sympathize with employer rights.

Congress should have realized each of these problems. For centuries there has been a conflict between employee rights to organize and employer rights. Throughout the nineteenth century courts found that employees who joined together to improve their working conditions were criminal conspirators. Judges regularly enjoined strikes, picketing, and boycotts based on only one-sided employer petitions. Injunctions were based on whether judges thought workers' actions were legitimate. Judges interpreted the antitrust laws, such as the Sherman Act of 1890 and the Clayton Act of 1914 to outlaw collective actions by employees. This was the case even though the Clayton Act stated it did not apply to unions and union activities. Just as Congress had enacted the Clayton Act to rein in judges' anti-union interpretations of the Sherman Act, in 1932 it passed the Norris-LaGuardia Act to overturn judges' anti-union interpretations of the Clayton Act.[34] The law enacted prior to the NLRA, the National Industrial Recovery Act, was struck down as unconstitutional.

When Congress enacted the NLRA just three years later, it had to know that judges would likely not be the new law's friends. There was no reason to believe that judges would stop sympathizing with employers. Indeed decades of anti-NLRA decisions and attitudes demonstrate that these ways of thinking have not disappeared. This history shows us that those views and legal interpretations will be carried over to any new law.

We could stop here on a hopeless note, that history tells us that workplace laws' will be subverted by judicial interpretation. But I argue there is another message: we can learn from this history. So far, we have explored the components that can be used to construct a litigation strategy to take back the Workers' Law. We now have an understanding of forces that affect how judges see cases. We have sketched out a new way of trying cases by presenting detailed evidence that speaks directly to the NLRA's policies and explains them to judges. The last chapter advocated grounding litigation in NLRA policies, rights, and values. This chapter showed what happens when cases are tried without presenting a clear case about NLRA rights, policies, and values: in critical areas judges reflexively let employer rights trump NLRA rights. Creating a record that demonstrates how NLRA policies affect a case is critical, but more is required than simply declaring which NLRA values and policies are involved in every case. How employer rights apply to the specific case also needs to be clearly identified and analyzed. Then courts must be guided as to how to make room for both. Each case is, of course, unique, but it can be helpful to identify issues that commonly appear and devise a general system for dealing with them. The next chapter begins that work.

5

LITIGATION THEMES

This chapter builds on the insights of the last chapter by examining common clashes of rights so that cases can be tried in a way that makes them visible. The key areas where clashes can be expected include the following: (1) Who owns the job? (2) How should a case be constructed to make clear the rights involved in a case? (3) How can the content of the rights in a case be dissected? (4) How can the case be structured so as to help judges find a way to accommodate rights? (5) How can the court be persuaded to focus on the actual parties in the case before it?

Property Rights in the Job

Every time NLRA rights are enforced, they diminish traditional employer rights. Some courts react to the NLRA as a fundamental violation of employer's liberty and property rights. This deep reluctance to lessen employer rights is so fundamental that it can influence the outcome of cases, unless there is a strong commitment to address these prejudices directly. To do this, though, we first need to understand the way judges and lawyers think about rights.

Judges and lawyers often talk about rights as if they were as solid and real as a brick. They talk about the content of a right or its weight. But legal rights have only the reality and weight that judges give them. Property rights in land, for example, exist solely because the law says they do and because courts and police enforce those rights.[1] Land itself is concrete and real in the way that a brick is, so most property rights in land can actually be measured. For example, if a stranger walks on to your front yard, you can see the stranger and your yard and know that the stranger does not belong there.

Today, however, most important property rights are not tangible, that is, they are not something that can be seen or touched. We speak of property rights in a job, but these are far more difficult to measure and define than are rights in land. In addition, while it is likely that most people will agree on the boundaries of land and whether these boundaries have been invaded, in the case of a job, agreement is far less likely. Furthermore, we can see some parts of a job, but important parts are not visible. Some are abstract, existing only in people's minds, and people are likely to give them different weights.

Rights involved in NLRA cases are not fixed; they can be expanded. The first step in doing this is to think about what is involved in the right. To go back to a property right in land, at one time, no one owned land, but at some point this changed. When property ownership came into existence, the law had to define what it meant to own land. The most basic quality of property ownership is the right to exclude others. Someone who trespasses owes the owner damages. Even with land it may be difficult to say that a trespass has occurred or that damages are owed. What happens if my neighbor's cow comes onto my property, eats my flowers, and dies? What happens if water flows from my neighbor's property to mine and causes damage? Over the centuries, the courts faced many such cases and had to decide what legitimate rights the owner had. It is exactly this issue that must be addressed with respect to the question of who has property rights in a job.

The NLRA provides the starting point for challenging the idea that employer rights are sacrosanct. Section 1 says that corporation law had unbalanced workplace rights by giving employers too much power. The NLRA was intended to restore the balance of power in the workplace. The starting point, then, is to ensure that judges understand the NLRA as the quid pro quo for the continued existence of corporation law and that Congress enacted the NLRA to restore the balance of power within the workplace. In other words, under the NLRA employers have rights but not absolute ones. However, most judges and, even worse, labor lawyers and union representatives try NLRA cases as if they were ignorant of the NLRA's reordering of rights. This is unfortunate. Employee rights cannot be enforced if no one argues for Section 1's rebalancing workplace power whenever cases are tried.

We all need to be reminded that the NLRA

> was passed at a time in our Nation's history when there was considerable legal debate over the constitutionality of any law that required employers to conform their business behavior to any governmentally imposed standards. It was seriously contended that Congress could not constitutionally compel an employer to recognize a union and allow his employees to participate in setting the terms and conditions of employment.[2]

The U.S. Supreme Court rejected these ideas when it upheld the NLRA's constitutionality[3] and when it rejected the claim that contracts, including employment contracts, can trump laws.[4] The Court said in 1959 that "the due process clause is no longer to be so broadly construed that the Congress and state legislatures are put in a strait jacket when they attempt to suppress business and industrial conditions which they regard as offensive to the public welfare."[5] Judges, workers, employers, union leaders, and lawyers need to know that employer rights are not inviolate.

The question, by what right can the law regulate employers, needs to be restated as: Who owns a job?[6] This question of abstract property rights has real consequences. Most of us will automatically say that the employer owns the job.[7] The answer seems so obvious that the question seems absurd. The sophisticated, including judges, will say that the ultimate owner is the shareholder.[8]

The question is not absurd. It is complex. How do we measure the dimensions of job ownership? Is the owner the one who made the investment that created the job? Does ownership include those who have invested in the job since it was created? Without continuing investments, jobs do not exist, and those investments include both money and effort. Certainly jobs cannot exist without a person who performs the job's duties—an employee—as much as the job's existence depends on financial investors. In fact, a job's existence depends on the efforts of all who help the business succeed and grow. In other words, job ownership can be based on sweat equity: the employee's work and commitment to the job generate capital for the employer to invest, distribute as dividends, or use as profits. When employers use the return on the employee's investment to create new jobs, the employer and new employees pay back the investment other employees made in creating that job.

Moreover, workers pay a price for their jobs when they suffer from a job's impact on their bodies and minds. These, too, are investments. Employees may own a job by adverse possession, through their years of work. Staying in a job and putting one's heart and soul into it make an employee less able to find another job. These kinds of investments are far more personal and costly than money. If employees have ownership rights in the job, then those property rights must be protected by the law, just as the law protects employer property rights. An employer may argue that it has a right to conduct its business in an orderly manner without being subjected to arbitrary restraints. That may be true, but being free of arbitrary restraints is not the same as being free of all restraints. Employees have the legal right to organize for the purpose of securing the redress of grievances and to negotiate agreements with employers relating to the conditions of work. That this may affect employer rights does not mean that employees do not have the right to organize.[9]

Although we are not accustomed to thinking that labor and employment laws protect employee property rights in the job, we need to change this perception to take into account the reality of employee investments in their jobs.

Society also has a right to ownership rights in jobs. Jobs cannot exist without society's investments. Many states make outright investments to lure companies by providing tax rebates, zoning, financing, and other subsidies. Society invests in jobs by paying for critical infrastructure that directly benefits employers. These include the right to use the air waves, copyright and patent protections, contract law, and corporation law. Society gives employers streets, highways, and supports for subway, bus, rail, and air traffic so workers can reach their jobs and the employer can market its goods and services. Communities provide sewage, trash pickup, and public health services so employers can have healthy workers. Society provides schools and other training to create an educated, productive workforce. Employers depend on the support of police, law, and courts to enforce and define their rights. Add to this what society does to make markets function. Jobs could not exist without these investments, and employers depend on communities to make them. No individual employer could afford to create them, and some cannot exist on an individual basis. For example, a section of roadway built in front of one's business is of little use by itself. As a result of all these investments, society owns jobs and has a right to regulate them in the public interest and to protect the community from injuries an employer might cause by the way it conducts its business.[10]

The reality is that all jobs in this country are public-sector jobs. This is as true of widget makers or programmers who work for Pixar as it is of firefighters or prosecuting attorneys, even if we are unaccustomed to seeing the investments society makes in jobs. If we were to examine and account for the true dollar value of all types and levels of public support provided to create and support jobs, the truth of this statement would be obvious.

In short, if job ownership were based on a full accounting for investments in jobs, there are many claimants. This more comprehensive view of job ownership and corporate debt to society is embodied in the NLRA. Some managers also see corporations as social institutions that form a corporate community made up of employees and suppliers.

> The medical company Johnson & Johnson even carved a credo in stone at its New Jersey headquarters, stating that shareholders would get a fair return only after the company had ensured outstanding value to customers, employees, suppliers, and the communities where the company operated.
> If one goes back to the classic study *The American Business Creed*, one finds striking evidence of a managerial philosophy that would today be considered heretical. As the authors observed: "Corporation managers generally claim that they have four broad responsibilities: to consumers, to employees, to stockholders, and to the general public . . . each group is on an equal footing; the function of management is to secure justice for all and unconditional maxima for none. Stockholders have no special priority; they are entitled to a fair return on their investment, but profits above a so-called fair level are an economic sin."[11]

The NLRA says that the way workers are treated within the workplace inevitably affects society as a whole. Just as workers' minds and bodies are marked by their commitments to their jobs, so, too, is society affected by the jobs it provides. Communities come to depend on their employers and can be devastated when they close or move. Employers that offer good jobs with good pay help to support vibrant communities that attract and retain people. But employers that offer poor jobs impose costs on their communities.[12] Because it is impossible to confine what happens within a workplace to the workplace, a society has an interest in its jobs. This gives its communities legally protected rights in connection with those jobs. A community has a right both to oversee its investments in the workplace and to protect itself from harmful employer practices.[13] NLRA policies recognize that the claims of society and workers to ownership of jobs are as legitimate as those of employers. How do these ideas relate to NLRA litigation? Law, cases, and evidence that demonstrate that parties in addition to employers have bona fide rights must be brought into trials to assist the judge in assessing the legitimacy of the completing claims of employers, employees, and the public. We need to help judges try cases based on evidence as to legitimate rights and not mere claims to rights in a job.

Jones & Laughlin's lawyers argued, in 1937, that the NLRA should be held unconstitutional because its enactment would radically weaken employer rights. They said that the underlying philosophy of the NLRA was a threat to an employer's normal right to manage its own business. The Court, however, took the employer to task because it did not base its case on the evidence presented; rather, it only insisted on its constitutional rights.[14]

Judges have a "sworn duty to decide cases in accordance with the Constitution and the laws that Congress has enacted."[15] Thus judges have an obligation to enforce the NLRA and will uphold their duty more vigorously if they understand the policies and justifications behind the law. The Supreme Court endorsed the need to accommodate both NLRA and employer rights in *Phelps Dodge Corp. v. NLRB*,[16] one of its earliest decisions interpreting the NLRA:

> Congress explicitly disclosed its purposes in declaring the policy which underlies the Act. Its ultimate concern, as well as the source of its power, was "to eliminate the causes of certain substantial obstructions to the free flow of commerce." This vital national purpose was to be accomplished "by encouraging the practice and procedure of collective bargaining and by protecting the exercise by workers of full freedom of association." § 1. Only thus could workers ensure themselves economic standards consonant with national well-being. Protection of the workers' right to self-organization does not curtail the appropriate sphere of managerial freedom; it furthers the wholesome conduct of business enterprise. "The Act," this Court has said, "does not interfere with the normal exercise of the right of the employer to select its employees or to discharge them." But "under cover of

that right," the employer may not "intimidate or coerce its employees with respect to their self-organization and representation." When "employers freely recognize the right of their employees to their own organizations and their unrestricted right of representation there will be much less occasion for controversy in respect to the free and appropriate exercise of the right of selection and discharge." . . . Labor unions were organized "out of the necessities of the situation. . . . Union was essential to give laborers opportunity to deal on equality with their employer." . . . And so the present Act . . . leaves the adjustment of industrial relations to the free play of economic forces but seeks to assure that the play of those forces be truly free.[17]

Reordering the way we think about property rights in jobs has the potential to support a new understanding of the NLRA, one that sees the rights of employers, employees, and the public in a job as shared and not in conflict with one another. Cases must be tried so that judges are educated about these shared rights and understand their full meaning. This will help them see that legal collective activity by employees includes making common cause with those who work for other employers.[18] Cases that involve the right of employees to make common cause with one another include organizing and secondary boycotts.[19] The scope of legitimate activity in secondary boycotts can be expanded when judges understand that the NLRA speaks forcefully in support of the right of employees to support one another, even though not working for the same employer.

Being Clear About Rights

There are many NLRA policies and rights, just as there are many employer rights. Not all matter in each case. Being clear about which rights are involved, and how, helps judges understand why there is a violation. It also makes it easier to see how to resolve a case and how to accommodate employer and NLRA rights.

Vagueness and failing to communicate which NLRA and employer rights are relevant to a case only invites judges to draw conclusions based on their preconceptions about rights. Recall that in *Lechmere, Inc. v. NLRB*[20] the Court said that the conflict was between the employer's right to control access to its property and the employees' right to hear the union organizers' message. Notice that this set up a situation in which the employee right was far weaker than the employer's right. Contrast this with a case in which the employee rights were the core NLRA rights of employees to make common cause with one another to engage in mutual aid or protection, to select representatives of their own choosing, to improve their purchasing power, and to stabilize wages and working conditions within and between industries. These are strong rights. Add to this a plausible claim that political speech was involved, since the NLRA's policies can be read as endorsing the public and political nature of discussions about unions. It is fair to say that these were the rights involved in *Lechmere*.

The content of the employer's property right also needs to be dissected, to show which of the bundle of potential employer rights is involved. The property right in *Lechmere* was not the strong property right the Courts suggested. Rather, it was weakened by the company's open invitation to all—or almost all—of the public to enter.

Compare this with the way rights were articulated by the Court in *Republic Aviation Corp. v. NLRB*.[21] This case also involved asking employees to join a union and, in addition, to wear a union button while on employer property. In this case, the Supreme Court found that the employee right involved was the core NLRA right, "the right of employees to organize for mutual aid without employer interference."[22] In contrast, the Board and Court concluded that the employer right involved was not a property right; rather, it was merely a right to ensure order among its employees, a managerial right. It was easier for the Court to see that these rights were involved because the employer's own employees were asking fellow employees to support the union. But under the NLRA this should not make a difference. Section 2(3) says that employees have the rights of employees, regardless of who their employer is. In *Republic Aviation*, the Supreme Court endorsed the principle that employer rights do not automatically trump NLRA rights:

> "It is not every interference with property rights that is within the Fifth Amendment. . . . Inconvenience, or even some dislocation of property rights, may be necessary in order to safeguard the right to collective bargaining." The Board has frequently applied this principle in decisions involving varying sets of circumstances, where it has held that the employer's right to control his property does not permit him to deny access to his property to persons whose presence is necessary there to enable the employees effectively to exercise their right to self-organization and collective bar-

gaining, and in those decisions which have reached the courts, the Board's position has been sustained. Similarly, the Board has held that, while it was "within the province of an employer to promulgate and enforce a rule prohibiting union solicitation during working hours," it was "not within the province of an employer to promulgate and enforce a rule prohibiting union solicitation by an employee outside of working hours, although on company property," the latter restriction being deemed an unreasonable impediment to the exercise of the right to self-organization.[23]

These are not isolated views. Ten years earlier, the Supreme Court said that providing rights for both employers and employees so they could negotiate and confer was not "an invasion of the constitutional right of either." Rather, it "was based on the recognition of the rights of both."[24] Employer rights are not and cannot be inviolable and sacrosanct. The question of when property rights can be "inconvenienced" or "dislocated" comes down to what we recognize as important. If we value worker and community safety and health, freedom from fire hazards, or aesthetics—and we do—then we let the state override employer property rights through inspections, fines, disclosure laws, record keeping requirements, and zoning limits.

It cannot be said too strongly how critical it is that NLRA values are explicitly included in the theory, trial, and advocacy in a case. It is the job of the advocate to tell the judge which rights are at risk in a case and explain why. It is the job of the judge to react to the party's claims, evidence, and theories. Failing to do the job of presenting the case for NLRA and employer rights tailored to the issues in each case means that the advocate is to blame if a judge fails to consider NLRA rights in deciding the case.

Dissecting the Content of Rights in Each Case

Making a boilerplate statement that generic NLRA rights are at risk is useless. It is the rights bound up with the facts in the specific case that matter. This means demonstrating to the judges why finding a violation will promote the specific NLRA rights while not finding a violation undermines those rights. The same demonstration and connection must also be made with employer rights. Judges need to be shown that protecting these specific employee rights does not mean destroying legitimate employer rights.

At first this will be difficult, because it means thinking about cases in new ways and developing completely new ways to try cases. Most important, it means fighting the inertia that has prevented the NLRB from being an effective champion for NLRA rights. Most fundamentally, it means trying to see the case through the judge's eyes: What will persuade the judge to accept your version of the facts, the policies, the rights, and how to accommodate them?

I came away from two weeks of teaching labor law to a group of trade unionists with a box of paints and a calendar with dog pictures. In class, I had urged them to be clear when they tried cases, to paint a clear picture of what had happened. I told them: If you try a case about a dog, remember that everyone carries around a mental picture of a dog, and that is the dog they will think of. So while you are talking about Fluffy, a sweet lap dog, the judge is thinking of Brutus, the dog who bit her last week. Perceptions and personal experiences are the foundations on which reality is built.

We all carry around assumptions. It is easy to dispel prejudices about concrete things like dogs, but assumptions about workplace rights, employees, and employers are a real challenge. Assumptions affected the outcome of each of the cases discussed in prior chapters. A failure to educate the judge about the people, events, rights, and policies in a case and how they tie together will mean a trial by assumptions.

Rights are abstract ideas, even though they have real consequences. When people hear abstract ideas such as freedom of speech, due process, and democracy, they will project their own experiences and ideas onto those rights. It is impossible to predict how people will feel about legal rights, even constitutional rights, so to prevent trial by assumptions, the content of those rights involved in the case must be part of the proofs.

The federal building where I worked for the NLRB was, naturally enough, the site for demonstrations. The building was an important symbol of the government the protesters were trying to speak to, and it had a broad plaza that gave demonstrators space to march or protest. You might assume that federal employees would understand and value constitutional rights. However, word of even a very small demonstration tended to throw my fellow government employees into a tizzy. They reacted as though they were under siege and in danger. Yet those demonstrators were doing no more than peacefully exercising their First Amendment rights of assembly, speech, and petition, rights I think my fellow workers would have endorsed in the abstract—at least I hope so. Similarly, judges may not always understand the exercise of NLRA rights and respect them as the embodiment of core American values; a successful litigation strategy can help them do so by carefully dissecting the exercise of the employer and NLRA rights in the case, by making them conscious of their decision-making processes, including their biases and preconceptions, and by giving them a guide for weighing and comparing the rights.

One way a conscious litigation approach can be used to expand rights to organize and bargain collectively is by building on judges' existing worldviews. Judges are likely to understand constitutional rights, and constitutional rights can be used to illuminate analogous NLRA rights and their content. For example, if employees are passing out handbills to urge a boycott in support of union activity, remind judges how analogous boycotts, such as civil rights boycotts, have been treated.[25] Civil rights boycotts have received far more favorable treatment than have labor boycotts. Show judges how the two are similar, and ask the courts to rethink that different treatment. Tie this to NLRA policies, and show what decision promotes those policies. Or consider making a case that provides record evidence for courts to consider how constitutional rights of free speech and assembly support expanding employees' NLRA rights to discuss issues that concern them and to organize or picket.

Section 8(c) of the NLRA also deals with speech.[26] It is commonly referred to as a free speech right for employers, even though it does not mention employers and nothing in it suggests that it cannot be used by unions. Section 8(c) gives no affirmative rights. It simply says that certain sorts of speech cannot be a violation of the NLRA. Compare its wording with that of Section 7, which says: "Employees *shall have the right . . .*" (emphasis added). Section 8(c) says:

> The expressing of any views, argument, or opinion, or the dissemination thereof, whether in written, printed, graphic, or visual form, shall not constitute or be evidence of an unfair labor practice under any of the provisions of this Act, if such expression contains no threat of reprisal or promise of benefit.

If Section 8(c) is understood to create an affirmative right—but the language does not say that—and it said to protect only employer anti-union speech—but it says nothing about employers, unions, or employees[27]—

what explains this? The answer seems to be that everyone has come to assume what Section 8(c) says, and this assumption has overwritten its plain words. As a result, unions bitterly condemn Section 8(c). Failure to read the actual words of Section 8(c) has left unions unable to think of strategies to expand its meaning to protect union and employee rights. Yet since many union violations are based on speech, unions stand to benefit from expanding Section 8(c) to protect worker and union speech rights.

Finally, judges are likely to assume that the NLRA's only concern is what happens in a workplace. However, a plain reading of the NLRA's policies demonstrates that its concerns are far broader. Unless cases are litigated in a way that includes a focus on the interconnection between work and society, this linkage will be lost. Seeing the issues as confined to a struggle between employers and unions also limits the palette of values judges can draw from in trying cases. These values might be expanded, to the benefit of unions, if the dissection of rights shows that NLRA rights are more than a struggle between employer and employees for control of the workplace. The NLRA exists to promote society's well-being, which includes not only economic well-being but also the promotion of democracy and social peace. Reminding judges that these are the values at stake may make it more likely that they will want to enforce the NLRA.

Helping Judges Find a Way to Accommodate Rights

It is critical to assist judges in reaching decisions that accommodate all legitimate rights—both NLRA and employer rights. Consider a judge deciding a case like *Lechmere*. The judge might decide that the union organizers should have been treated as employees under Section 2(3) with the rights and protections the NLRA gives employees. It is possible to win on this issue but gain no meaningful rights. This depends on what content the judge decides to give the right and how employer rights are treated. In other words, what matters is what access the organizers get to the employer's property and what they are allowed to do there. Employers have managerial rights when dealing with their own employees' exercise of NLRA rights. An employer should also have a managerial right with regard to union organizers, even ones who have the full rights of employees. If the judge has no help in accommodating the organizers' employee rights with the employer's need to run its business, the judge may decide that the only option is to exclude the organizers.

What can be done to help judges with these conflicts of rights? The person trying the case needs to figure out the questions the judge must consider and provide an answer for each of these. Most judges will probably be concerned that organizers not have free run of the employer's premises. In the *Lechmere* situation, for example, would the organizers have access to none of the employer's property, only to the parking lot, or, as statutory employees, could they enter all areas Lechmere employees could? If the latter, could they talk to the employer's employees and distribute literature to them on the same basis as a Lechmere employee could? Is there an appropriate distinction that gives employees of an employer more access rights than those who are not employees of this employer?

Is the employer right in the case of union organizers—who are statutory employees, but not of this employer—an employer property right or only a lesser managerial right? If it is a property right, is it a right to totally exclude or some lesser property right? If it is a managerial right, is it limited to excluding employees from access only to the extent necessary to effectively manage the workplace?

Given these conflicting rights, what is the best way to accommodate them with the least harm to each party? Could the organizers have rights on a par with shoppers' access rights? Should the employer's employees have rights to invite others, such as union organizers, in to protect their rights or to help them exercise their rights? Would this mean that Lechmere's employees could invite in an OSHA inspector over the employer's objection?[28]

These are not hypothetical questions. They are issues that judges will have to decide and ones employers will raise to support limiting organizer and employee rights. The employer has the edge if the NLRB or union attorney fails to present the case for how to accommodate NLRA rights with the employer's rights.

Focusing on the Parties in the Case

In every case—not just NLRA cases—the identity of the parties is always a critical issue. In criminal cases, the jury must not decide a case based on prejudices or stereotypes. It should not matter that the defendant is a member of a group likely to commit this sort of crime or is a bad person in general. The jury must decide whether the defendant committed the specific crime charged. This is also true of employers, employees, and unions in NLRB cases. What should matter is the question of what this employer, employee, or union did and why they did it. Decisions should not be made on the basis of stereotypes or prejudice.

While NLRA cases are civil cases, they are similar to criminal cases in the way they are investigated and tried. They are not mere personal disputes but, rather, the cases are brought to vindicate public rights. In NLRA cases the government prosecutes someone for violating the law. NLRA remedies are supposed to promote the policies of the Act rather than to make an injured party whole. It is, however, easy to lose sight of the fact that NLRA cases are public cases whose concern is with the social impact of what happens in each workplace. Instead, cases may appear to be about no more than a mere workplace disagreement.

NLRA cases must be tried using a sort of double vision. One eye must be focused on the facts of the case; the other must be concerned with whether the employer, union, or employee in the specific case is a fair representative of employers, employees, and unions in general, for other judges who are deciding later cases will be bound by the case's outcome and analysis or will use it as a guide. Thus evidence must be presented on the history of the parties' interactions and motivations. Information must be provided to help the judge overcome biases about employers, employees, or unions.

Judges seem to decide cases by taking only one party's rights into account. The *Darlington, Adkins, Mackay,* and *Lechmere* cases discussed in chapter 4 are examples. They also may fail to take into consideration how the parties' interactions have led to the problem. This makes it more likely that only one party will be seen as responsible and whether a remedy is needed.

Consider the facts in *Elk Lumber Co.*,[29] decided in 1950. When the employer changed the way it loaded lumber onto boxcars, the work was easier and the flow steadier. As a result, it cut the wages of its five loaders so that they went from a piece rate that averaged about $2.71 an hour to $1.52 an hour, a cut of about $61 a week. Put another way, for what it used to pay the five loaders, the company could now hire 8.8 loaders. The employees calculated that their per-car rate had been cut from $14.45 per car to $12.20 per car. They also knew what the quota of work was at other plants in the area. So they decided to cut the number of cars loaded in a day to reflect the wage cut and what other plants required. The employer fired them, and the Board decided this was lawful.

The Board held that this was a slowdown and that a slowdown was not protected. It said that the only way employees can exert pressure on an employer is to strike. The Board saw this case as an employer's legitimate right to get a full day's work versus employees' illegitimate attempt to control their wage-effort bargain.[30] It saw the employees as masquerading as loyal employees by continuing to work while defrauding their employer of wages.

To see the case this way means seeing only one side of the case and ignoring the parties' interactions. The employees did not simply decide they were going to change their wages. They were responding to their employer's unilateral change in their rate of pay by keeping the ratio of their pay to amount of work in status quo. From their point of view, the employer had changed the terms of the parties' wage-effort bargain, and the employees were trying to keep the terms the parties had originally agreed to.

In the pre-NLRA world, the employer had the right to unilaterally change the terms of work. In the NLRA world, the employees have the right to join together to support one another and to negotiate the terms under which they work and even to use coercion in that effort. The employer violates the law if it fires them for doing this. In *Elk Lumber,* the employer made a unilateral change, behaving as if this were a pre-NLRA workplace, but the employees' attempts to get the employer to discuss their pay was just what the NLRA promoted. The Board showed no concern about whether the decision promoted NLRA policies and paid no attention to who the parties really were, why they acted as they did, and how they were interacting with one another.

Contrast this with NLRB v. *Fansteel Metallurgical Corp.,*[31] decided in 1939. There the Board found that the employees' sit-down strike was a reaction to employer provocation. It ordered the employer to reinstate the discharged sit-down strikers. The Supreme Court, however, said that employer's actions were irrelevant and did not override the employer's legal rights to possession and protection of its property. The employees' NLRA rights were invisible. The Court did not consider the parties' interaction to be relevant and never explained why discharge was necessary to protect the employer's rights.

This tunnel vision is not an isolated problem. Bargaining impasses are another example. Impasses figure into strikes, striker replacement, and the employer's right to implement its final offer. One party can create an impasse by being unreasonable, but it is fair to assume that most impasses are caused by both parties' failing to agree. Agreement is a good outcome for many reasons. Failure to reach agreement disrupts the workplace relationship, in both the short and long term, and can also harm society, while agreement lets the parties tailor work conditions to their needs and allows them to get back to work. Furthermore, reaching an agreement means that there is buy-in to the process.

There are two possible reasons for an impasse: either the parties are simply unable to reach an agreement, in which case the law should help them continue to negotiate and resolve their differences, or one party is at fault for causing the impasse and should be sanctioned—and certainly not rewarded. Thus when an NLRA case involves an impasse, the focus must be on what happened during the negotiations at issue to lead to this problem and on how this decision will affect the parties' future bargaining as well as bargaining in general.

The NLRA policy is to promote the "practice and procedure" of collective bargaining. It says nothing about actually reaching an agreement. Judges must avoid being so focused on an outcome that the process is harmed, and especially to avoid rewarding the party who is refusing to abide by that process.

> The object of this Act was not to allow governmental regulation of the terms and conditions of employment, but rather to ensure that employers and their employees could work together to establish mutually satisfactory conditions. The basic theme of the Act was that through collective bargaining the passions, arguments, and struggles of prior years would be channeled into constructive, open discussions leading, it was hoped, to mutual agreement. But it was recognized from the beginning that agreement might in some cases be impossible, and it was never intended that the Government would in such cases step in, become a party to the negotiations and impose its own views of a desirable settlement.[32]

But the courts have intervened to do just this, not by dictating specific terms but by setting up their own bargaining process, one that does not encourage employers and employees to work together to establish mutually satisfactory conditions. When there is an impasse, judges allow an employer to implement its final offer. When an impasse causes a strike, employers are allowed to permanently replace the strikers with nonunion workers and to implement any terms they like for those replacement workers. These put a thumb on the employer's side of the scale, in defiance of NLRA policy to promote equality of bargaining power and divert the parties from focusing on reaching a bargained agreement. The drafters of the NLRA believed that legal rules structured any market, and they chose rules to create a market that would redistribute power from employers toward employees.[33] These judicial doctrines, however, reward the employer who can reach an impasse while taking away the union's power to say no.

These doctrines grow out of judges' stereotypes about the roles of employers, employees, and unions in bargaining and are built on assumptions about the relative rights of the parties. Judges are never required to consider the parties' bargaining interactions or to make findings as to what decision will promote NLRA policies. They ignore the obvious: the very purpose of a union's existence is to bargain better terms for its members. If it cannot do this, then it has little reason to exist. The union and employer both know that when a union has trouble getting an agreement, the employees may decide that there is no point in having union representation. As a result, these doctrines ignore the fact that the union is more likely to want an agreement than the employer, and the employer is more likely to gain from having no agreement. Only when an employer's behavior is particularly egregious are its rights to implement workplace terms and permanently replace strikers lost. And even when their conduct is grossly illegal, employers never lose the right to replace strikers.

Judges must be helped to focus on the natures of the specific parties in the case before them. They need to be shown how their behavior complied or did not comply with the NLRA and how it goaded the other side to react. Judges also need to know how the parties compare with other employers, employees, and unions so they can tailor the remedy to fit a particular case while also developing legal doctrine that promotes the NLRA's policies. Research shows that compliance is affected by how a rule of law is chosen and the message it sends with regard to deviant behavior. When there is no risk of punishment, evasion becomes commonplace among dedicated cheaters. This demoralizes those who want to comply with the law and goads them to evade it. Therefore, judges must send a message that law evaders are deviants, not normal citizens, and will be punished.[34]

Examining which sort of party this is—law abider or shirker—and creating legal doctrine that punishes the shirker and supports the law abider is the best way to support the behavior of those who want to comply with their legal obligations. Pushing judges to focus on the identity and behavior of the parties in each case is a fundamental problem. For many judges, these stereotypes may be built on ideas that getting rid of unions is key to economic prosperity and advancement.[35] The ease with which collective bargaining rights were taken from the employees of the Department of Homeland Security is a matter for concern. The fact that it was on the grounds that collective bargaining rights endanger national security tells us that stereotypes about employers, employees, and unions have a firm grip.[36]

6

NLRA RIGHTS WITHIN OTHER LAWS

The idea that workers' legal rights are inferior to those of employers is one that must change for the good of society. This new way of thinking about employer and worker rights has been championed by former Secretaries of Labor and by major labor and legal thinkers,[1] and these ideas may be found in both U.S. and international law. In other words, NLRA values of equality of bargaining power and social and economic justice are not unique. There is a web of laws that embody the same principles and that can be used to support and give content to NLRA policies and to guide courts in interpreting them. The authority of these sources of law is at least equivalent to—if not greater than—the common-law concepts judges draw on when they overturn the NLRA's intent. These rights are found within our country's fundamental documents and in law created by the community of nations to which we belong.

United States courts have tended not to turn to sources such as international law in interpreting workers' rights, but this is changing.[2] The pedigree and weight of many of the laws discussed in this chapter are greater than the common-law tradition that infuses judges' thinking about workplace rights. Some might argue that, if these other laws were sources for worker rights, we would have already seen them used in interpreting workplace rights. But so far these other laws have not been made part of NLRA litigation, and they have not been championed in a strategic way. As a result, we do not know their full potential.

In addition to their legal weight, these laws can inspire a campaign to remake our understandings about how work and society fit together. They speak of work as a source of dignity and self-fulfillment. They promote the rights of worker voice, association, participation, equity, and equality of opportunity. They link economic welfare with social welfare. Their message is a counterpoint to, and different from, that of the cost-benefit analysis and its illusory fairness.[3]

This chapter sets out the text of many of these sources from U.S. and international law and suggests possible legal contexts in which they can be used.

The NLRA's Ancestors

NLRA rights evolved from ideas that existed long before 1935. Thomas Kohler says:

> The meanings and understandings that informed this scheme were by that time well-known and broadly accepted. . . . They constantly had been reiterated "in reports of industrial commissions, court decisions, rulings of administrative bodies, and legislation"; Congress merely "gathered up the . . . threads" and wove the statute from them. In short, labor law was not a congressional invention. The threads in the legislative loom had been spun by many hands, and of these, many never had held a law book.[4]

The Clayton Antitrust and Norris-LaGuardia Acts are NLRA antecedents whose values influenced the drafting of the NLRA. This means that these statutes are evidence that should be used in interpreting the NLRA.[5]

The Clayton Antitrust Act, enacted in 1914, declares: "the labor of a human being is not a commodity or article of commerce." It supports the role of labor organizations in providing mutual help.[6] In 1932, in the Norris-LaGuardia Act, Congress said:

> Whereas under prevailing economic conditions, developed with the aid of governmental authority for owners of property to organize in the corporate and other forms of ownership association, the individual unorganized worker is commonly helpless to exercise actual liberty of contract and to protect his freedom of labor, and thereby to obtain acceptable terms and conditions of employment, wherefore, though he should be free to decline

to associate with his fellows, it is necessary that he have full freedom of association, self-organization, and designation of representatives of his own
choosing, to negotiate the terms and conditions of his employment, and
that he shall be free from the interference, restraint, or coercion of employers of labor, or their agents, in the designation of such representatives or in
self-organization or in other concerted activities for the purpose of collective bargaining or other mutual aid or protection. . . .[7]

Norris-LaGuardia also protects collective action and limits judicial power
over collective action. It recognizes that labor disputes affect far more than
just conditions between an employer and its employees.[8]

When it enacted the NLRA three years later after the Norris-LaGuardia
Act, Congress repeated the point that worker and employer rights must be
brought into balance. By restating these same principles, Congress demonstrated that employees were to have a wide range of protected legal interests, including an interest in the working conditions of employees outside
their own workplace. This idea is fundamental to the interpretation of
union access to organize a workplace, the obligation to pay union dues,
and limits on secondary boycotts.

The United States Constitution

The United States Constitution has the potential to be a support for
worker rights. The Constitution is the supreme law in this country, and,
therefore, no state or federal law can conflict with it. Its protections for freedom of speech and association are similar to NLRA policies to promote and
protect rights of freedom of association, freedom of speech, and collective
action.[9] These constitutional doctrines may be useful in expanding rights
in many areas. Two areas in which there has not been success in urging First
Amendment rights, though the issue is still worth pursuing in the future, are
secondary boycotts[10] and recognitional picketing[11] in Sections 8(b)(4) and
(7).[12] Each of these violations depends on speech and association issues and
thus has an uneasy fit with the First Amendment. Congress eventually included special provisos to avoid having them held unconstitutional.

It is unfortunate that, in this critical area of speech and associational
rights, the Supreme Court has had a difficult time applying constitutional
rights in a consistent way in both the private and public sector. For exam-

ple, in *Smith v. Arkansas Highway Employees, Local 1315*,[13] the Court decided that, while public employees had a First Amendment right to join and be represented by a union, their employer could refuse to let a union representative take part in the employer's grievance procedure. The Court admitted that this holding would tend "to impair or undermine—if only slightly—the effectiveness of the union in representing the economic interests of its members." But, it found, this impairment is not prohibited by the Constitution. The Court issued this decision without holding a hearing and even admitted it was making assumptions instead of relying on evidence. While the Court might be correct that an employer has no constitutional obligation to meet with a union in general, it failed to consider the question whether the employer can deny public employees the right to choose to associate with a union as a representative in presenting a grievance. Justice Marshall dissented and said:

> Now this Court is deciding vital constitutional questions without even a plenary hearing. I dissent.
> This Court has long held that the First Amendment protects the right of unions to secure legal representation for their members. . . . Based on this precedent and on Arkansas' recognition of public employees' right to organize and join a union, . . . the Court of Appeals concluded that the First Amendment also encompasses respondent union's right to file grievances on behalf of its members. If a public employer may not refuse to entertain a grievance submitted by a union-salaried attorney, it is not immediately apparent why the employer in this case should be entitled to reject a grievance asserted by the union itself.[14]

The erratic line of cases on access to shopping malls is a second area that demonstrates the uneasiness the Court feels in finding a principled way to apply the First Amendment to labor rights.[15] In each of these areas, the Court's inconsistency means there is space to make the case for a principled application of First Amendment rights.

James Pope has argued eloquently for using the Thirteenth Amendment's protections against involuntary servitude and badges and incidents of slavery as a basis for remaking labor law.[16] This amendment has been so little used that it has unexplored potential for expanding workplace rights.

We should also consider turning to the fundamental policies set out in the Preamble to the Constitution of the United States. The Preamble says that this country is founded on values of justice, social welfare, and liberty, thus affirming ideas that were first expressed in the Declaration of Independence. The Preamble states:

> We the People of the United States, in Order to form a more perfect Union, establish Justice, insure domestic Tranquility, provide for the common defence, promote the general Welfare, and secure the Blessings of Liberty to ourselves and our Posterity, do ordain and establish this Constitution for the United States of America.

The Declaration of Independence states: "We hold these truths to be self-evident, that all men are created equal, that they are endowed by their Creator with certain unalienable Rights, that among these are Life, Liberty and the pursuit of Happiness."

The drafters of the Declaration chose these words carefully. They understood that the right to the pursuit of happiness is not a right to be in a state of happiness but rather it meant that every person has a right to conditions that can ensure a meaningful chance to seek and achieve happiness. These conditions include ensuring that the basic needs for material comfort, food, shelter, clothing, and education are provided so that poverty does not make it impossible to engage in the pursuit of happiness.[17] The signers of the Declaration were not opposed to happiness, but they understood that happiness cannot be guaranteed. On the other hand, it is possible to guarantee that a person's basic needs have been provided. In addition, while material comfort cannot guarantee happiness, it is difficult to be happy when basic needs have not been met. The NLRA reflects these ideas when it links inadequate wages and working conditions with strife.

To these ideas add those President Franklin Roosevelt expressed in 1944, nine years after the NLRA was enacted. Roosevelt asked Congress to implement an economic bill of rights and argued that it was "definitely the responsibility of the Congress to do so." His ideas reflect and expand the NLRA's linking of material well-being, social justice, and democratic governance:

> It is our duty now to begin to lay the plans and determine the strategy for the winning of a lasting peace and the establishment of an American standard of living higher than ever before known. We cannot be content, no matter how high that general standard of living may be, if some fraction of our people—whether it be one-third or one-fifth or one-tenth—is ill-fed, ill-clothed, ill-housed, and insecure.

This Republic had its beginning, and grew to its present strength, under the protection of certain inalienable political rights—among them the right of free speech, free press, free worship, trial by jury, freedom from unreasonable searches and seizures. They were our rights to life and liberty.

As our nation has grown in size and stature, however—as our industrial economy expanded—these political rights proved inadequate to assure us equality in the pursuit of happiness.

We have come to a clear realization of the fact that true individual freedom cannot exist without economic security and independence. "Necessitous men are not free men." People who are hungry and out of a job are the stuff of which dictatorships are made.

In our day these economic truths have become accepted as self-evident. We have accepted, so to speak, a second Bill of Rights under which a new basis of security and prosperity can be established for all—regardless of station, race, or creed.

Among these are:

The right to a useful and remunerative job in the industries or shops or farms or mines of the nation;

The right to earn enough to provide adequate food and clothing and recreation;

The right of every farmer to raise and sell his products at a return which will give him and his family a decent living;

The right of every businessman, large and small, to trade in an atmosphere of freedom from unfair competition and domination by monopolies at home or abroad;

The right of every family to a decent home;

The right to adequate medical care and the opportunity to achieve and enjoy good health;

The right to adequate protection from the economic fears of old age, sickness, accident, and unemployment;

The right to a good education.

All of these rights spell security. And after this war is won we must be prepared to move forward, in the implementation of these rights, to new goals of human happiness and well-being.

America's own rightful place in the world depends in large part upon how fully these and similar rights have been carried into practice for our citizens. For unless there is security here at home, there cannot be lasting peace in the world.

One of the great American industrialists of our day—a man who has rendered yeoman service to his country in this crisis—recently emphasized the grave dangers of rightist reaction in this Nation. All clear-thinking businessmen share his concern. Indeed, if such reaction should develop—if history were to repeat itself and we were to return to the so-called normalcy of the 1920s—then it is certain that, even though we shall have conquered our enemies on the battlefields abroad, we shall have yielded to the spirit of fascism here at home.[18]

International Law

International law also embodies values and legal rights similar to those of the NLRA. Recently Justice Ruth Bader Ginsberg explained why it is right and appropriate for U.S. laws to be interpreted in light of international law.[19] She and fellow Justices Rehnquist and O'Connor have endorsed the value of learning from others who have given thought to the same issues. Ginsberg cited a long tradition in this country for doing so, going back to the founding of the United States. The Declaration of Independence, for example, placed its case for separating from Great Britain before the world. The Constitution was drafted by drawing on the insights of philosophers from Europe. Article I, Section 8, Clause 10 grants Congress the power "to define and punish . . . Offences against the Law of Nations." Ginsberg says:

> John Jay, one of the authors of The Federalist Papers and our first Chief Justice, wrote in 1793 that the United States, "by taking a place among the nations of the earth, [had] become amenable to the laws of nations." Eleven years later, Chief Justice John Marshall cautioned that "an act of Congress ought never to be construed to violate the law of nations if any other possible construction remains."[20]

It is hard for Americans to understand just how highly international law is regarded by other countries. Within the United States, we rarely hear any international law mentioned outside trade treaties. Indeed, the United States is unique among westernized countries in tending to pay little attention to international law. For example, it has refused to ratify most of the International Labor Organisation's (ILO) workplace conventions.

However, this does not mean the ILO conventions cannot be an important source of rights and aid in a campaign to take back the Workers' Law.[21] They can be a tremendous resource because the international community has spoken clearly and forcefully in support of broad worker rights, including freedom of association and collective bargaining. Even conventions that have not been ratified by the United States may be used as evidence of international norms. Indeed, a stronger argument can be made for them as binding law. In 1998, the ILO made its fundamental conventions binding on all member countries, even those that had not ratified them. The ILO Declaration on Fundamental Principles and Rights at Work Section 2 says

> that all Members, even if they have not ratified the Conventions in question, have an obligation arising from the very fact of membership in the Organization to respect, to promote and to realize, in good faith and in accordance with the Constitution, the principles concerning the fundamental rights which are the subject of those Conventions, namely:
> (a) freedom of association and the effective recognition of the right to collective bargaining;
> (b) the elimination of all forms of forced or compulsory labour;
> (c) the effective abolition of child labour; and
> (d) the elimination of discrimination in respect of employment and occupation.[22]

As a result, because the United States is a member of the ILO, it is bound to abide by the key conventions of freedom of association and collective bargaining even though it has not ratified them.

ILO Convention 87 on Freedom of Association and Protection of the Right to Organise states: "Each Member of the International Labour Organisation . . . undertakes to take all necessary and appropriate measures to ensure that workers and employers may exercise freely the right to organise."[23] ILO Convention 98 on the Right to Organise and Collective Bargaining states:

> 1. Workers shall enjoy adequate protection against acts of anti-union discrimination in respect of their employment.
> 2. Such protection shall apply more particularly in respect of acts calculated to—
>   (a) make the employment of a worker subject to the condition that he shall not join a union or shall relinquish trade union membership;
>   (b) cause the dismissal of or otherwise prejudice a worker by reason of union membership or because of participation in union activities outside working hours or, with the consent of the employer, within working hours.[24]

The United States has ratified the United Nations' International Covenant on Civil and Political Rights.[25] This Covenant declares that "everyone shall have the right to freedom of association with others, including the right to form and join trade unions." It requires that governments must "respect and . . . ensure to all individuals within its territory and subject to its jurisdiction the rights recognized in the present Covenant" and requires governments "to ensure that any person whose rights or freedoms . . . are violated shall have an effective remedy."

Add to these the ILO's Declaration of Philadelphia, whose preamble says:

> The Conference reaffirms the fundamental principles on which the Organization is based and, in particular, that—
> (a) labour is not a commodity;
> (b) freedom of expression and of association are essential to sustained progress;
> (c) poverty anywhere constitutes a danger to prosperity everywhere;
> (d) the war against want requires to be carried on with unrelenting vigor within each nation, and by continuous and concerted international effort in which the representatives of workers and employers, enjoying equal status with those of governments, join with them in free discussion and democratic decision with a view to the promotion of the common welfare.[26]

The United Nations itself, in its Universal Declaration of Human Rights[27] calls on "all peoples and all nations" to strive . . . to promote respect for these rights and freedoms." Its declaration of work rights states:

> Article 23.
> (1) Everyone has the right to work, to free choice of employment, to just and favourable conditions of work and to protection against unemployment.
> (2) Everyone, without any discrimination, has the right to equal pay for equal work.
> (3) Everyone who works has the right to just and favourable remuneration ensuring for himself and his family an existence worthy of human dignity, and supplemented, if necessary, by other means of social protection.
> (4) Everyone has the right to form and to join trade unions for the protection of his interests.
> Article 24.
> Everyone has the right to rest and leisure, including reasonable limitation of working hours and periodic holidays with pay.
> Article 25.
> (1) Everyone has the right to a standard of living adequate for the health and well-being of himself and of his family, including food, clothing, hous-

ing and medical care and necessary social services, and the right to security in the event of unemployment, sickness, disability, widowhood, old age or other lack of livelihood in circumstances beyond his control.[28]

Again, all these international provisions have insights and language that can be used to expand and strengthen NLRA rights.

The Law of Other Countries

It is worth taking a look at laws from other countries, even though they may not be binding law, since they may reveal new ways of looking at rights. It is common to look at the law of Canada, a neighbor with whom we share a history and tradition. But other countries can also be a source of ideas and a way to reflect on our own laws. For example, one of the purposes of New Zealand's State Sector Act 1988 is "to ensure that every employer in the State services is a good employer."[29] It requires that the chief executive of any public department must "operate a personnel policy that complies with the principle of being a good employer."[30]

> 2. . . . a "good employer" is an employer who operates a personnel policy containing provisions generally accepted as necessary for the fair and proper treatment of employees in all aspects of their employment, including provisions requiring—
> (a) Good and safe working conditions; and
> (b) An equal employment opportunities programme; and
> (c) The impartial selection of suitably qualified persons for appointment; and . . .
> (e) Opportunities for the enhancement of the abilities of individual employees; and
> (f) Recognition of the aims and aspirations, and the cultural differences, of ethnic or minority groups; and
> (g) Recognition of the employment requirements of women; and
> (h) Recognition of the employment requirements of persons with disabilities.

The ideas and sources presented here are not sufficient in themselves to change the law. They are included here as a resource and an inspiration to spur thinking about looking broadly for resources to press into a campaign to take back the Workers' Law. They are also intended to change ways of thinking about workplace rights. It is one thing to assume that the NLRA stands alone. It is quite another thing to understand it as just one of many laws, treaties, and documents that all have the same insights about the just treatment of workers and of how that treatment affects all of our society.

7

TRYING CASES—THE RULES

You would think that people in labor studies, labor history, labor sociology, industrial relations, human resources, labor economics, labor law, and corporate law would have a basic understanding about each of these areas. But nothing could be further from the truth. In fact, most people do not read research outside their area. For law reform to succeed, there must be more interaction and sharing of ideas.

This was brought home to me a few years ago when I was at a conference listening to three prominent labor historians talk about their ideas for labor law reform. The fourth person on the panel, an equally prominent labor law professor, was to comment on the proposals. I was sitting in the back row with another, more experienced labor law professor from another law school. As we listened to the historians' proposals, we kept whispering to each other, "You can't do that. It would violate the right to due process and the First Amendment." At one point, my colleague said, "I sure hope we don't sound this bad when we talk about labor history." The law professor/commentator looked increasingly distressed as he listened to the proposals. He had to handle the delicate and difficult situation of telling these rightly famous people that the proposals they were advancing with ardor and all seriousness were illegal and therefore useless.

Each discipline related to workplace issues has special knowledge, and law is no exception. For example, when I teach first-year students about burdens of proof, they have trouble grasping how this matters. I try to get my point across by telling them that if a party has the burden of proof, that means this is the party who has been picked to lose, all proof being equal. When I see them again in their second or third years, most have clerked and handled real cases. When we discuss burdens of proof in labor and employment law, they take notes. They understand that failing to carry your burden of proof means you lose, so it is important to know who has the burden of proof on what issue.

Many issues are critical to how a case is tried and who wins or loses. Often when labor cases are discussed by nonlawyers, I can see they don't realize the important role played by some legal concept. Constructing a successful litigation strategy means sharing information and educating one another. One part of a litigation strategy is dissecting the factors that go into judicial decision making and then deciding how to press them into service.

The ideas discussed in this chapter are mostly technical legal issues that are important to a litigation strategy. I hope nonlawyers will not decide that this is a chapter to skip. The issues discussed here are actually weapons both lawyers and nonlawyers will need for the struggle ahead. In addition, learning about them can be fun, because (1) understanding them is like finally figuring out a secret language; (2) they make a difference—sometimes they make all the difference; (3) you ignore them at your peril; and (4) knowledge is power. Once you appreciate these points of law, a new world will be open. You will never be satisfied with knowing only the outcome of a case; you'll want to understand the process that led to the result.

This chapter provides resources for dealing with procedural problems that are likely to arise in pursuing a litigation strategy.

Statutory Interpretation

For many reasons, deciding cases takes more than just applying the law as it is written. No statute or legal doctrine can predict all the complex situations that may arise. This means that decision makers are often on the edges of the law, trying to calculate whether a statute or doctrine should apply to certain facts. In the process, they slowly stretch the reach of the law. People constantly react to the law, and this contributes to its change and development. Finally, there are legal doctrines, such as burdens of proof, that play a critical role that is almost invisible to nonlawyers.

Lawyers and judges understand these dynamics of cases differently than nonlawyers do. Learning to see the law as lawyers do opens up ways to affect the NLRA's interpretation and development, case by case.

Law interacts with what happens outside the courtroom in complex and intriguing ways that ultimately affect how a statue is interpreted. Simply memorizing or studying law as nothing more than rules or "black letter" law is tedious and frustrating. It also makes law seem arbitrary. Over the decades, the way a law is interpreted seems to meander all over the place and for no clear reason. For example, graduate-student employees were for many years not considered employees under the NLRA and therefore had no NLRA rights. Then the NLRB decided graduate students at New York University were employees and protected under the NLRA.[1] A few years later, the NLRB decided that Brown University graduate students were not employees.[2]

This may look as if the Board has no consistency, or as if all decisions are solely a matter of politics. While there may be some truth to both these views, they offer little help in dealing with the *Brown University* decision. In fact, the immediate response by many in the labor movement has been to concede that no graduate students have a right to organize under the NLRA. However, there are other ways to look at what it has done. The Board majority in *Brown* certainly worded its decision as if it applied to all graduate students and meant that no graduate student could be an employee under the NLRA. But since accepting this claim only ensures it becomes a reality, why not take up the challenge and prove them wrong? In fact, if you are a union lawyer, officer, or member taking up challenges is in your job description.

Here are some examples of ways to use knowledge of law as a weapon in the struggle for labor rights. The *Brown* majority claimed two things: Brown University graduate employees were not employees under the NLRA and therefore, no graduate employees at any university could be employees. The Board had the legal power to make a decision about the employee status of the graduate students at Brown University. It had no power to extend that decision to graduate students at any other institutions, and it will not necessarily apply to even Brown graduate students for all time. It can legally only apply to the conditions of the graduate students at Brown who were involved in this case.

When the NLRB claimed that *Brown* applied to all graduate students, it misstated the extent of its legal authority. Section 9(b) limits Board decision- making power in election cases to deciding issues only in the case before it. Election case decisions are not supposed to be based on broad, sweeping generalities, as they were in this case. In other words, the issue the Board had the power to decide was not whether all graduate students can be employees but only whether these particular graduate students were employees. Thus the next case involving graduate students might prove they are employees by demonstrating that there are significant differences between them and the conditions of Brown students at the time their case was tried. In other words, the way people react to decisions affects what they mean.[3]

The *Yeshiva University*[4] case provides a good example that such a strategy is possible. In 1980, the U.S. Supreme Court decided that the Yeshiva University faculty were managers and therefore not employees under the NLRA. Though many thought this meant no faculty at private universities had the right to organize and be represented by a union, this was not the case. The Kendall College faculty were found to be employees just a few years later[5] by putting facts in the record that demonstrated that their working conditions were different than those at Yeshiva and that they were employees. Not only could there be a similar outcome for graduate students, the way the decision in *Brown* was written makes this even easier. The decision relies on a skimpy examination of the facts in the case. Instead, it asserts that the decision is being made for policy reasons but fails to demonstrate the basis for that policy.

Another example is *Lechmere, Inc. v. NLRB*,[6] in which the Supreme Court said that the union organizers had no legal right to enter an employer's property to talk with workers about unionization. Despite the Court's language, this is not a blanket prohibition. Its application depends on the property and freedom of speech laws of the state where the job site is—and potentially other laws and factors. As a result, whether union organizers have access depends on which state they live in.[7] In other words, a court or Board decision should not be taken as the final statement of rights. The way people react to case decisions is as much a part of statutory interpretation as the decision itself. Understanding this creates opportunities to change the law. It is part of what I call the Toothpaste Tube theory of labor law.

The Toothpaste Tube Theory of Labor Law

Under the toothpaste tube theory of labor law, employer and employee relations are always under pressure. Part of that pressure comes from law. A toothpaste tube bulges out in one place when pressure is exerted elsewhere. As case decisions change the balance of power among employers, employees, and unions, new opportunities or problems come into being. When the *Lechmere* decision excluded organizers from the parking lots of shopping malls, one method of organizing was limited. Unions reacted by sending in salts to be hired and organize employer workforces. Salts were fearless in their organizing, because they did not fear being fired. For the same reason, employers did not like salts. When some employers reacted by firing the salts, they found themselves in violation of the NLRA. Eventually, the Supreme Court decided in *NLRB v. Town & Country Electric*[8] that salts were employees and that firing or refusing to hire them violated the NLRA. That case strengthened the NLRA's definition of employee in Section 2(3), expanded *Lechmere's* limited definition, and endorsed core NLRA purposes and values.

Some employers then lobbied Congress to outlaw salting.[9] No such law has so far been enacted, so employers have tried to find holes in the case law to weed out salts while not being found to violate the NLRA. Because some have been successful, salting is now less useful or is used for different goals than in the past. This is part of the toothpaste tube dynamic. It is something to be prepared for and something to try to use to advantage while preparing for the reactions to any advantages that develop. Efforts to politicize the NLRB since 1980 have made the cases that come to and through the Board a battlefield on which a war over workplace rights is being fought. Cases can either drift through the process or be seized upon as opportunities to shift the law in a direction that restores the values and policies of the NLRA.

Judicial Activism or Statutory Interpretation?

Many people become frustrated when courts hand down different interpretations. Especially when two opinions come to directly opposite conclusions on similar facts or issues or when prior case law is reversed, it is hard to see how both can be valid interpretations of the law. It is possible, however, that both are valid. Differences in facts or in how cases are tried affect outcomes. In addition, changes in social values can compel the law to change. All this is part of the dynamic of interpreting the law. Interpretations of law change over time—and for perfectly valid reasons. As our society, technology, perceptions, and values change, the way we think about important issues changes, and our laws adjust to reflect this evolution. Some dismiss dissenting opinions as irrelevant, but because today's dissent may be tomorrow's law, the dissent's viewpoint may be useful in future litigation.

For example, slavery once was not only legal but widely accepted. Even the U.S. Constitution refers to slavery. One hundred fifty years ago slavery became illegal, and it is now seen as immoral. When the U.S. Constitution was enacted, only white males who owned large amounts of property were given the right to vote. Now universal suffrage is a fundamental value. Courts have to interpret law despite tidal changes in values and viewpoints such as these.

Different ways of interpreting a statute may also be valid because, no matter how carefully a law is drafted, unforeseen situations always arise. Congress may also have trouble getting agreement on controversial parts of a law, so they are left ambiguous or not included. Of course, where there is controversy, there will be litigation. Ultimately, the courts must interpret laws that are ambiguous or have gaps.

Interpreting statutes is part of what it means to be ruled by law,[10] but it is not an easy task. If the statute is not ambiguous, then there is no need for more analysis, but if a case has been filed, there is usually some disagreement about what a statute means or how it applies. When a judge decides a statute is ambiguous, the next step involves looking for guidance in interpreting it. This can come from the statute as a whole, from its stated purpose or policies, and from the law's legislative history. The goal is to find the legislature's intent and to interpret the statute to promote that intent. But there is no agreement on the weight to give each of these interpretive devices and even whether a statute is ambiguous and needs interpretation beyond its text.[11]

To make this even more difficult, statutory interpretation is constantly struggling against common social beliefs. This is especially the case with laws that govern the workplace, for they involve volatile systems where there are often clashes over rights. "Unlike mathematical symbols, the phrasing of such social legislation as this seldom attains more than approximate precision of definition. That is why all relevant aids are summoned to determine meaning."[12]

The problem is even more complex in the case of the NLRB. Although it decides cases, it is more than a court. It is an expert agency whose job it is to make policy decisions as it interprets the law in each case it decides. The appellate courts have trouble deciding how to treat the NLRA's policy decisions. The Supreme Court has said that the courts should normally defer to NLRB decisions:

> It is the Board on which Congress conferred the authority to develop and apply fundamental national labor policy. Because it is to the Board that Congress entrusted the task of "applying the Act's general prohibitory language in the light of the infinite combinations of events which might be charged violative of its terms," that body, if it is to accomplish the task which Congress set for it, necessarily must have authority to formulate rules to fill the interstices of the broad statutory provisions. . . . The Board is expert in federal national labor relations policy, and it is in the Board . . . that [Congress] . . . vested responsibility for developing that policy. . . . "The function of striking that balance to effectuate national labor policy is often a difficult and delicate responsibility, which the Congress committed primarily to the National Labor Relations Board, subject to limited judicial review." The judicial role is narrow: The rule which the Board adopts is judicially reviewable for consistency with the Act, and for rationality, but if it satisfies those criteria, the Board's application of the rule, if supported by substantial evidence on the record as a whole, must be enforced.[13]

But the reality is that, all too often, appellate courts ignore judicial deference and substitute their judgment for that of the NLRB. In a study of court of appeals decisions in cases in which the NLRB had ordered an employer to bargain over a decision to subcontract or relocate work, the courts reversed the NLRB about 80 percent of the time to find no duty to bargain. In addition, the courts' decisions showed contempt and extreme hostility to the NLRB and made no effort to apply the careful deference the Supreme Court has mandated.[14] To be successful, a litigation strategy must take this tendency of courts into consideration.[15] Merely reminding them of their duty to defer is not enough.

Burdens of Proof

Burdens of proof can make the difference between winning and losing. In an NLRB hearing, the Board attorney has the burden of proving an unfair labor practice. What this means is that the Board has the odds stacked against it in every case. On the other hand, some NLRB burdens should normally help a union. For example, whoever files an election petition—usually a union—lists the job classifications to be included in the bargaining unit. Whoever objects to that unit—usually the employer—has the burden of proving that the unit the union requested is not *an* appropriate bargaining unit. It is not on the union to prove that the unit it has filed for is *the* only appropriate unit, as some believe. This means that if the union and employer both present evidence of equal weight, the employer loses, and the election will be held in the unit the union requested. The employer cannot win by showing the unit it wants is better. Put another way, the employer can win only if it shows that the unit the union wants is not a legal unit, that it is not *an* appropriate unit because it does not promote "the purpose of collective bargaining." Proving that the union asked for a unit that is *not* appropriate at all is a hard burden to carry. So the effect of putting the burden of proof on the employer combined with what it must prove means the union should normally get the unit it asks for.

Burdens also play a role in unfair labor practice cases. In 1991, in *Dubuque Packing Co.*,[16] the NLRB created a complex test for proving that an employer violated its obligation to bargain about a decision to relocate work. *Dubuque* uses "shifting burdens of proof." This means that on some issues the NLRB's attorney has the burden and, on other issues, the employer bears the burden. Here is how it works in a relocation case under *Dubuque*.

The NLRB attorney begins with a burden of producing evidence to prove that (1) the employer refused to bargain with the union about a decision to relocate work away from the unionized workers, that is, from the bargaining unit, and (2) relocating the work meant the same work was being done in a new location. In other words, moving the work was not a basic change in the nature of the employer's operation. If the NLRB lawyer proves these two things, she will have made a prima facie case that the employer violated its duty to bargain about the relocation. If the NLRB attorney fails to make a prima facie case, the administrative law judge (ALJ) can dismiss the case, even if the respondent presents no evidence.

If, and only if, the NLRB attorney carries this burden of proof does the burden shift to the employer. The employer must prove either that (1) the work at the new plant is not the same as the work at the old plant—in other words, work at the old plant was not moved to the new plant—or that (2) the work at both plants is the same, but moving the work was the result of an entrepreneurial decision to change the scope and direction of the business and (a) labor costs were not *a* factor in the decision or (b) if labor costs were *a* factor, bargaining would have failed, because the union could not have offered enough concessions to change the decision.

During the trial, both the NLRB and the employer's attorneys will present evidence on every issue mentioned above. The judge will decide the case by essentially putting each side's evidence on a scale and determining which weighs more. If a party has the burden of proof on an issue, that party's evidence must outweigh the other's. The scale is, of course, an abstract scale so it is up to the judge to determine weight. In cases with clear cut evidence, all judges should agree on who wins, but in cases where evidence is harder to assess, the way the judge understands the evidence is critical. The NLRB is most at risk of losing in cases with more subjective evidence. The *Dubuque* test and its burdens are not in the NLRA. All the NLRA says is that an employer violates the law if it "refuses to bargain collectively with the representatives of [its] employees." The NLRB created this test in reaction to a series of court cases that progressively removed any obligation for an employer to bargain on fundamental decisions about where work is performed. These decisions let employers easily take work where prices are lower and labor more docile. Those cases are a clear victory of employer property and managerial rights over NLRA rights. The *Dubuque* test makes it somewhat more likely that an employer might have an obligation to bargain over a decision to relocate work from one place to another.

Proving cases also means thinking about the types of issues that must be proved. Some kinds of evidence are easier to produce than others. Evidence that is objective is easier to prove than subjective evidence. For example, if I want to prove that it rained on a certain day at a certain place, I can call eyewitnesses or use weather records. These are types of objective evidence. But if I want to prove that the reason you did not go for a swim was because you thought it would rain at that time and place, I have a much harder job. People's intentions, beliefs, and motives are kinds of subjective evidence. I could potentially ask witnesses whether you said it would rain, but you might have been joking, or they might have misheard you. I could call witnesses to testify that you took an umbrella with you that day, but perhaps you were giving it as a gift or taking it to keep the intense sun off. Or I could call you as a witness and ask you, but you might lie, and I would have to prove you were lying.

The *Dubuque* test has both objective and subjective factors, and examining them reveals something about what the NLRB was thinking as well as what the prospects are of winning the case. The objective factors under *Dubuque* include proving whether there has been a basic change in the nature of the employer's operation, that the work performed at the two plants differs significantly, and that the old work was discontinued and was not moved. Subjective factors include whether labor costs were part of the decision and whether or not the union could have offered sufficient concessions to change the employer's mind.

It is hard to say who has the more difficult job of carrying the burden of proof. The employer has the burden of proving its defenses using subjective evidence and thus should have the more difficult burden of proof. Some of the factors seem unprovable. For example, proving whether bargaining would have been futile because the union could not have offered sufficient concessions to have changed the employer's decision means proving what the union would have offered (but did not because it was not given the chance) and proving what the employer's reaction would have been had such an offer been made. But aside from trying to prove events that never happened, the employer is in the driver's seat because it can testify as to its own state of mind and say that it planned to move no matter what the union offered. It also knows what records it has and has the key witnesses on its payroll.

Proving these cases is so complex that it is easy to lose sight of how any of them are connected with the NLRA's policies and values. Potentially relevant NLRA policies are promoting collective bargaining and stabilizing competitive wages and working conditions within and between industries. The *Dubuque* test does not seem to promote those values. In fact, the test exists only as a reaction to a series of cases that give primacy to employer entrepreneurial rights over collective bargaining rights. Unions lose about 250,000 members a year, many of them as the result of subcontracting, relocations, and closings. These cases and issues present a real challenge for a litigation strategy and an important target.

Before leaving the subject of burdens of proof, a few more ideas are important. First, there are different types of burdens and different consequences of failing to meet them. There is a burden of pleading in either a complaint or an answer. These documents frame the issues in a case. If the NLRB or plaintiff in a civil case fails to carry the burden of pleading, the judge can dismiss the case. Next there is a burden of production, of producing witnesses or documents as evidence on an issue. A failure to carry this burden means having the judge find against you on that issue. Finally, there is a burden of proof. If you fail to prove that the evidence you have produced should be believed, then you will lose. Normally a party has the burden of pleading, production of evidence, and proof on an issue. It is unusual to assign the various burdens on an issue to more than one party.

Second, there are reasons courts or the law imposes a burden on a party. Some burdens are assigned according to tradition. Plaintiffs or, in NLRB cases, the NLRB normally carry the burden of proving the elements of a violation. In addition, the legislature may enact a law that assigns the burden of proof. A burden of proof may also be assigned to the party who has the easiest access to information or control of the information, basically for reasons of fairness. Notice that in the *Dubuque* test, the employer bears the burden of proving facts about its decision-making process. Burdens of proof mean picking winners and losers, so there may be policy reasons to make it easier or harder for one party to win. Finally, burdens may be assigned based on probabilities—that is, the party who is asserting the improbable may be assigned the burden of proof.

As new case law develops through a litigation strategy, attention needs to be paid to technical issues such as burdens of proof. It is impossible to appreciate how a case is tried or even the Board's decision to issue a complaint without taking burdens of proof into consideration. NLRB attorneys may believe that certain events occurred and that there is a violation. They may be frustrated by the difficulty—or even impossibility—of proving something they believe is true. Nonetheless, they have to face the reality of what must be done to win a case. This affects NLRB Regional Office decisions whether to issue a complaint. Burdens are an interpretation of the law. They can and should be changed if necessary to promote NLRA policies.

The Process of a Litigation Strategy

The NLRB is a gatekeeper and controls its cases. Using a litigation strategy to take back the Workers' Law means mastering and controlling NLRB procedure to achieve better law from the time an NLRB charge is filed, through investigation, decision to issue a complaint, hearing, ALJ decision, Board decision, and court of appeals decision. Legal change means shepherding the charge through each of these steps.

Some NLRB and court rules and regulations give a party some ability to shape a case, while others create impediments. The most difficult regulations are those that affect the time from filing the charge through the trial before the ALJ, where the record is created. Trying to overcome procedural roadblocks is more difficult if the NLRB Regional Office is unwilling to pursue a theory. The discussion that follows provides guidance for moving through those obstacles.[17]

From Charge to Hearing

Unions have the initial control of NLRB cases, because they decide whether and when to file a charge. If a union wants to seek novel remedies or is asking for a complaint to be issued based on a novel theory, ideally the request should be made in the charge. It is important to bear in mind that, if a complaint is issued, its allegations will have to track the allegations of the charge. The case can be dismissed for failure to meet this requirement.[18] Therefore, the charging party should compare the allegations of the complaint and charge and, if necessary, amend the charge.

When a charging party files a charge that is intended to change the law, special precautions must be taken. For example, giving all parties notice that an innovation is being sought gives them an opportunity and even a requirement to respond early in the process. There is usually no discovery in NLRB cases, so anything that helps uncover the other party's positions is helpful. In addition, NLRB procedures now require that any differences between the charging party and the NLRB about the appropriate remedy must be presented to the Regional Office and resolved before the hearing. If no agreement can be reached, the Board attorney will argue only for the Regional Office's views. The charging party will have the responsibility for presenting its case and views on the novel issue to the ALJ and the Board.[19]

These details need to be worked out as early as possible so the hearing can run smoothly. Board investigations run on a short time frame, so failing to resolve these issues early leads to delay.

The Regional Director normally has discretion whether to issue a complaint and as to what is alleged in a complaint.[20] If a case involves novel or complex issues, however, the Regional Director must submit the case to the NLRB Division of Advice before issuing a complaint.[21] The complaint must "be sufficiently detailed to enable the parties to understand the offenses charged and the issues to be met. The complaint should be sufficiently specific to defend against a Motion for a Bill of Particulars . . . Careful drafting of the complaint . . . avoids many problems during trial and time-consuming briefs and arguments. The failure to properly draft or amend complaints can result in the loss of substantive rights."[22]

The Board has been open in recent years to seeking innovative or special remedies.[23] Unions need to be aware that special procedures apply when seeking these kinds of remedies and must make certain they are followed both when the NLRB seeks a special remedy and when the union—but not the NLRB—does so.

For example, when the remedy sought is novel or unique, the NLRB must give adequate notice to all parties that such a remedy is being sought as a matter of due process. This lets all parties know they need to be prepared to present evidence on the issue. This notice can be contained in the NLRB complaint. The NLRB's *Casehandling Manual* for unfair labor practices says that the complaint should contain a separate request for the specific novel relief and "should specifically reserve the General Counsel's right to subsequently seek, and the Board's right to ultimately provide, any other appropriate remedy."[24]

It may seem odd, but the charging party is not a party to the case unless it asks to become one. Once a complaint has been issued, the charging party should move to intervene as a party. The NLRB ULP *Casehandling Manual* explains how to intervene. The first step is to file a written motion with the Regional Director before the trial or move to intervene at the start of the hearing. The motion must explain why the person who wants to intervene claims she has an interest in being part of the hearing. Normally, it is obvious that a charging party has an interest. The NLRB ULP *Casehandling Manual* says that the NLRB "should not oppose intervention by parties or interested persons with direct interest in the outcome of the proceeding. . . . Otherwise, counsel for the General Counsel should oppose such intervention."[25]

It is important to be aware that intervention may not give the intervener the full-party rights possessed by the NLRB and the respondent. The intervener's rights may be limited to the terms the Regional Director or ALJ thinks are proper.[26] The motion to intervene should therefore include a request for full-party status and provide evidence and arguments why that status should be granted.

It is especially important to intervene to become a party if the NLRB issues a complaint that is not based on the theory of violation the charging party advocates or if the charging party is seeking a remedy that has not been alleged or if no remedies have been alleged.[27] Having party status can help the charging party preserve its right to advocate the theory or remedy it thinks appropriate. The regulations do not require a charging party or intervener to file a pleading, but they do not forbid it either. The wisest course is to file a formal pleading to advise all parties about a novel remedy or theory. The pleading could be titled as an intervener's response to the complaint. This is a critical step. Failure to request an innovative remedy and inform all parties it is being sought before the hearing can be grounds for denying it.[28] One additional reason to provide early notice of an innovative remedy or theory is to avoid trial delay. NLRB hearings are scheduled to last a set number of days based on the regional office's estimate of the time needed to try the issues in the case. If the NLRB is unaware that a novel remedy or theory will be tried—and especially that it will require the presentation of expert witnesses—the NLRB will underestimate the hearing length. When a trial exceeds the number of days scheduled, it can take months before a new trial date can be set that will accommodate the schedules of all parties. In addition, the respondent employer will protest that it has been surprised and needs additional time to prepare its case. If no notice or late notice has been given, the ALJ will grant the respondent's request.

If no complaint is issued and the reason is that the theory of violation is contrary to precedent, the charging party should request review through the NLRB General Counsel's Division of Advice.

Procedural Issues during the Hearing

The issues most likely to arise during a hearing are technical procedural issues and issues involving the presentation of evidence. Both are discussed here.

Normally, the NLRB's case is tried by an attorney in the Regional Office where the case was filed. That attorney is responsible for presenting evidence in support of the complaint.[29] However, all parties to the proceeding, including the charging party and any interveners, may call, examine, and cross-examine witnesses and introduce evidence into the record; submit briefs; engage in oral argument; and submit proposed findings and conclusions to the ALJ.[30] The NLRB's rules state that "every party has the right to present his case or defense by oral or documentary evidence, to submit rebuttal evidence, and to conduct such cross-examination as may be required for a full and true disclosure of the facts."[31]

When a special remedy is sought, the Board attorney is advised to "explain to the Administrative Law Judge and the parties that the recommended special remedy is not a limitation as to normal Board remedies, but needs to be granted in addition to such remedies. Counsel for the General Counsel should always request the ALJ and Board to provide 'any further relief as may be appropriate.'"[32] A charging party who is seeking a special remedy or pursuing a novel theory should follow a similar process, especially when the region has chosen not to follow that course.

A second problem that is likely to arise at trial is getting evidence admitted. No one has been using a litigation strategy based on NLRA values or requesting the admission of expert testimony or exhibits demonstrating that a change in the law is needed. As a result, it is likely that the respondent-employer will object both to the innovation being sought and to trying a case by presenting data, expert witnesses, and other evidence in support of the change. The ALJ also will not be used to thinking about cases and evidence in this way and may be concerned that this will lengthen the hearing. In order to build a record that supports a particular result, you must persuade the ALJ that the evidence is relevant to your case and therefore should be admitted into the record. Eventually it means persuading the ALJ that the evidence supports your claims and therefore you have met your burden of proof.

NLRB hearings use the Federal Rules of Evidence.[33] Getting evidence admitted hinges on proving that it is relevant to the issues in the case. All relevant evidence is admissible; evidence that is not relevant is not admissible.[34] The Federal Rules of Evidence define relevant evidence as "evidence having any tendency to make the existence of any fact that is of consequence to the determination of the action more probable or less probable than it would be without the evidence."[35] This means that to have evidence admitted, a party must be prepared to demonstrate its relevance to an issue or issues in the case.

To do this means first constructing a theory about why certain actions violate the NLRA or why a certain remedy is required to further the policies of the NLRA. You must then show how the evidence supports these theories. The theory of a case is like the plan for building a house. The facts are the materials used in building it. Proving the relevance of evidence means showing how and where testimony or other evidence fits into the building plan. The details will vary depending on the specific case. To give an example, evidence that would be relevant to proving that interest arbitration should be ordered instead of a bargaining order would be evidence that demonstrates how a bargaining order does not promote the NLRA's purposes and policies or evidence that demonstrates that interest arbitration does promote the NLRA's purposes and policies. Part of the argument for admitting the evidence is that Section 10(c) itself requires that NLRA remedies promote the NLRA's policies.

The most difficult situations will be those where there is no explicit statement such as Section 10(c) provides in the statute and where there is Supreme Court precedent to the contrary. Even here, an argument should be made connecting express NLRA policies to the issues in the case and demonstrating why the evidence is relevant. The judge may reject the theory in such a situation as barred by case law. This means being prepared with fallback arguments and strategies for getting evidence admitted. If the ALJ refuses to admit any evidence, she should be asked to place it in the "rejected exhibits file"[36] and an objection to the ruling should be stated on the record.[37] This decision can then be appealed.

There is currently some movement by the Republicans on the Board and also the influential D.C. Circuit[38] to require a case-by-case analysis in support of remedies. This can be used as support for seeking innovative, individualized remedies and presenting a record that demonstrates the need for a specific remedy.[39]

This is a quick overview and introduction to some highly technical concepts. They cannot be mastered or used to their best advantage without study, thought, and practice. However, simply grasping the basics means having a greater understanding of the challenges and potential involved in taking back the Workers' Law. It means being able to participate more fully in this strategy to, at last, achieve Wagner's vision of what the workplace and this society should be.

8

USING THE NLRB AS
A RESOURCE

The National Labor Relations Board is one of the most important resources now available to unions. Although many unionists may reject this idea, this chapter offers them reasons to rethink their position. It offers an invitation to consider ways to exploit the NLRA and NLRB as resources in the cause of worker organization.

The Cost of Not Using the NLRA/NLRB

There are real costs to unions in not using the NLRA and NLRB. Most criticisms of the NLRA and NLRB have centered around elections, but unfortunately these criticisms are usually expressed as a blanket condemnation of the Board. Even when unions are clear that they are criticizing the NLRB only for failures related to elections, most people will not understand the distinction between organizing and unfair labor practices. Indiscriminate anti-NLRB rhetoric is a positive disservice to workers, unions, and their goals. Important rights can be attained only through the NLRB—for example, rights to reinstatement and backpay for workers who have been fired or not hired for union activity. It is true that the backpay remedy is woefully inadequate and can be slow in coming, but there is no alternate remedy. Furthermore, the NLRB handles cases and provides attorneys at no cost. In other words, there is a possibility of gain from a small investment in worker and union time and money. For a worker financially on the edge these NLRB remedies have some value. I have seen workers who have accepted anti-NLRB rhetoric and been persuaded there is a better remedy somewhere else, only to learn, too late, that there is no other law to protect or help them.[1]

Organizers tell workers they can depend on the union when they risk their jobs to organize a union. They tell them that an employer's threats and intimidation are illegal and that the law forbids firing a worker for union activity, and this is true. But if the union then refuses to file an NLRB charge when the employer violates the law, out of anti-NLRB animus, it betrays the trust of the workers. What is more, unions that fail to act on NLRA violations reinforce the employer's message that unions are impotent.

Strategic use of the NLRB can enhance union organizing success.

Using the NLRB

There has been so much angry denunciation of the NLRB in recent years that, before talking about strategies, it makes sense to lay out some facts and statistics about how the NLRB functions. Some of the information is drawn from my experience as an NLRB attorney in a busy Regional Office.

What Is the NLRB?

People often talk about the NLRB as if it were one monolithic entity. Thinking about it this way can lead to mistakes in strategy and missed opportunities.

The NLRB is a complex organization—not just in the way it is set up—but also in terms of the people who work there. Different divisions of the Board tend to attract different sorts people, and each division has a different focus. Some divisions may even be antagonistic to one another. At the simplest level, the NLRB is divided into three main parts: (1) the General Counsel's side; (2) the Board side; and (3) the Division of Judges. The General Counsel's side includes the Regional Offices that are located throughout the country and other functions that are mainly located in Washington, D.C. Some are administrative, policymaking, and supervisory. Others handle appeals from election cases; appeals from the dismissal of an unfair labor practice charge; special litigation projects, such as contempt litigation; and arguments in appeals before the U.S. circuit courts of appeals.

The NLRB employees most people and union organizers interact with are the investigators and attorneys in a Regional Office. They come to work for the Board for many reasons. Some are timeservers who want to get by with as little effort as possible. Some want to do whatever it takes to get good casehandling statistics, even if it means cutting corners. In my experience, however, most people are at the NLRB because they want to "do justice." They know that they have a duty of loyalty to the NLRB and that, as government employees, they are required to demonstrate fairness and evenhandedness to all sides. They are federal government employees— not union agents, attorneys, or cheerleaders. As government employees, sometimes they have to take actions they do not personally support, something that is true of most jobs at times. All of them, even the best, will be under pressure to meet NLRB time goals, because meeting them affects their evaluations, tenure, and pay. In short, NLRB agents face pressures different from those of union representatives. What may come across as a lack of interest in the case may actually be an effort not to appear biased.

Unions need to think about how to speak to the person and not just the government official. At the same time, they need to be aware that the job of the NLRB agent is not to represent the union; it is to promote the NLRA's polices. Most of the time these policies promote union interests and goals. In all cases, an agent will be less effective at promoting NLRA policies if she is seen as biased. In other words, good agents try to maintain a neutral stance so their impartiality cannot be questioned.

It is also important to understand the problems Board employees have faced in recent years. The NLRB has been under assault from the right and the left since the early 1980s. Most Board agents at some point have probably been accused of being an enemy of workers. For those who went to work for the Board as a calling, this can be painful.

The NLRB has also been hard put to add new agents or replace departing agents. There has been insufficient money for support services, computers, online research services, training, and travel for investigations and trial. The number of professional staff in all Regional Offices across the country in the years 1994–2004 has varied from 874 to 1,004, a peak that was reached in September 2001. In fiscal year (FY) 2004, it was 928.40 employees. These very low numbers are the result of severely restricted budgets, which necessitate increasing agent's caseloads. When agents carry high caseloads, either they or the agency must cut corners. Understanding the stresses that NLRB agents face and recognizing the differences among NLRB agents allow union representatives to take a strategic approach to interactions with the Board.

Is the Board as Bad as They Say?

What people know about the NLRB is often based on anecdotes that fail to reveal how the agency performs overall. Given that fewer than one thousand NLRB Regional Office employees handle all the cases and public questions, the volume and quality of work are impressive. It would be better if there were lobbying to press for more resources.

The most common contact Regional Offices have with the public is through calls or visits from members of the public with questions about their rights. NLRB agents answer these questions and help route people to the proper agency to assist them, if there is one.[2] In FY 2004, Regional Office agents handled 204,855 callers, an increase of 8.5 percent from the 188,751 inquiries received during FY 2003. The FY 2003 number was an increase of 19.9 percent over the prior year. This is about 221 information calls or visits a year for each agent in the Regional Offices, in addition to all their other work.

Agents may help callers in drafting and filing charges if the facts suggest the NLRA was violated.

> If an individual describes circumstances which may indicate a violation of the Act, the Board agent should advise such individual of the right to file a charge. The Board agent should assist in the preparation of any charge to the extent necessary. Such assistance may include identifying the sections of the Act involved and the basic theory of the allegations, furnishing the appropriate charge form and reasonable clerical assistance, and drafting the language of the charge itself.[3]

Much of the NLRB's work involves investigating and prosecuting unfair labor practices. The NLRB has no power to initiate its own investigations. The process can begin only when someone files a charge.[4] All charges are investigated by an NLRB agent, including NLRB attorneys. The NLRB's *Casehandling Manual* says:

Although the charging party should be asked to specify the allegations of the charge and the facts in support of them, many individual charging parties and others do not possess the knowledge or expertise to identify all possible issues. While the Board agent must remain neutral and not be an advocate for either party, the agent should provide assistance in identifying issues. In this regard, the Board agent should candidly apprise the charging party of any potential issues and provide the charging party an opportunity to amend the charge in a timely fashion, if necessary, in order to pursue additional allegations.[5]

In FY 2004, Regional Office investigations found reasonable cause to believe a violation had been committed in 37.7 percent of charges filed. Since 1980, this percentage, known as the merit factor, has fluctuated between 32 and 40 percent.[6] In other words, about 60 percent of cases are found not to have merit after they are investigated. Some argue that the NLRB should go to complaint on all charges filed. They say that failing to do so demonstrates bias against unions and workers. That claim fails to consider what leads to these statistics.

The truth is that not all charges filed have merit. For example, the NLRB *Casehandling Manual* states: "If an individual presents a situation that is clearly not covered by the Act, the Board agent should so indicate and discourage the filing of a charge. If an individual asserts, however, the right to file a charge, the Board agent should take a charge."[7] While the agents might have been wrong, they are trained professionals and are likely to have been right about whether the facts showed a violation. The NLRB investigation process is similar to that in criminal cases. There would be a public outcry if prosecutors indicted defendants without any investigation into the merits of the case. Charges can be filed against unions, and obviously unions would not want the NLRB to prosecute them on all charges filed against them, especially ones with no merit. It would be wrong to require that only charges filed against employers get tried without investigation.

There is a cost to issuing complaint in a case in which an investigation shows lack of probable cause. The case is likely to be lost at trial and cost the government and respondent money, time, and stress for no good reason. Union representatives know that they themselves would not take every grievance to arbitration.

If the NLRB had to try cases that had no merit, this would have an impact on its overall effectiveness. When I went into trial, I knew I had a good case, and so did the party I was prosecuting. This made it easier to get settlements, and settlements are good for all parties. They get backpay and other relief to workers sooner than would be the case with a full trial, and they allow everyone to move on with their lives more quickly. Had my cases not been investigated and found to have merit, I would not have been able to go into trial with as much confidence in my cases and would have had a harder time getting settlements, even for the strong cases. That said, I have to admit that when I settled a case I was always happy, relieved, and sad. I was happy because everyone had reached a resolution, and that was best for them. I was relieved, because, even with the best of all cases, there is always the possibility of losing. Settling meant the case would not be lost. And I was sad, because all settlements mean compromises. The standard Board settlement for a discharge case was reinstatement and 80 percent of backpay. It is hard to take less than 100 percent for many reasons. If a case seems very good, it is hard to accept less than everything. This is especially the case when the backpay remedy is so low that even 100 percent backpay does not make the employee whole. I know that the workers whose cases I handled felt some of these same emotions and certainly disappointment at having to compromise when they were smarting from unfair treatment.

Trying bad cases means taking money away from good cases. It tarnishes the Board's reputation and makes it less effective in pursuing its mission. No ethical, competent lawyer takes all cases. In addition, when the government prosecutes a case, there is, literally, a price to pay for taking bad cases—payments to the respondent under the Equal Access to Justice Act (EAJA). The NLRB is underfunded, and losing cases and making EAJA payments further depletes agency resources. There is empirical evidence that supports taking only meritorious cases. In FY 2004, NLRB Regional Offices settled 96.1 percent of the cases in which the region had found merit. Over the last ten years the settlement rate has ranged from 91.5 to 99.5 percent.[8] In other words, the vast majority of unfair labor practice cases settle and settle quickly. For the small percentage of cases that did not settle and that went to trial, the NLRB won 82.7 percent, in whole or in part, at the NLRB and administrative law judge levels in FY 2004.[9]

Making NLRB Charges Count

What is the most effective way to approach the NLRB concerning unfair labor practice cases? Of most importance, all agents appreciate a union representative who is prepared to make a fast start in an investigation. The Board's time limits, the agent's caseload, and the lack of support resources are always in an agent's mind. When a charging party is not prepared to pursue the case, it affects how well the agent can do the job.

When a union is the bargaining representative, it should consider whether the employer has information related to the dispute before filing a charge. A union has a right to information reasonably necessary to its role as the employees' representative. Union representation includes filing legal claims when there appears to be a violation of the law. If the employer fails to provide the information the union has requested, this also violates the NLRA, and a charge should be filed for refusing to provide it.

Before filing a charge, but particularly ones involving bad faith bargaining, unions should think about whether they have or can develop evidence that can be used in a hearing that uses the litigation strategies I advocate. For example, if an employer presents an offer that includes severe cutbacks, the union may believe—and be correct—that the employer is trying to force an impasse. Having impasse as a goal is bad faith bargaining. The problem is how to demonstrate that the employer has this intent, rather than just hard bargaining. The law permits both parties to play hardball as long as they do so in good faith. An impasse is a bona fide impasse only if there is a deadlock despite the parties' efforts to reach agreement.

Give some thought to ways to illustrate the employer's motive during bargaining and before there is a declaration of impasse. One possibility is to present evidence during negotiations to show how such an offer would harm the bargaining relationship and push the employer to respond. Think of how to demonstrate that the employer's purpose is to destroy the union as the employees' representative and to put an end to the employer's obligation to bargain.

Traditionally, an employer was allowed to implement a final offer on reaching an impasse only if it was done in way that did not disparage the collective bargaining relationship or denigrate the bargaining partner.[10] This requirement has never been overruled, but it has fallen into disuse. Bad faith bargaining cases traditionally talked about offers that no self-respecting union could accept as evidence of bad faith bargaining. Therefore, one strategy during negotiations is to spell out how the employer's offer disparages the union and destroys collective bargaining. For example, make a formal information request asking how this course of bargaining will not undermine unionization. Bring in an expert—perhaps union representatives from this and other unions or a researcher—to present data during bargaining to show why no self-respecting union could accept this offer and why and how it denigrates the bargaining process. Push the employer to respond.

The stakes are high when bargaining appears to be heading toward impasse and implementation. Many unions try to prevent impasse by making a series of mini-concessions or taking actions, such as information requests, to claim there is no impasse. Ultimately this is not a winning strategy. It weakens the union, bargaining, and contract terms. It certainly does not prevent implementation and involves, at best, a long legal battle. Taking the course I suggest may make it difficult or even impossible to deny that the parties are on track to an impasse. It attempts to make visible what everyone knows is happening by calling the employer on its motives for pushing negotiations in that direction.

The chief advantage of confronting the real issue—an employer's strategy to use impasse to destroy unionism—is that, if it does not push the employer to negotiate in good faith, it at least creates evidence that can be used during the investigation and at trial to demonstrate bad faith bargaining. It also pulls back the curtain to enlighten the judges who may ultimately hear this case. This creates a very different record from today's bad faith bargaining cases. Most cases put together evidence of bad faith bargaining from an after-the-fact analysis of evidence that had no great significance at the time events occurred. Evidence that reveals the motives of the parties during negotiations should make it easier to prove a violation. It also demonstrates that the employer's right to implement upon reaching an impasse must be overturned because it undermines NLRA policies. But caution is called for. Each set of negotiations is unique. Do not pursue this tactic without a lot of advance thought, discussion with people knowledgeable about law and bargaining, and a well-thought-out strategy.

In my experience, unions that were particularly successful in NLRB cases made special efforts to support their witnesses. One union, for example, got jobs for the discharged workers they filed charges for. This gave their witnesses backbones and demonstrated the union's trustworthiness. Of course, not all unions can do this, but they can do many things to ensure the success of a charge. Being prepared to file a charge means having records and evidence in good shape and ready to go. This includes having a list of witnesses and contact information ready, helping ensure workers are available to the agent and cooperative, and tracking down documents and information as the investigation progresses. All too many workplaces have their "Big Red"—no real name, no phone number, and no address— who was privy to key events and thus is an essential witness. The time a Board agent spends tracking down contact information and arranging appointments with reluctant witnesses is time taken away from the core of the investigation.

Many common problems could be overcome with small changes in union practices. For example, proving that the employer knew an employee was engaged in union activity is critical in a Section 8(a)(3) case and usually difficult. Some unions send letters to the employer, as employees sign cards, saying that the named employees are on the organizing committee and that if anything happens to them, such as discipline or discharge charges will be filed alleging anti-union discrimination. Some union organizers always wear union jackets and hats and drive cars with large union signs. I am told that in at least one case, company supervisors walked into a restaurant while employees were meeting with such union organizers. This makes it easy to prove that the employer knew that the employees were engaged in union activity. Union representatives should get copies of all literature handed out in an organizing campaign and save it, along with information about the date it was distributed, where, by whom, and to whom.

All election campaigns should be conducted as if a *Gissel* bargaining order[11] or a challenge to union card solicitation and signing is likely. When it is necessary to prove a card's authenticity[12] or the conditions under which it was signed at trial, the worst scenario is having to call each person to authenticate his or her own card. It is much easier and cuts trial time to call just those who asked employees to sign cards and have them testify to authenticate the cards they collected and the conditions under which they were collected. In a large unit, organizers may not recall which cards they got signed, as well as the conditions under which they were collected. One way to clear this up is to have each person passing out cards witness each card's signing by countersigning the card. This means instructing the card solicitors to initial or sign each card and list date, time, and place after an employee signs a card.

Doing this takes very little time as each card is signed. If this is a uniform practice, it will be easy to identify who is to be the witness for each card and may help jog the solicitor's memory. Anyone who has ever had to try a case where it was necessary to prove the authenticity of cards after the fact knows that it takes an enormous amount of time to sort the situation out. The problem is magnified as the unit grows larger. This is time better spent, especially in this kind of a case, on developing the evidence. In the context of a petition for a Section 10(j) injunction[13]—a likely context for a *Gissel* case—the time to prepare for the hearing is so short and the workload so high that the problem of card authentication can become a real impediment to preparing to try the case.

Each time a union begins to bargain it should bear in mind that it may be faced with filing a charge. Bad faith bargaining law is difficult, and the outcome depends on being able to reconstruct the complex events that occurred over many bargaining sessions and away from the table. It is hard to keep track of the give-and-take after the fact. Most negotiators take notes for their own needs, but unfortunately, it is difficult to negotiate and also take the detailed notes needed for a charge and trial. Assigning a member of the bargaining team to make a good detailed record that include phrasing, explanations, and other nuances, makes it possible to reconstruct what has happened and is helpful for negotiations and to the NLRB. I won't paint in the details of the union representative who, at the end of a two-hour appointment, was still unable to figure out what had happened when during just three bargaining sessions and who summed things up by apologizing and saying that next time he went into bargaining he would take better notes.

The NLRB agent assigned to investigate an unfair labor practice case normally asks the charged party to voluntarily respond to the allegations against it.[14] Board agents have no power to compel information from the charged party or witnesses without an investigative subpoena. Section 11(1) of the NLRA[15] has long given authority to use subpoenas to get information from charged parties, but until recently Regional Offices were reluctant to use them. Investigative subpoenas had to be authorized by NLRB headquarters, and this slowed investigations.[16] In 2000, General

Counsel Leonard Page gave Regional Directors or their designees authority to issue investigative subpoenas for witnesses and documents to charged parties and third-party witnesses when evidence was needed to determine whether a charge had merit but the evidence could not be obtained voluntarily.[17]

The default, however, remains to investigate without using investigative subpoenas:

> During certain investigations, in both R and C cases, resort to subpoenas will be necessary in order to ascertain the facts on which to base an administrative decision on the merits.
>
> Investigative subpoenas, however, are no substitute for a promptly initiated, dogged, and thorough pursuit of relevant evidence from cooperative sources.[18]

A Regional Director now has discretion to issue investigative subpoenas for witness testimony or documents from parties or third-party witnesses whenever the evidence would materially aid in investigating a charge but cannot be obtained voluntarily.[19] The only exception to this discretion is in the case of a serious legal problem, such as when a witness is likely to raise a serious constitutional defense or a claim of privilege.[20]

In sum, unions can expect to play a critical role whenever they file a charge. A charge is most likely to be found to have merit when the charging party works with the Board agent to get the case investigated, tried, and settled, and to obtain the best remedy available.

Undervalued Remedies.   Earlier chapters have talked about ways to use litigation to strengthen NLRA remedies. There are ways unions can benefit now by using NLRA remedies. Unions speak of NLRB notices as mere pieces of paper. Ironically, any NLRB agent knows that employers fight hard to keep from posting a notice and fight over every word in it. Why is this, if notice posting is nothing more than a piece of paper and a waste of time? From the employer's point of view posting a notice is indeed a very big issue. It means publicly and visibly admitting wrongdoing, and this is true even if the notice includes a nonadmission clause. It means admitting that the employer is subordinate to the law. It means posting the fact that employees have statutorily protected rights. Unlike other government agencies, the NLRB does not require employers to post notices of NLRA rights on a regular basis where employees can see them. Thus only when an NLRB notice is posted are these rights made visible. Rather than dismiss the value of notice postings, it makes more sense to see a notice posting through the employer's eyes and devise ways to exploit it.

Bad faith bargaining cases are difficult to prove, and it is fair to say that a bargaining order remedy is of little value in and of itself. However, it should be borne in mind that bargaining orders and findings of bad faith bargaining have important consequences. A finding of bad faith bargaining can mean that a strike is an unfair labor practice strike and not an economic strike. Such a finding means strikers cannot be permanently replaced. It can also determine that there was not a valid impasse and thus the employer cannot implement its final offer.

Any order, including a bargaining order, can be a basis for a contempt finding. Contempt can mean imposing heavy remedies. In my experience, unions rarely ask for a contempt order. Of the times I saw the NLRB pursue contempt, the initiative came from the NLRB. Contempt is a powerful tool to ensure compliance, and it is worthwhile being vigilant in pursuing it. The groundwork for it must be laid in each case where an order is issued. This means paying attention to the wording of cease-and-desist orders. When an employer violates a court order, it has potentially engaged in contemptuous behavior. A finding of contempt expands the range of remedies available. These can include payment of costs and attorney fees, compensatory damages, and coercive remedies imposed to ensure compliance.[21]

The wording of the NLRB order is key to finding a party in contempt for later conduct, as well as its being enforced by a court of appeals. An enforced cease-and-desist order does not expire. The question is whether the new action violates the language of the order. A narrow cease-and-desist order—one that uses the language "like or related"—will cover later violations that violate the same sections of the NLRA or that undermine the effectiveness of an order—for example, discharging union supporters to undermine a bargaining order. Broad cease-and-desist language such as "in any other manner" may reach any future violation.[22]

Orders bind only a party to the case, as a matter of due process. Sometimes entities other than a single employer have committed the unfair labor practice or may be responsible for remedying it. There are many forms of "derivative liability" that unions should be aware of for these can expand who is liable for an unfair labor practice. When there are more pockets to pay backpay it is easier to get a complete remedy. Those liable can include someone who buys a business or even the owner of a corporation under certain circumstances.[23] It is worthwhile for union agents to study the legal requirements for liability and keep members vigilant in collecting and reporting information. If the information is available, alternate respondents should be included when filing a charge. If it is learned later that an employer is selling or merging its business, the union should immediately notify the NLRB. The NLRB will notify any potential successor employer that it may be liable to remedy unfair labor practices.[24]

Some of the "persons" who may also be liable for remedying an unfair labor practice include (1) entities that appear distinct but are actually alter egos or disguised continuances of the one who committed the unfair labor practice; (2) affiliated groups of business entities that may be found to be a single employer and liable for the remedy; (3) "Golden State successors,"[25] who include purchasers who continue a business in substantially the same form, but only if the successor knew about the unfair labor practices before buying the business; (4) corporate shareholders, who may be found personally liable for a corporation's unfair labor practices (known as "piercing the corporate veil") if the corporate form is being used to perpetrate a fraud, evade legal obligations, or produce injustice or when the corporation's principals have essentially used the corporate form as their private bank by intermingling personal and corporate assets and property for personal purposes; (5) piercing the corporate veil is also allowed against a parent corporation that treats a corporate subsidiary as if it had no separate legal personality, thus making the parent liable for the subsidiary's actions; (6) "officers, agents, successors, and assigns, " which can include an officer who fails to ensure the corporation complies with an NLRB order when the order's language states that it binds them; and (7) one who transfers an asset fraudulently when litigation is pending or likely (under certain circumstances the transfer may be set aside).[26]

NLRB Elections. Most criticism of the Board is based on election case procedure. Board election processes can be complex. As a result, there are opportunities to create delay, and this gives employers time to mount an anti-union campaign and tends to work against a union victory. Delay can arise from hearings, appeals from a Decision Directing an Election, post-election challenges and objections, tests of certification, and appeals to the courts of appeals. In the worst case, it can be years before all appeals are exhausted and a final decision is issued. Fortunately, not all cases are worst-case.

In FY 2004, elections were conducted in a median time of thirty-nine days from the filing of the petition, and 93.6 percent of elections were held within fifty-six days of filing. In other words, there was some delay, but only a small minority—6.4 percent of cases—took more than fifty-six days to hold an election. Most cases (89 percent) took place based on agreements between the union and employer. Regional Directors issued 328 decisions in contested representation cases after hearing in a median of thirty-five days from the filing of the petition.[27] In other words, most NLRB elections were without the hearings that can cause delay.

If unions lobbied for more financial support and staff and then pressed the NLRB to institute new procedures to shorten election times, delay could be decreased even more. Unfortunately, NLRB resources have long been under severe strain:

> The average professional staff handling the workload in the Regional Of-
> fices remained virtually level during FY 2004, with 928.40 employees as
> compared to 927.56 in FY 2003. As of the end of September 2001 the pro-
> fessional workforce in the Field was 1004. As a result of severely restricted
> budgets in Fiscal Years 1994 through 1999 the NLRB was not able to hire
> sufficient numbers of investigators and attorneys and as a consequence the
> average professional staffing level for the Regional Offices declined from
> 930 to 874. In FY 2000 and FY 2001 more substantial budgets were provided
> to the Agency supporting hiring increases to process both current case in-
> take and the backlog of cases that had developed during the years of bud-
> get shortfalls. Only limited hiring took place in FY 2002 and FY 2003
> because of delay in the enactment of our final budget. In fact, in FY 2003
> Agency funding, along with funding for a number of other government
> agencies, was delayed until February, when a final appropriation was ap-
> proved by Congress. As a result of this delayed and reduced hiring, we ex-
> perienced an increase in situations pending under investigation from 4796
> at the end of FY 2002 to 4893 at the end of FY 2003. After a year of level
> staffing, however, the Regions were able to reduce the number of situations
> pending from 4893 at the end of FY 2003 to 4175 at the end of FY 2004, a de-
> crease of 14.7 percent.[28]

Recently, General Counsel Arthur Rosenfeld testified that one reason the NLRB supports voluntary recognition of unions is that the agency does not

have enough money to conduct secret ballot elections in every unionization campaign. He said: "'We could not continue day-to-day operations if
there weren't voluntary recognitions.'"[29] Rep. Charles Norwood (R-Ga.),
the sponsor of the Secret Ballot Protection Act (H.R. 4343), a bill intended
to mandate NLRB elections, responded that "he would support increased
funding for the National Labor Relations Board to facilitate secret ballot
elections in every unionization campaign."[30] Maybe unions should take
him up on this promise.

One criticism of the NLRB is that the Board decides the unit for an election. This is not completely accurate. The party that files the election petition—usually the union—has a presumption in favor of the unit that it has
selected. The employer must prove that the unit the union asked for is not
appropriate. The NLRA does not require that a unit petitioned for be *the*
most appropriate unit. It only has to be *an* appropriate unit.[31] In other
words, many different sorts of units can be appropriate. The point of asking whether a unit is appropriate is to ensure that the unit is one that has
cohesion, in which bargaining can reasonably occur and in which unions
can easily represent the interests of the employees. This means that the
NLRB and a union are not likely to be at cross-purposes here. Obviously
all would be well if employers, unions, and the Board merely engaged in
a rational process of determining whether the unit was an appropriate one.
The reality is that the unit configuration is a battleground on which a
shadow war is being fought. The real issue is what unit makes a union win
more or less likely. For the union, that may mean it wants a unit where it
has support. For the employer that may mean it does not want a unit where
the union has support.

One strategy worth considering in a tough election situation in which
the employer is likely to contest the unit is to consider whether it is possible to go into an election hearing by being flexible in the choice of unit. Having a fallback position can be a way to insure the union achieves a good
unit. A good example was a case in which the union petitioned to represent employees at several—but not all—metropolitan cable television facilities. On the first day of the hearing, the employer put on a strong case
demonstrating that the only appropriate unit was employer-wide. On the
second day, the union filed an amended petition seeking an employer-wide
unit. The employer then tried valiantly to demonstrate that this was not an
appropriate unit, but it had fallen into a trap and could not win. Clearly,

not everyone can petition for an array of units, but it is worth thinking about what options and potential fallback positions exist.

It is also helpful to bear in mind that the unit in which an election is held is not necessarily the unit that must exist for all time. Units can change as new job classifications are created. Some changes can come through negotiations. Others occur through less frequently used processes, such as unit clarification petitions.[32]

The biggest issue about NLRB elections for unions is opposition to them and demand for legislation for card-check recognition. Even if law reform were possible, it still might not remedy problems of delay. Something that is not discussed in the ongoing campaigns for card-check recognition, but needs to be, is that even card-check agreements cannot prevent litigation[33] and delay.[34] The courts are likely to decide that U.S. constitutional due process rights require permitting appeals to card-check results. After all, the NLRA says nothing about court challenges or appeals from elections. Despite this, over time, processes to allow employers to appeal or challenge election results have been developed.

Card-check success in some Canadian jurisdictions may say more about the differences between the U.S. and Canadian societies and relations between unions and employers than about our labor laws.[35] Most card-check agreements include neutrality agreements as well. It may be that it is the neutrality agreement that is more important than card check. If this is true, then getting a neutrality agreement as part of an NLRB campaign may prevent delay and lead to a better relationship. It may also be that card-check-with-neutrality agreements succeed because the employers who agree to them are more likely be the employers who are less adamantly anti-union.

In any case, as long as we have the current system, how can a union representative weave a path through the Board's election processes? In both representation and unfair labor practice cases, there is no substitute for having strong organization, whether that comes about through a slow, organic process or through a blitz.

Unions fear that an employer can thwart worker desires by misusing Board processes to drag out the process, to increase costs, and to force an election in a unit configuration that ensures a union loss. The AFL-CIO Organizing Department and others have responded to these problems by urging unions to boycott Board elections. The Board itself has lately been making efforts to discourage abuse of its processes. The NLRB recently introduced a "Full Consent Election Agreement" in order to minimize and eliminate delay while providing due process rights. It allows for a pre-election hearing but makes the Regional Director's decision final and binding.[36] This eliminates the major cause of delay. The Board needs to be encouraged to continue efforts to prevent misuse of its processes. A Board avoidance strategy has succeeded in some cases, but it is too early to say whether this is clearly superior in every case or will prove superior in the long term. It is certain that employers will respond to this strategy and develop methods to deal it. Rather than advocating only one organizing strategy there is an important discussion yet to be had on identifying strategies and determining which work best in which situations.

There may be reasons a union may prefer a Board election, oversight, and certification. In the long run, government-run elections are best for unions and workers. Government involvement transforms representation from a private transaction into a public process with the sanction of law. It says that our society supports the right to union representation. Americans see elections as a fundamental part of a democracy. Opponents of unions understand this. They use the campaign for card check to demonstrate that unions are undemocratic organizations. The response to these charges is complicated and difficult to make. Given this difficulty and given the value of an officially sanctioned secret-ballot election, it makes sense to work toward making this process a good one.

The focus on card check has also meant losing sight of the greatest threat to union membership in the United States: losses of union members when their companies close, contract work out, or relocate. This creates a membership deficit of about 200,000 every year. Unions just cannot organize out of this hole, so it hard to understand why there is so little attention to this steady erosion compared to the campaign for card check.

Using the NLRB Strategically.   There are many reasons and ways for unions to use the NLRB strategically. It can be used to build solidarity and demonstrate that the union will stand with the workers and fight for their rights. NLRB remedies provide a means to educate members, workers who might one day be members, and employers about the law. NLRB charges can be used to highlight problems with lower-level management and make their superiors aware of problems within the company.

NLRB charges have some similarities to corporate campaigns. They cost companies time and money when they investigate and respond to them. Some unions have used corporate campaigns to expose misconduct and bring economic pressure on employers to reform their behavior. Although charges should not be filed for merely coercive reasons, the fact is that unfair labor practice cases create economic pressure and expose employer misconduct. Charges can be used to build union bargaining power. For example, a union may agree to settle NLRB cases in exchange for employer bargaining concessions.

Board charges can play a useful role in organizing. Filing a charge may refocus the course of bargaining or forestall future illegal terminations, threats, interrogations, or other unfair labor practices. The charge makes it clear that the union is aware of what is happening to the employees and vigilant. It can be used to rally workers and pressure the employer to make a quick resolution. Sometimes settlements come about with the mere filing of a charge. When the NLRB issues a complaint, it sends a message that the government has found that an employer is not just treating its workers badly but is actually a law breaker. This may encourage community members and organizations to support the workers publicly. It may also change the employer's behavior. In a bitter bargaining-lockout case involving International Paper's taking aggressive actions, for example, the employer changed its behavior in some critical ways as soon as it learned that the NLRB was issuing a complaint.[37]

In an election or contract campaign, a union can use the filing of a charge as a rallying point and to demonstrate it is actively supporting the workers. Actions can range from distributing informational flyers to bringing workers as a group to the Board offices to file the charge and then to present a copy of the charge to management. Filing a charge can take place with a press release or press conference. The same thing can be done when the Board issues a complaint.

Unions should be on the outlook for common unfair labor practices. Often these are illegal nonsolicitation or nondistribution rules, such as forbidding employees to talk to fellow employees about their pay and other working conditions. These are often easy violations to prove, and, again, they send an important message to workers the union is trying to organize. If an employer has an illegal nonsolicitation or nondistribution rule, employees may be afraid to be involved in a union campaign. A charge filed early in an election campaign can remove the illegal rule, inform the workers of their rights, expose the employer as a lawbreaker, and demonstrate that the union is vigilant. An illegal rule may even be grounds for over-turning an election the union has lost.[38]

In my experience unions are far too reluctant to file charges. They often seem to assume that they must have enough evidence to prove a violation. This is not necessary. Charges can't be filed in bad faith; the charge form it-self makes this clear. They may be filed, however, if there is a good faith be-lief that an unfair labor practice has been committed. The union may be unable to develop sufficient evidence on its own, but the Board agent may develop it during the investigation.

When a charge is filed, especially in the midst of a campaign, a union needs to be prepared for the possibility that it will be found not to have merit. Just as its filing or the issuance of a complaint may buoy the union, a dismissal may have a depressing effect. When the charge is filed, then, it is important to have a plan for handling a dismissal. It may be that when the Board decides that there is insufficient evidence to support a charge, the union will be given a choice whether to take a dismissal or withdraw the charge. If the union is given advance notice of a dismissal, it may want to reach a quick settlement with the employer.

It may be helpful to bear in mind that dismissing a charge does not mean there has been a final and binding decision. A dismissal means only that, at this time, sufficient evidence has not been uncovered to conclude that an unfair labor practice has been committed. This means that the charge can be refiled and should be refiled if additional evidence is found within the period of the statute of limitations. The underlying evidence can also be background evidence of animus for a later-filed charge, even one filed af-ter the six-month statute of limitations period has expired.

Stop Avoiding the Board

Unions are better off if the NLRB is a strong agency. Ultimately, union energy is better spent strengthening the NLRA and NLRB than finding ways to avoid them. Beyond the daily problems unions face, there is room for long-term strategies that can generate valuable resources in labor's ar-senal.

There is, of course, only so much that can be done against a virulently anti-union employer whose goal is a scorched-earth war. That means a long, hard battle, where it is good to have allies, resources, and alternative strategies. The NLRB should be included among these. But unfortunately for unions, the Board has been seriously depleted since 1981 through neglect and outright attack by conservative presidents and Congresses. It has suffered from the appointment of officials whose stated mission was to eliminate the Board. Through this difficult time, it has not been able to count on support from unions because this would conflict with their public position that the Board is an enemy of unions and workers.

Anti-union employers benefit from a Board under attack and neglected by its natural constituents. Unions and workers will benefit from a Board that receives adequate funding, full staffing, and good leadership. This is not to say that the Board and its decisions cannot be criticized, but criticism—even vigorous criticism—is not the same as rejecting and undermining the Board. Criticism can promote improvement, and thoughtful criticism should continue.

The historical record demonstrates that the NLRA and NLRB have been essential to sustained union organization. Letting the NLRB be destroyed gives aid and comfort to the enemies of unions and risks returning us to the world in which unions had no legal support.

9

AN INVITATION

Just as law is not the whole world, a litigation strategy, by itself, is not enough to take back the Workers' Law. It is true that individual cases can be litigated using the ideas I have presented here and those cases could, over time, make a difference. But to make a real change, there must be a larger strategy. Law matters, but law is only one of the many parts that must be brought together in this campaign.

Both work and law play pivotal roles in shaping our societies, but both are often invisible. A successful strategy to take back the Workers' Law must make both of these visible.

Most of us see law as rules, more or less like traffic laws. They are written in books and tell us what we can and cannot do. But that is not the way law really operates. It is intimately connected to the structure of our lives. Law affects how we behave and how this society and our relationships to one another are structured. Our attitudes also affect how successful a law is. To take back the Workers' Law, we must change understandings about the legal rights employers, workers, and society have to control what happens in the workplace. These understandings will help us see that the private workplace does not exist in isolation. What happens there affects our society, and society provides the infrastructure that the workplace needs to exist. We must make these interconnections visible.

Work is also invisible. It plays a pivotal role in society. It shapes our days, our prospects, our views, and our economy. Yet we tend to give little thought to the relationships among work, our lives, and our communities, except when things go wrong at our jobs or when unemployment is high— or when firefighters dash into burning buildings. To take back the Workers' Law, we must make work visible in all its dimensions—legal, moral, social, political, and personal. We must understand that everything connected with work involves moral and political choices and personal and public responsibility.

Labor and employment law can be a lens though which to see the struggles in our society. Seeing through that lens is, at first, demoralizing. The default option for workplace rights is at-will employment, a system with no rights for workers, except the hollow right to quit a job. But most Americans believe that, in a great country like this, the law treats them fairly. They think law gives them seniority, severance pay, and a right to just cause for termination. But no law gives them these rights.[1] Even union members do not understand that these rights come through collective bargaining, not from law.

These are things people value, but as long as workers think they already have these rights, or as long as they believe they have no better prospects, they will see no reason to take action to get them. Thus there needs to be an education strategy to let workers know what rights they actually have and how to get the rights they want. We all need to learn that it is unions that have most consistently fought to win these rights for all of us. Unions have fought to get workplace due process and industrial justice for unionized workers through collective bargaining agreements. And they have fought just as hard for all us—workers or not, union or not—through laws to make work better—for civil rights, Title VII, OSHA, living wages, pension protections, and the minimum wage. These are but a few of the actions that constitute a track record of siding with workers by acting to benefit society as a whole. Unions have acted to promote respect for human work that is not just intellectual or philosophical, that contributes to the welfare of all in our society.

But most Americans think that unions work only for union members. Fifty-four percent think unions mostly hurt workers who are not unionized. Only 35 percent of unorganized Americans think that unions help them, while only 54 percent of union members think that unions help the unorganized.[2]

This should not be surprising. "Concerted activity by employees, unions, and the employer-union relationship [is] considered an alien presence in the U.S. landscape."[3] As a whole, we continue to believe that jobs must be controlled by master-and-servant law, that economic survival depends on workplaces that are totalitarian, and that democratic values are dangerous. This is not an environment in which unions can thrive or even survive. It is not a good environment for work and workers.

This book advocates using a litigation strategy to take back the Workers' Law, but the best lawyering in the world, by itself, cannot make this a society rooted in the NLRA values of democracy, solidarity, social and economic justice, fairness, and equality. The NAACP Legal Defense Fund did not overthrow legalized apartheid in this country just by winning cases. Its success depends on a moral and mental transformation.

The truth is that American workers today are not ready to seize their rights. Rather, just the opposite. Gallup polls since 1937 have shown that most Americans approve of labor unions. Even today, about 65 percent say they approve of unions,[4] but, as a 1999 study[5] shows, worker support is for a weak form of unionization, in which the union cooperates with the employer. This is not evidence that if only employer opposition could be eliminated (as through neutrality agreements) or evaded (as through card check or a blitz organization), labor's numbers would soar. The results seem to mean that workers accept management's right to call the shots.

This interpretation fits with what we see every day about how most people feel about employers, unions, and the social order. If union numbers depend only on eliminating or evading employer opposition, then it makes sense to focus on technical fixes, such as card-check and neutrality agreements. But if the situation is more dire, if employer opposition is but a symptom of a wider problem, then the remedy must be more global. I see the situation as more pervasive. I think the solution has to be a campaign to transform this society into a community that is infused with NLRA values.

We are engaged in a war of ideas. Radically conservative think tanks and advocacy groups around the world are colonizing our minds and the way we think by changing our very language. Even labor and its allies now use the language of commerce and economics as the way to explain the world. When we come to believe it is not legitimate to speak in moral and social language, then we lose the ability to see our moral and social reality.

Employers ship jobs off to impoverished—and thus supine—workers in

India, China, Malaysia, or the Dominican Republic. No one calls them "runaway shops." They use the sterile word "outsourcing." Those in the know are replacing the word "citizen" with "customer." We celebrate "creative destruction." We accept that corporations must be able to move where and when they wish, and therefore that cities, states, and countries must compete with one another, even when this risks financial, environmental, and community ruin. On my way to work, I pass parts of a once vital city where abandoned businesses and homes are turning into burned-out junk piles and urban forests. Rural towns are returning to wilderness as work leaves and the inhabitants follow.

We face a much more deeply rooted problem than just employers who hate unions enough to wage total war. Employer anti-union campaigns do hurt organizing success, but if workers did not fear their employer's power over them, if workers were not afraid of losing their jobs, then employer anti-union campaigns would have no power over them. In addition, if workers truly believed that unions would and could stand by their side when they needed an ally, then more workers might be willing to risk losing their jobs.

But the truth is that workers do fear their employers, and rightly so. And workers, as part of the public, are more likely to think of union corruption, union bosses, and union self-interest than "Solidarity Forever."

This is a country that has moved so far to the right politically that laws passed during the Nixon Administration could not be proposed today even by Democrats. It was not always this way, and it does not have to stay this way. It is possible to make it respectable to support values other than corporate values.

To make this happen there must be a campaign by land, sea, and air—using targeted litigation, social science research, liberal think tanks, investigative reporting, education, and activism to replace corporate values with the NLRA values of solidarity, social and economic justice, democracy, equality, and fairness. Labor must play a part in this campaign at each of these levels.

Those who join in this campaign to take back the Workers' Law and our society as a whole must be tireless. This campaign must speak clearly and forthrightly about who gains and who loses from conservative economic policy. The message must be in terms the public understands and is ready to hear. Most workers today are not the converted, so we need to paint a clear picture that explains why people are living the lives they do. We need to present a stirring vision of how those lives and our communities can be made better. Most important, the language and vision must be matched with honest and consistent actions.

If we want to remake this society into one whose values are the values of solidarity, fairness, social and economic justice, and democracy, we need a multipronged campaign. Law is a part of that campaign but only one part. Each piece of this effort is important if labor's power is to be restored and if the United States is to return to the democratic values it once espoused.

This book is an invitation to begin that effort.

NOTES

Introduction

1. *See* Michael D. Yates, *Naming the System: Inequality and Work in the Global Economy* (2003).

2. Barry T. Hirsch & David A. MacPherson, *How Unions Help Bring Low-Wage Workers Out of Poverty: Pay of Union and Nonunion Workers in Selected Occupations 2002*, http://www.aflcio.org/joinaunion/why/uniondifference/uniondiff11a.cfm; Lawrence Mishel & Matthew Walters, *How Unions Help All Workers* (Aug. 2003), http://www.epinet.org/content.cfm/briefingpapers_bp143.

3. Richard Kluger, *Simple Justice* (1975).

4. NLRA § 1; 29 U.S.C. § 151 (emphasis added).

5. Wade Rathke, Majority Unionism: Strategies for Organizing the 21st Century Labor Movement (June 2002) (unpublished paper); *see also* Barbara Ehrenreich & Thomas Geoghegan, *Lighting Labor's Fire*, The Nation, Dec. 23, 2002, http://www.thenation.com/doc.mhtml?i=20021223&s=ehrenreich.

6. Michelle Amber, *AFL-CIO Convenes Organizing Summit to Find New Ways to Expand Membership*, Daily Lab. Rep. (BNA), C-1 (Jan. 14, 2003).

7. *Kirkland Calls for Excluding Employers From Election Process*, Daily Lab. Rep. (BNA), D8 (June 18, 1993); *Kirkland Says Many Unions Avoiding NLRB, Calls Board an "Impediment" to Organizing*, Daily Lab. Rep. (BNA), A-11 (Aug. 30, 1989); *Senate Labor Subcommittee Holds Hearing on Organizing Rights Under Taft-Hartley Act*, Daily Lab. Rep. (BNA), A-11 (Feb. 1, 1988).

8. Richard Trumka, *Build Rank-and-File Activism*, in *The Future of Labor* 64 (Labor Research Association 1992).

9. Richard Trumka, *Why Labor Law Has Failed*, 89 W. Va. L. Rev. 871, 881 (1987):

> If section 7 of the Wagner Act were repealed, unions would be thrust back into the common-law regime existing in the 1920s. The common-law doctrines of property, contract, and tort law used by employers' lawyers have never been repudiated by the courts. They are not applied today for the simple reason that statutory

rights have taken precedence over them. In the absence of the protections provided by section 7, however, twenty-first century courts would apply existing common law doctrines.

Janice R. Bellace, *The Future of Employee Representation in America: Enabling Freedom of Association in the Workplace in Changing Times Through Statutory Reform,* 5 U. Pa. J. Lab. & Emp. L. 1, 7 (2002).

10. Karl E. Klare, *Judicial Deradicalization of the Wagner Act and the Origins of Modern Legal Consciousness, 1937–1941,* 62 Minn. L. Rev. 265 (1977–1978); Karl Klare, *Critical Theory and Labor Relations Law,* in *The Politics of Law* 61, 62–63 (David Karirys ed., rev. ed., 1990). David Brody points out: "[The judicial] work of interpreting labor's rights out of existence has steadily proceeded. The incremental dismantling of the duty to bargain . . . can be replicated many times over in the case law governing interrogations, captive audience meetings, union access, coercive speech, you name it." David Brody, *Labor vs. the Law: How the Wagner Act Became a Management Tool,* 13 New Lab. Forum (Spring 2004).

11. For examples of this discussion, see *Labor Notes Roundtable, Organizing: What's Needed* (Nov. 2002–Apr. 2003), http://www.labornotes.org/archives/2003/organizing .html.

12. "In a variety of contexts, the Supreme Court, often with the prodding of the circuit courts, and sometimes, particularly in the 1980s, even the Board itself, has provided cramped and narrow interpretations of the Act that have countered its basic policy contained in the preamble." William B. Gould, *Labor Law and Its Limits: Some Proposals for Reform,* 49 Wayne L. Rev. 667, 674–75 (2003).

13. Human Rights Watch, *Unfair Advantage: Workers Freedom of Association in the United States Under International Human Rights Standards* (2000). See ILO Convention No. 98, Right to Organise and Collective Bargaining Convention, 32d Sess., art. 1 (1949); ILO Convention No. 87, Freedom of Association and Protection of the Right to Organise Convention, 31st Sess., art. 11 (1948); *see also* ILO Convention No. 154, Collective Bargaining Convention, 67th Sess. (1981); ILO Declaration on Fundamental Principles and Rights at Work, 86th Sess. (1998).

14. Michael LeRoy, *Lockouts Involving Replacement Workers: An Empirical Public Policy Analysis and Proposal to Balance Economic Weapons under the NLRA,* 74 Wash. U. L. Q. 981 (1996).

15. "The remedies, along with substantive law, have been fashioned without regard to the broad equitable purposes of remedial authority, i.e, to act as both a prophylactic and to reorder the employment relationship." Gould, *Labor Law and Its Limits,* 675.

16. *Id.* at 676–77; United Automobile Workers, *Community Action Program, Labor Laws: Assaults on the National Labor Relations Act* (2001), http://www.uaw.org/cap/01/issue/ issue06-2.html

17. Office of the NLRB General Counsel, *Memorandum GC 03-01: Summary of Operations Fiscal Year 2002* (Feb. 4, 2003), http://www.nlrb.gov/gcmemo/gc03-01.html.

18. For a description of pre-NLRA judicial values, see Reinhold Fahlbeck, *The Demise of Collective Bargaining in the USA: Reflections on the Un-American Character of American Labor Law,* 15 Berkeley J. Emp. & Lab. L. 307, 312–15 (1994).

19. In 2002, 13.2 percent of workers were union members, down from 13.4 percent in 2001. The number of persons belonging to a union in 1983 fell by 280,000 to 16.1 million in 2002. Department of Labor Bureau of Labor Statistics, *Union Members in 2002,* USDL 03–88 http://www.bls.gov/cps/ (Feb. 25, 2003).

20. *See* Valerie E. Lee & David T. Burkam, *Inequality at the Starting Gate: Social Background Differences in Achievement as Children Begin School* (2002); Lawrence Mischel et al., *The State of Working America, 2002/2003* (2003).

21. Michael D. Yates, *Why Unions Matter* 81–103 (1998).

22. Human Rights Watch, *Unfair Advantage.*

23. Staughton Lynd, *Communal Rights,* 62 Tex. L. Rev. 1417, 1424 (1984).

24. NLRB v. Town & Country Elec., Inc., 516 U.S. 85 (1995).

25. *Rep. Johnson Issues Statement on Emerging Trends in Labor Laws in U.S.,* U.S. Fed News, May 10, 2004; *Salting: A House Bill Blocking Companies from Having to Hire Union Organizers,* 54 Underground Construction 8 (July 1, 1999); James Worsham, *House-Passed Bill Would Help Firms Resist Union Organizing,* Nation's Business, June 1998, at 8; *Prepared Statement of Associated Builders and Contractors ABC Before the House Small Business Committee,* Federal News Service, Mar. 4, 1998.

26. 502 U.S. 527 (1992).

27. § 2(3); 29 U.S.C. § 152(3) (2002).

28. In fact, Congress rejected limiting the definition of employee to the employees of a particular employer and even to those in the same industry, a limitation found in the Norris-LaGuardia Act, 29 U.S.C. § 113(a) (2002). Richard Michael Fischl, *Self, Others, and Section 7: Mutualism and Protected Protest Activities under the National Labor Relations Act,* 89 Colum. L. Rev. 789, 852 (1989); George Feldman, *Workplace Power and Collective Activity: The Supervisory and Managerial Exclusions in Labor Law,* 37 Ariz. L. Rev. 525, 526 (1995).

29. Ellen Dannin, *Finding the Workers' Law,* 8 Green Bag 19 (2004).

30. William R. Corbett, *Waiting for the Labor Law of the Twenty-First Century: Everything Old Is New Again,* 23 Berkeley J. Emp. & Lab. L. 259, 287 (2002).

31. For some recent examples, see Office of the General Counsel, Division of Operations-Management, *Administrative Investigations vis-à-vis Hearings in Post-Election Proceedings,* Memorandum OM 04–26 (Feb. 12, 2004), http://www.nlrb.gov/nlrb/shared_files/ommemo/ommemo/om04-26.pdf; Office of the General Counsel, Division of Operations-Management, *"Test of Certification" Bargaining Order Summary Judgment Cases,* Memorandum OM 04–25 (Feb. 12, 2004), http://www.nlrb.gov/nlrb/shared_files/ommemo/ommemo/2004index.asp.

1. Why Judges Rewrite Labor Law

1. Richard N. Block, *Rethinking the National Labor Relations Act and Zero-Sum Labor Law: An Industrial Relations View,* 18 Berkeley J. Emp. & Lab. L. 30, 34–35 (1997); *see also* David Card & Richard Freeman, *Small Differences That Matter: Labor Markets and Income Maintenance in Canada and the United States* (1993).

2. William R. Corbett, *The Need for a Revitalized Common Law of the Workplace,* 69 Brooklyn L. Rev. 91, 96–97, 134–35 (2003); Joseph Slater, *The Rise of Master-Servant and the Fall of Master Narrative: A Review of Labor Law in America,* 15 Berkeley J. Emp. & Lab. L. 141, 147–51 (1994). Consider the experience of seeking labor rights provisions in trade agreements. Lance Compa & Jeffrey S. Vogt, *Labor Regulation and Trade: Labor Rights in the Generalized System of Preferences: A 20–Year Review,* 22 Comp. Lab. L. & Pol'y J. 199 (2001).

3. Common law, as used here, refers to the process of making law through judicial decisions. The common-law system was developed in England many centuries ago. Countries that were once English colonies, such as the United States, have inherited the common law system. Law students in common law countries study court cases in order to learn what the law is. They also study the process of reasoning judges use in applying and developing the law. In order to find what the law is on a specific subject, a lawyer in a common-law country must examine judicial decisions. In the last century, particularly since the New Deal, legislatures have become more important in the lawmaking process. Judges still play a key role in lawmaking when they interpret and apply statutes in cases that come before them.

4. Corbett, *The Need for a Revitalized Common Law of the Workplace*, 96–97, 152.

5. *Id.* at 157.

6. McClatchy Newspapers, Inc. v. NLRB, 131 F.3d 1026 (D.C. Cir. 1997).

7. NLRB v. Mackay Radio & Tel. Co., 304 U.S. 333 (1938).

8. There is a special procedural problem when the NLRB has ruled that certain facts cannot be a violation. In those cases, it is difficult to get the NLRB General Counsel to issue a complaint, and it is difficult to appeal that decision. General Counsel Arthur Rosenfeld stated that he can issue a complaint and argue for reversal. He also said that as General Counsel he has a duty to present the Board with new and developing workplace issues so the Board can consider whether it should reverse itself. *Board GC Addresses Prosecutorial Discretion, Asks Board to Re-examine Previous Rulings*, 72 Law Week (BNA) 2111 (Aug. 26, 2003).

9. McClatchy Newspapers, Inc. v. NLRB, 131 F.3d 1026 (D.C. Cir. 1997).

10. United Food & Commercial Workers Union, Local 1036 v. NLRB, 307 F.3d 760 (9th Cir. 2002) (en banc), *cert. denied sub nom.* Mulder v. NLRB, 537 U.S. 1024 (2002).

11. Michael J. Hayes, *After "Hiding the Ball" Is Over: How the NLRB Must Change Its Approach to Decision-Making*, 33 Rutgers L. J. 523, 525 (2002) (appellate courts reverse dozens of Board decisions every year).

12. James J. Brudney et al., *Reflections on Group Action and the Law of the Workplace*, 74 Tex. L. Rev. 1563, 1572–73 (1996).

13. *Id.* at 1581–83.

14. James J. Brudney et al., *Judicial Hostility Towards Labor Unions? Applying the Social Science Background Model to a Celebrated Concern*, 60 Ohio St. L.J. 1675 (1999) (judicial bias study); Joseph Slater, *The Rise of Master-Servant and the Fall of Master Narrative: A Review of Labor Law in America*, 15 Berkeley J. Emp. & Lab. L. 141, 167–68 (1994).

15. *See* Richard Michael Fischl, *Some Realism About Critical Legal Studies*, 41 U. Miami L. Rev. 505, 526–27 (1987); Brudney, *Reflections on Group Action*, 1589.

16. James A. Gross, *Incorporating Human Rights Principles into U.S. Labor Arbitration: A Proposal for Fundamental Change*, 8 Empl. Rts & Empl. Pol'y J. 1 (2004); James Gray Pope, *How American Workers Lost the Right to Strike, and Other Tales*, 103 Mich. L. Rev. 518 (2004)

17. *See* Karl E. Klare, *Judicial Deradicalization of the Wagner Act and the Origins of Modern Legal Consciousness, 1937–1941*, 62 Minn. L. Rev. 265 (1977–1978).

18. Clyde W. Summers, *Employment at Will in the United States: The Divine Right of Employers*, 3 U. Pa. J. Lab. & Emp. L. 65, 68, 78 (2000).

19. Pauline T. Kim, *Bargaining with Imperfect Information: A Study of Worker Perceptions of Legal Protection in an At-Will World*, 83 Cornell L. Rev. 105 (1997).

20. Richard Epstein, *In Defense of the Contract at Will*, 51 U. Chi. L. Rev. 947 (1984).

21. Jesse Rudy, *What They Don't Know Won't Hurt Them: Defending Employment-at-Will in Light of Findings That Employees Believe They Possess Just Cause Protection*, 23 Berkeley J. Emp. & Lab. L. 307 (202); Pauline T. Kim, *Norms, Learning, and Law: Exploring the Influences on Workers' Legal Knowledge*, 1999 U. Ill. L. Rev. 447; Kim, *Bargaining with Imperfect Information*, 83 Cornell L. Rev. 105.

22. *See, e.g.*, Skagerberg v. Blandin Paper Co., 266 N.W. 872 (Minn. 1936).

23. Peter Linzer, *The Decline of Assent: At-Will Employment as a Case Study of the Breakdown of Private Law Theory*, 20 Ga. L. Rev. 323, 377 n.256 (1986).

24. Jay Feinman, *The Development of the Employment at Will Rule*, 20 Am. J. Leg. Hist. 118 (1976); *but see* Epstein, *In Defense of the Contract at Will*, 951–52.

25. NLRB v. Jones & Laughlin Steel Corp., 301 U.S. 1 (1937) (extract from Respondent's brief).

26. *See* Lord Wedderburn, *Labour Law: From Here to Autonomy?*, 16 Indus. L. J. 1, 4–7 (1987); Thomas Barton, *Book Review: Expectations, Institutions, and Meanings*, 74 Cal. L. Rev. 1805, 1823 (1986).

27. James Atleson, *Values and Assumptions in American Labor Law* (1984); James Brudney, *Of Labor Law and Dissonance,* 30 Conn. L. Rev. 1353 (1998); Julius Getman, *Of Labor Law and Birdsong,* 30 Conn. L. Rev. (1998). A study of a campaign to alter views in order to change labor law reform found that one of the few groups not influenced was the judiciary. Ellen Dannin, *Hail, Market, Full of Grace: Buying and Selling Labor Law Reform,* 2001 L. Rev. Mich. St. U.–Det. Coll. L. 1090.

28. Janice R. Bellace, *The Future of Employee Representation in America: Enabling Freedom of Association in the Workplace in Changing Times Through Statutory Reform,* 5 U. Pa. J. Lab. & Emp. L. 1, 5, 9–10 (2002).

29. Two cases that present this issue of jobs as property are *NLRB v. Adkins Transfer Co., Inc.,* 226 F.2d 324 (6th Cir. 1955), and *Textile Workers Union v. Darlington,* 380 U.S. 263 (1965). In both cases, the courts felt the employer had an unfettered right to make decisions about its property. *See also* Richard Michael Fischl, *Self, Others, and Section 7: Mutualism and Protected Protest Activities under the National Labor Relations Act,* 89 Colum. L. Rev. 789, 798–800, 803–09 (1989).

30. Sanford M. Jacoby, *Employee Representation and Corporate Governance: A Missing Link,* 3 U. Pa. J. Lab. & Emp. L. 449, 450–51 (2001).

31. "Companies that sweeten executive compensation with unusually large bonuses or options plans tend to have deeper and more frequent credit downgrades and higher bond-default rates than those that don't offer such plum packages, according to a Moody's Investors Service report." *Moody's Study Links CEO Packages to Default Rates,* FXStreet.com, July 25, 2005, http://www.fxstreet.com/nou/noticies/afx/noticia.asp?pv_noticia=1122312608-e04f0f08-34099#; Claudia H. Deutsch, *Executive Pay; My Big Fat C.E.O. Paycheck,* New York Times, April 3, 2005, at 1–1; *United Chief Was Paid $366,000 Bonus in 2004,* New York Times, March 17, 2005, at C-3; *Workplace Fairness,* http://www.workplacefairness.org/index.php?page=paywatch; AFL-CIO, *Executive PayWatch* http://www.aflcio.org/corporateamerica/paywatch/

32. Karl Klare, *The Horizons of Transformative Labour Law and Employment Law,* in *Labour Law in an Era of Globalization: Transformative Practices & Possibilities* 3, 11 (Joanne Conaghan et al. eds., 2002); Cynthia L. Estlund, *Labor, Property, and Sovereignty After Lechmere,* 46 Stan. L. Rev. 305 (1994).

33. Bellace, *The Future of Employee Representation,* 12, 17 n.74.

34. Klare, *Horizons of Transformative Labour Law,* 3, 13.

35. Atleson, *Values and Assumptions,* 13–14.

36. Mark Barenberg, *The Political Economy of the Wagner Act: Power, Symbol, and Workplace Cooperation,* 106 Harv. L. Rev. 1379, 1475 (1993).

37. Leo E. Strine Jr., *The Inescapably Empirical Foundation of the Common Law of Corporations,* 27 Del. J. Corp. L. 499, 514–15 (2002).

38. David Brody, *Labor vs. the Law: How the Wagner Act Became a Management Tool,* 13 New Lab. Forum 9, 14 (Spring 2004); *see also* Karl Klare, *Critical Theory and Labor Relations Law* in *The Politics of Law* 61, 64 (David Kairys ed., rev. ed., 1990).

39. Corbett, *The Need for a Revitalized Common Law of the Workplace,* 98–99.

40. NLRA § 10(e), (f); 29 U.S.C. § 160(e), (f).

41. Cynthia L. Estlund, *The Ossification of American Labor Law,* 102 Colum. L. Rev. 1527, 1597–99 (2002).

42. Brudney et al., *Judicial Hostility Towards Labor Unions?* 1704–05, 1720, 1726–27.

43. 226 F.2d 324 (6th Cir. 1955). *See also* Cynthia L. Estlund, *Economic Rationality and Union Avoidance: Misunderstanding the National Labor Relations Act,* 71 Tex. L. Rev. 921 (1993).

44. Textile Workers Union v. Darlington, 380 U.S. 263 (1965).

45. Robert S. Vance, *A View from the Circuit: A Federal Circuit Judge Views the NLRA Appellate Scene,* 1 Lab. Law. 39, 40 (1985).

46. "If judges become too wedded to previous judicial conceptions of reality, they may resist accepting different conceptions that have evolved in a dynamic marketplace. Instead of shaping a common law that fits the circumstances . . . as they exist here and now, judges may be tempted to adhere to precedent rigidly, lest they be seen as engaged in unprincipled (and somewhat daunting) acts of lawmaking." Strine, *The Inescapably Empirical Foundation,* 501.

47. The law of personal jurisdiction (when a defendant can be forced to be a defendant in a state where he or she is not a citizen) has gone through periods of development leading to highly technical and complicated dogmas that become impossible to apply. These have been followed by radical changes to realign the law with the requirements of the due process clause.

48. 115 F.3d 1045 (D.C. Cir 1997).

49. *Id.* at 5.

50. For a longer discussion of this issue, *see* Ellen Dannin, *From Dictator Game to Ultimatum Game . . . and Back Again: Judicial Amendment Posing as Legal Interpretation,* 6 U. Penn. J. Lab. & Empl. L. 241 (2004).

51. Bellace, *The Future of Employee Representation,* 17.

52. Estlund, *The Ossification of American Labor Law,* 1532–44.

53. Ralph K. Winter, *Judicial Review of Agency Decisions: The Labor Board and the Court,* 1968 Sup. Ct. Rev. 53, 65.

54. Testimony of Sidney Hillman, 1 *Legislative History of the National Labor Relations Act* 149–150 (1935).

55. "Nothing in this Act shall be construed to authorize the Board to appoint individuals for the purpose of conciliation or mediation, or for economic analysis." NLRA § 4(a); 29 U.S.C. § 154(a). Mediation is available through the Federal Mediation and Conciliation Service but only if the parties request it.

56. Testimony of Elinore Herrick. 1 Legislative History, 211 (emphasis added); *see also* 2 *Legislative History of the National Labor Relations Act* 2312, 2321 (1935); *see also* Ellen Dannin & Clive Gilson, *Getting to Impasse: Negotiations Under the National Labor Relations Act and the Employment Contracts Act,* 11 Am. U. J. Int'l L. & Pol'y 917 (1996).

57. For a brief history of these laws, see Robert A. Gorman, *Basic Text on Labor Law: Unionization and Collective Bargaining* 1–4 (1976). For a book length discussion, see Charles O. Gregory & Harold A. Katz, *Labor and the Law* (3d ed. 1979).

58. Winter, *Judicial Review of Agency Decisions,* 57–58.

59. NLRA § 10(c); 29 USC § 160(c); *see* H.K. Porter Co. v. NLRB, 397 U.S. 821 (1970).

2. Developing a Strategy to Take Back the NLRA

1. James J. Brudney et al., *Judicial Hostility Towards Labor Unions? Applying the Social Science Background Model to a Celebrated Concern,* 60 Ohio St. L.J. 1675, 1681, 1704–05, 1720, 1726–27 (1999).

2. 347 U.S. 483 (1954). Howard University School of Law has created a Brown@50 Web site with information about the cases that led to Brown v. Board, http://brownat50 .org/.

3. 169 Md. 478, 182 A. 590 (Ct. App. 1936).

4. Robert J. Cottrol et al., *NAACP v. Jim Crow: The Legal Strategy That Brought Down "Separate but Equal" by Toppling School Segregation,* 28 American Educator 9, 21, 26–27 (Summer 2004); Richard Kluger, *Simple Justice: The History of Brown v. Board of Education and Black America's Struggle for Equality* 185–93 (2004).

5. Kluger, *Simple Justice* 315–45.

6. Richard Michael Fischl, *Self, Others, and Section 7: Mutualism and Protected Protest Activities under the National Labor Relations Act,* 89 Colum. L. Rev. 789, 798–800, 862 (1989).

7. Michael J. Hayes, *After "Hiding the Ball" Is Over: How the NLRB Must Change Its Approach to Decision-Making,* 33 Rutgers L. J. 523, 561–62 (2002).

8. Robert S. Vance, *A View from the Circuit: A Federal Circuit Judge Views the NLRA Appellate Scene,* 1 Lab. Law, 39, 39 (1985).

9. Professor Matthew Finkin gives some examples of cases in which state and federal judges permit blatant violations of the NLRA out of their ignorance of labor law. Matthew W. Finkin, *The Marginalization of Academic Labor Law in the United States: A Footnote to Estlund and Summers,* 23 Comp. Lab. L. & Pol'y J. 811, 814 n.10 (2002).

10. Mark Barenberg, *The Political Economy of the Wagner Act: Power, Symbol, and Workplace Cooperation,* 106 Harv. L. Rev. 1379, 1423 (1993).

11. Vance, *A View from the Circuit* 39.

12. NLRA § 10(e), (f); 29 U.S.C. § 160(e), (f); ABA Section of Labor and Employment Law, *The Developing Labor Law* 2582–92 (4th ed., American Bar Association 2001); Robert Gorman, *Basic Text on Labor Law, Unionization, and Collective Bargaining* 10–14 (1976).

13. 307 F.3d 760 (9th Cir. 2002), *cert. denied sub nom.* Mulder v. NLRB, 537 U.S. 1024 (2002).

14. *Id.* at 769.

15. 287 N.L.R.B. 1080 (1988).

16. *See, e.g.,* Microimage Display Div. of Xidex Corp., v. NLRB, 924 F.2d 245, 255 (D.C. Cir. 1991); *Cherokee Marine Terminal,* 287 N.L.R.B. 1080 (1988).

17. *Cherokee Marine Terminal,* 287 N.L.R.B. at 1080.

18. 347 U.S. 483 (1954).

19. Cottrol et al., *NAACP v. Jim Crow,* 28–29.

20. NLRB v. Jones & Laughlin Steel Corp., 301 U.S. 1 (1937). The extract from the Petitioner's brief stated: "These facts are clearly shown by a survey of the results of individual disputes, the statistics with regard to the total number of such disputes, and repeated federal activities in connection with industrial strife." *Id.* at 6. NLRB member Peter Hurtgen dissented from a change in NLRB policy because no data supported the need to alter the policy. Levitz Furniture Co., 333 N.L.R.B. 717, 731 (2001).

21. *Jones & Laughlin Steel Corp.,* 301 U.S. at 29.

22. Judge Strine also cautions: "Even when that technique is used to improve the judge's ability to assess empirical claims based on social science research, common sense and modesty still counsel against the adoption of eternal verities supposedly premised on the latest . . . scholarship." Leo E. Strine Jr., *The Inescapably Empirical Foundation of the Common Law of Corporations,* 27 Del. J. Corp. L. 499, 516–17 (2002).

23. I discuss these issues in more detail in chapter 7.

3. NLRA Values, American Values

1. Cynthia Estlund, *Reflections on the Declining Prestige of American Labor Law Scholarship,* 23 Comp. Lab. L. & Pol'y J. 789, 792 (2002).

2. Michael Zweig argues that "union organizing will largely fail unless it is conducted in the context of a broad social movement for worker rights, which in turn needs to be embedded in a broad class-based social movement that challenges capitalist power if not the capitalist system itself. Such a movement will need to assert directly and openly the interests of workers as a class in opposition to the interests of capitalists, also taken as a class." Michael Zweig, Class-Based Union Organizing (Oct. 11–12, 2002) (unpublished paper delivered at Worker's Rights Conference, East Lansing, Michigan).

3. Lee Modjeska, *In Defense of the NLRB,* 33 Mercer L. Rev. 851, 855 (1982).

4. Unbelievable, Inc. v. NLRB, 118 F.3d 795, 810 (D.C. Cir. 1997) (Wald, J., dissenting in part).

5. Phelps Dodge Corp. v. NLRB, 313 U.S. 177, 191, 194 (1941); *see also* Republic Aviation Corp. v. NLRB, 324 U.S. 793, 798 (1945).

6. 305 U.S. 197 (1938). *See also* James Gray Pope, *How American Workers Lost the Right to Strike, and Other Tales,* 103 Mich. L. Rev. 518, 534 – 39 (2004). David Brody contends that "the right to organize in the specific sense of the individual right of workers to associate" should be used to secure "penalties that actually deter employers and enable workers to organize without fear." David Brody, *Labor vs. the Law: How the Wagner Act Became a Management Tool,* 13 New Lab. Forum 9, 13 (Spring 2004).

7. The Supreme Court has held that an order requiring the inclusion of a specific term in an agreement is not permissible. H.K. Porter Co. v. NLRB, 397 US 99 (1970). The decision did not consider whether its ruling promoted NLRA policies, other than Section 8(d)'s statement that the obligation to bargain does not compel agreement on a proposal or a term. There was a strong dissent in the case. It may be that creating a record that demonstrated the appropriateness of imposing a remedy would persuade the court to revisit this issue.

8. 494 U.S. 775, 796 (1990).

9. 489 U.S. 426 (1989).

10. *Id.* at 463.

11. For discussions on the state of contemporary corporate law, see Daniel J. H. Greenwood, *Democracy and Delaware: The Mysterious Race to the Bottom/Top,* 23 Yale L. & Pol'y Rev. 381 (2005); Dalia Tsuk, *From Pluralism to Individualism: Berle and Means and 20th-Century American Legal Thought: Adolf A. Berle, Jr., and Gardiner C. Means. The Modern Corporation and Private Property,* 30 Law & Soc. Inquiry 179 (2005).

12. Frank W. Munger, *Social Citizen as "Guest Worker": A Comment on Identities of Immigrants and the Working Poor,* 49 N.Y.L. Sch. L. Rev. 665, 668 – 71 (2004/2005).

13. The link http://workingamerica.org/jobtracker/index.cfm allows users to find out which jobs in any zip code, state, or industry have been sent overseas.

Today, corporation law, technology, and trade agreements have removed barriers to the movement of goods, services and money, thus making it easier for corporations to outsource work. This forces workers in high-wage countries to compete against huge workforces in low-wage countries.

Importing manufactured products from low-wage countries has helped to reduce prices paid by consumers. However, it has also helped to lower wages in high-wage countries like the U.S. In addition, studies show that the benefits of globalization have tended to flow primarily to the educated economic elites: "Economists also generally accept that trade liberalization has been one of the factors increasing inequality, redistributing wage income from workers without college degrees to workers with college and advanced degrees, in addition to shifting income from wages generally to profits." Dean Baker & Mark Weisbrot, *Will New Trade Gains Make Us Rich?* http://www.cepr.net/will_new_trade_gains_make_us_ric.htm.

14. Katharine Bradbury, *Additional Slack in the Economy: The Poor Recovery in Labor Force Participation During This Business Cycle* (Fed. Res. Bank Boston Pub. Pol'y Brief No.05–2), http://www.bos.frb.org/economic/ppb/2005/ppb052.htm.

15. http://stats.bls.gov/news.release/realer.to2.htm.

16. Census Bureau, *Income, Poverty, and Health Insurance Coverage in the United States: 2004* 8–15 (August 2005), http://www.census.gov/prod/2005pubs/p60-229.pdf.

17. According to the U.S. Bureau of Labor Statistics, average hourly earnings in May 2005 of private sector production or nonsupervisory workers in constant dollars has de-

clined by .4 percent from one year ago, http://stats.bls.gov/news.release/realer.t01.htm. In addition, the percent change in seasonally adjusted average weekly earnings from the same month a year ago for private sector production or nonsupervisory workers shows that in each of the months from May 2004 to May 2005, 11 of the 13 months have had negative changes. Those declines have been as much as 1.6 percent.

18. Sarah Anderson, et alia, Executive Excess 2005 (Aug. 30, 2005), http://www .fairecomony.org/press/2005/EE2005_pr.html; Sarah Anderson, et alia, *Executive Excess 2004* (Aug. 31, 2004), http://www.faireconomy.org/press/2004/EE2004.pdf.

19. It is generally agreed that economic inequality in the U.S. has increased in recent decades. The percentage of national income flowing to the bottom first, second, third, and fourth quintiles is lower now than it was in 1980, while only the highest quintile has experienced an increase, http://www.epinet.org/datazone/05/inc_share.pdf.

20. "Economists assume that faster productivity growth generates higher living standards through higher average wages" but "only a small proportion of the increase in productivity growth since early 2001 has flowed to wages and compensation, implying that working families are not benefitting much from this improved output per hour." Economic Policy Institute, Economic Snapshot (April 21, 2005), http://www.epinet .org/content.cfm/webfeatures_snapshots_20050421.

21. David K. Shipler, *The Working Poor: Invisible in America* (2004).

22. William R. Corbett, *Waiting for the Labor Law of the Twenty-First Century: Everything Old Is New Again,* 23 Berkeley J. Emp. & Lab. L. 259, 286–87 (2002).

23. Section 2(3) defines employees as including any employee and not limited to the employees of a particular employer. Only employees have rights under the NLRA. As a result, anyone who does not fall into the definition of employee is not protected, and there are limits on protections for making common cause with someone who is not an employee. Could these limits be overcome by proving that making common cause with a nonemployee was necessary to promote the employee's NLRA rights? One example would be raising wages for domestic workers, people not defined as employees. Increasing their wages might make it easier raise those of other workers in the community. *See, e.g.,* United Food & Commercial Workers Union, Local 1036 v. NLRB, 307 F.3d 760 (9th Cir. 2002), *cert. denied sub nom.* Mulder v. NLRB, 537 U.S. 1024 (2002).

24. Staughton Lynd, *Communal Rights,* 62 Tex. L. Rev. 1417, 1423–24 (1984); *id.* at 1425– 26; Lee Modjeska, *The NLRB Litigational Processes: A Response to Chairman Dotson,* 23 Wake Forest L. Rev. 399, 403–04 (1988).

25. When courts are guided by these principles it makes a difference. In NLRB v. *Town & Country Electric, Inc.,* the Supreme Court had to decide whether salts sent in to be hired and organize a workplace were protected as employees. The Court found salts were employees and protected because this interpretation was "consistent with several of the Act's purposes, such as protecting 'the right of employees to organize for mutual aid without employer interference,' and 'encouraging and protecting the collective-bargaining process.'" *NLRB v. Town & Country Electric, Inc.,* 516 U.S. 85, 91 (1995). Contrast this with the Supreme Court's earlier decision in *Lechmere, Inc. v. NLRB,* 502 U.S. 527 (1992).

Another example is *Fall River Dyeing & Finishing Corp. v. NLRB,* 482 U.S. 27 (1987), the Court endorsed certain presumptions created by the Board as necessary to protecting union representation in order to achieve the Act's goal of industrial peace. In *Steele v. Louisville & Nashville Railroad Co.* 323 U.S. 192 (1944), the Court refused to permit the union to exercise the rights that the law seemed to give it, because this would have undermined the intent and operation of the Railway Labor Act.

26. Mark Barenberg, *The Political Economy of the Wagner Act: Power, Symbol, and Workplace Cooperation,* 106 Harv. L. Rev. 1379, 1423 (1993).

27. *Id.* at 1423–24.

28. Emporium Capwell Co. v. Western Addition Community Organization, 420 U.S. 50, 62 (1975).

29. NLRB v. Jones & Laughlin Steel Corp., 301 U.S. 1, 42 (1937); *id.* at 45–46; Phelps Dodge Corp. v. NLRB, 313 U.S.177, 182 (1941).

30. *Phelps Dodge,* 313 U.S. at 194; *see also* Republic Aviation Corp. v. NLRB, 324 U.S. 793, 798 (1945).

31. For alternate views of Congress's intent, see Janice R. Bellace, *The Future of Employee Representation in America: Enabling Freedom of Association in the Workplace in Changing Times Through Statutory Reform,* 5 U. Pa. J. Lab. & Emp. L. 1 (2002).

32. For an extended discussion on subjects related to this, see Cynthia L. Estlund, *Working Together: The Workplace, Civil Society, and the Law,* 89 Geo. L.J. 1 (2000).

33. *Jones & Laughlin Steel,* 301 U.S. at 33.

34. Dana Muir, *Groundings of Voice in Employee Rights,* 36 Vand. J. Transnat'l L. 485, 521 (2003).

35. Mark Barenberg, *The Political Economy of the Wagner Act: Power, Symbol, and Workplace Cooperation,* 106 Harv. L. Rev. 1379, 1422–23 (1993).

36. Union members vote in percentages far exceeding nonunion members, and unions work to encourage new voters. In the 2000 elections, for example, unions registered 2.3 million new voters, made 8 million phone calls to get out the vote, passed out more than 14 million leaflets, emailed people urging them to vote, and supported hundreds of candidates and issues in elections. *People-Powered Politics,* http://www.aflcio .org/aboutaflcio/about/convention/2001/ecreport/ppp.cfm; see also *Winning for Working Families: Recommendations from the Officers of the AFL-CIO for Uniting and Strengthening the Union Movement* (Apr. 2005), http://www.aflcio.org/aboutaflcio/ ourfuture/upload/executive_officers.pdf; *Recommendations from AFL-CIO Officers for Strengthening the Union Movement,* Daily Lab. Rep. (BNA) E-1 (Apr. 29, 2005).

37. Samuel Issacharoff, *Reconstructing Employment Governing the Workplace: The Future of Labor and Employment Law,* 104 Harv. L. Rev. 607, 626 (1990).

38. Of course, this is not the only way to think about the power the NLRA gives workers and unions and its impact on society. Some see the NLRA as special-interest legislation that lets one group act against the rest of society. Ralph K. Winter, *Judicial Review of Agency Decisions: The Labor Board and the Court,* 1968 Sup. Ct. Rev. 53, 58; *see also* Reinhold Fahlbeck, *The Demise of Collective Bargaining in the USA: Reflections on the Un-American Character of American Labor Law,* 15 Berkeley J. Emp. & Lab. L. 307 (1994).

39. Barenberg, *The Political Economy of the Wagner Act,* 1492; *see also* Karl E. Klare, *Judicial Deradicalization of the Wagner Act and the Origins of Modern Legal Consciousness,* 62 Minn. L. Rev. 265 (1977–1978).

40. Barenberg, *The Political Economy of the Wagner Act,* 1391–92.

41. *Id.* at 1413–14 (1993).

42. Ellen Dannin, *Contracting Mediation: The Impact of Different Statutory Regimes,* 17 Hofstra Lab. & Empl. L.J. 65, 109–10 (1999); Corbett, *Waiting for the Labor Law of the Twenty-First Century,* 276–77.

43. For an in-depth exploration of the meaning of freedom of association, see Sheldon Leader, *Freedom of Association: A Study in Labor Law and Political Theory* (1992).

44. NLRB v. Jones & Laughlin Steel Corp., 301 U.S. 1, 43–44 (1937).

45. *Id.* at 33–34.

46. Statement of Daniel V. Yager, Senior Vice President and General Counsel LPA, the Labor Policy Association before the Senate Health, Education, Labor and Pensions Committee Hearing on Workers' Freedom of Association: Obstacles to Forming a Union (June 19, 2002).

47. Brody, *Labor vs. the Law.*

48. 29 U.S.C. § 157 (1994).

49. The story of this and related events is told in Ellen Dannin, *Working Free: The Origins and Impact of New Zealand's Employment Contracts Act* (1997). Other factors also led to this decline. The law provided for minority representation. Employers used this to play members off against one another. This problem of minority unions was one that concerned Robert Wagner. He told Congress that the provisions for majority rule were fundamental, that "without them the phrase 'collective bargaining' is devoid of meaning and the very few unfair employers are encouraged to divide their workers among themselves." 79 Cong. Rec. 2372 (1935).

In addition, some unions consolidated in order to have more resources and because the Council of Trade Unions demanded that there be fewer, industry-focused unions; however, they lost strength through the process of integrating different organizations.

50. Michael H. Gottesman, *Wither Goest Labor Law: Law and Economics in the Workplace,* 100 Yale L.J. 2767, 2789 (1991).

51. Dan M. Kahan, *The Logic of Reciprocity: Trust, Collective Action, and Law,* 102 Mich. L. Rev. 71, 75–80 (2003); *see also* Frans B. M. de Waal, *How Animals Do Business,* 292 Sci. Am. 73 (2005).

52. United Food & Commercial Workers Union, Local 1036 v. NLRB, 307 F.3d 760 (9th Cir. 2002), *cert. denied sub nom.* Mulder v. NLRB, 537 U.S. 1024 (2002).

53. *See, e.g.,* Briggs Mfg. Co., 75 N.L.R.B. 569, 570 n.3 (1947).

54. Congress "adopted a definition of 'labor dispute' in Section 2 (9) for the Wagner Act that eliminated even the 'same industry' limitation imposed by Norris-LaGuardia." Richard Michael Fischl, *Self, Others, and Section 7: Mutualism and Protected Protest Activities under the National Labor Relations Act,* 89 Colum. L. Rev. 789, 852 (1989).

This issue of mutual aid or protection and the ability of employees to make common cause with one another is now being fought out over the issue of who must pay union dues and in what amount. The NLRA requires the assessment of "uniform" dues, but the Supreme Court has created a number of exceptions and limitations. One limitation that wholly ignores NLRA policies for mutual aid or protection and worker solidarity leading to the elimination of wage competition within and between industries is the requirement that dues dissenters have to pay dues only for actions that are sufficiently local. Douglas E. Ray et al., *Understanding Labor Law* 387–89, 429 (1999).

55. 29 U.S.C. § 152(3) (1994).

56. Eastex, Inc. v. NLRB, 437 U.S. 556 (1978). This was a major break in philosophy with the Norris-LaGuardia Act. Norris LaGuardia protects labor disputes whether the act is done "singly or in concert." 29 U.S.C. § 104.

57. Lynd, *Communal Rights,* 1429–30.

58. James J. Brudney, *Reflections on Group Action and the Law of the Workplace,* 74 Tex. L. Rev. 1563, 1565–66 (1996); *see also* Sharon Rabin Margalioth, *The Significance of Worker Attitudes: Individualism as a Cause for Labor's Decline,* 16 Hofstra Lab. & Emp. L.J. 133 (1998). Many scholars would dispute this view.

59. Mark A. Rothstein, *Employment Law* 698–709. (2d ed. 1999). Two recent examples in Title VII cases include *Flowers v. Columbia College Chicago,* 397 F.3d 532 (7th Cir. 2005), and *Konits v. Valley Stream Central High School District,* 394 F.3d 121 (2d Cir. 2005).

60. Lynd, *Communal Rights,* 1427.

61. *See* Alvin E. Roth, *Bargaining Experiments,* in *The Handbook of Experimental Economics* 253 (John H. Kagel & Alvin E. Roth eds. 1995); Dan M. Kahan, *The Logic of Reciprocity: Trust, Collective Action, and Law,* 102 Mich. L. Rev. 71, 71–72 (2003); George Feldman, *Unions, Solidarity, and Class: The Limits of Liberal Labor Law,* 15 Berkeley J. Emp. & Lab. L. 187 (1994).

62. These ideas are borrowed from Michael H. Gottesman, *Wither Goest Labor Law: Law and Economics in the Workplace*, 100 Yale L.J. 2767, 2790–93 (1991); *see also* Cass Sunstein, *The Second Bill of Rights: FDR's Unfinished Revolution and Why We Need it More than Ever* (2004).

63. Barenberg, *The Political Economy of the Wagner Act*, 1417.

64. Kohn v. Southwest Reg'l Council of Carpenters, 289 F. Supp. 2d 1155 (C.D. Cal. 2003).

65. Issacharoff, *Reconstructing Employment Governing the Workplace*, 625–26; *see also* NLRB v. Adkins Transfer Co., Inc., 226 F.2d 324 (6th Cir. 1955).

66. Kahan, *The Logic of Reciprocity*, 74–77.

67. Thomas C. Kohler, *Propter Honoris Respectum: The Disintegration of Labor Law: Some Notes for a Comparative Study of Legal Transformation*, 73 Notre Dame L. Rev. 1311, 1327 (1998).

4. Litigating the NLRA Values

1. Ellen Dannin, *Hail, Market, Full of Grace: Buying and Selling Labor Law Reform*, 2001 L. Rev. Mich. St. U.–Det. Coll. L. 1090; Ellen Dannin, *Consummating Market-Based Labor Law Reform in New Zealand: Context and Reconfiguration*, 14 B.U. Int'l L.J. 267 (1996).

2. 380 U.S. 263 (1965); *see* James Gray Pope, *How American Workers Lost the Right to Strike, and Other Tales*, 103 Mich. L. Rev. 518, 544–50 (2004).

3. *Darlington*, 380 at 270.

4. Clyde W. Summers, *Employment at Will in the United States: The Divine Right of Employers*, 3 U. Pa. J. Lab. & Emp. L. 65, 79 (2000).

5. NLRB v. Adkins Transfer Co., Inc., 226 F.2d 324 (6th Cir. 1955).

6. 304 U.S. 333 (1938); *see* Pope, *How American Workers Lost the Right to Strike*, 527–34.

7. Section 13. Taft-Hartley added at the end "or to affect the limitations or qualifications of that right."

8. Robert A. Gorman, *Basic Text on Labor Law: Unionization and Collective Bargaining* 342 (1976).

9. Gangaram Singh and I are currently analyzing data that examines the impact permanent and temporary striker replacement and implementation upon impasse have on bargaining power and bargaining strategies. Preliminary data show a strong impact.

10. Summers, *Employment at Will in the United States*, 80–81.

11. Cynthia Gramm, *Empirical Evidence on Political Arguments Relating to Replacement Worker Legislation*, 42 Lab. L.J. 491 (1991); *see, e.g.* Julius Getman, *The Betrayal of Local 19* (1998); Peter Rachleff, *Hard-Pressed in the Heartland: The Hormel Strike and the Future of the Labor Movement* (1993).

12. Michael Yates, *Power on the Job: The Legal Rights of Working People* 121–26 (1994).

13. 489 U.S. 426 (1989).

14. 502 U.S. 527 (1992).

15. Pope, *How American Workers Lost the Right to Strike*, 539–44; *see also* ITT Indus. Inc., 341 N.L.R.B. No.118 (May 13, 2004); Cleveland Real Estate Partners v. NLRB, 95 F.3d 457 (6th Cir. 1996).

16. The issue of rights of access to malls has had a complicated constitutional law history. The dissent points out that the majority is highly selective in its discussion of that history and of precedent concerning access to employees on employer property. The dissent also argues that the majority was not bound by any precedent to reach the outcome it did, although the majority speaks as though it had no choice. *See* 502 U.S. at 542–45.

17. *See* Arindrajit Dube & Ken Jacobs, *Hidden Costs of Wal-Mart Jobs: Use of Safety Net Programs by Wal-Mart Workers in California*, UC Berkeley Labor Center Briefing Paper Series (Aug. 2, 2004), http://laborcenter.berkeley.edu/lowwage/walmart.pdf.

18. A secondary boycott occurs when a union exerts pressure on an employer indirectly by targeting a "secondary" employer who is not involved in the dispute. Secondary boycotts were made illegal when Section 8(b)(4)(B) was added to the NLRA in 1947.

19. H. K. Porter Co. v. NLRB, 397 U.S. 99, 103 (1970); *see also* Ellen Dannin, *Legislative Intent and Impasse Resolution Under the National Labor Relations Act: Does Law Matter?* 15 Hofstra Lab. & Empl. L.J. 11 (1997).

20. Ellen Dannin, *From Dictator Game to Ultimatum Game . . . and Back Again: Judicial Amendment Posing as Legal Interpretation,* 6 U. Penn. J. Lab. & Empl. L. 241 (2004); James J. Brudney, *To Strike or Not to Strike,* 1999 Wis. L. Rev. 65, 85–86. For a discussion of how the doctrine arose, see Ellen Dannin, *Collective Bargaining, Impasse and the Implementation of Final Offers: Have We Created a Right Unaccompanied by Fulfillment,* 19 U. Tol. L. Rev. 41 (1987).

21. Morris Kleiner, *Intensity of Management Resistance: Understanding the Decline of Unionization in the Private Sector,* 22 J. Lab. Res. 519 (2001).

22. *See, e.g.,* Unbelievable, Inc. v. NLRB, 118 F.3d 795 (D.C. Cir. 1997); Don Lee Distrib. v. NLRB, 145 F.3d 834 (6th Cir. 1998), *cert. denied,* 525 U.S. 1102 (1999); Don Lee Distribs., 322 N.L.R.B. 470 (1996). *See also* Ellen Dannin & Terry Wagar, *Lawless Law? The Subversion of the National Labor Relations Act,* 34 Loyola (L.A.) L. Rev. 197, 200–02 (2000).

23. First Nat'l Maint. Corp. v. NLRB, 452 U.S. 666 (1981); Fibreboard Paper Prods. v. NLRB, 379 U.S. 203 (1964).

24. 452 U.S. at 679.

25. Catherine R. Fayette, *Judicial Decisions on an Employer's Duty to Bargain: Balanced Analyses or Personal Bias?* 51 Wayne L. Rev. 1221 (2004).

26. 115 F.3d 1045 (D.C. Cir. 1997).

27. Dannin & Wagar, *Lawless Law,* 210–12.

28. Summers, *Employment at Will in the United States,* 80.

29. *First Nat'l Maint. Corp,* 452 U.S. 666.

30. 233 F.3d 831 (4th Cir. 2000).

31. The district court denied relief based on speculation as to whether the workers had found other jobs. Hirsch v. Dorsey Trailers, Inc., 147 F.3d 243, 248 (3d Cir. 1998) (10(j) injunction case).

32. *Dorsey Trailers Contemplates Bankruptcy, Refrigerated Transporter,* Dec. 1, 2000, http://www.keepmedia.com/ShowItemDetails.do?itemID=216357&extID=10030.

33. *Dorsey Trailers Inc. Agrees to Sell Assets,* Apr. 1, 2001, http://trailer-bodybuilders.com/mag/trucks_dorsey_trailers_inc/; *Dorsey Trailers Selling Cartersville Assets,* Atlanta Business Chronicle, Mar. 28, 2001, http://www.bizjournals.com/atlanta/stories/2001/03/26/daily29.html

34. Charles O. Gregory & Harold A. Katz, *Labor and the Law* (3d ed. 1979); Robert A. Gorman, *Basic Text on Labor Law: Unionization and Collective Bargaining* 1–6 (1976); Lee Modjeska, *The NLRB Litigational Processes: A Response to Chairman Dotson,* 23 Wake Forest L. Rev. 399, 401–09 (1988); Ralph K. Winter, *Judicial Review of Agency Decisions: The Labor Board and the Court,* 1968 Sup. Ct. Rev. 53, 59 n.5.

5. Litigation Themes

1. Cass Sunstein, *The Second Bill of Rights: FDR's Unfinished Revolution and Why We Need It More Than Ever* 17–34 (2004).

2. H. K. Porter Co. v. NLRB, 397 U.S. 99, 104–05 (1970).

3. NLRB v. Jones & Laughlin Steel Corp., 301 U.S. 1 (1937).

4. Lincoln Fed. Labor Union v. Northwestern Iron & Metal Co., 335 U.S. 525, 536–37 (1949).

5. *Id.* at 537.

6. *See* Michael H. Gottesman, *Wither Goest Labor Law: Law and Economics in the Workplace*, 100 Yale L.J. 2767, 2790–93 (1991).

7. Reinhold Fahlbeck, *The Demise of Collective Bargaining in the USA: Reflections on the Un-American Character of American Labor Law*, 15 Berkeley J. Emp. & Lab. L. 307, 314 (1994).

8. Sanford M. Jacoby, *Employee Representation and Corporate Governance: A Missing Link*, 3 U. Pa. J. Lab. & Emp. L. 449, 453 (2001).

9. NLRB v. Jones & Laughlin Steel Corp., 301 U.S. 1, 43–44 (1937).

10. *See* Sunstein, *The Second Bill of Rights.*

11. Jacoby, *Employee Representation and Corporate Governance*, 454.

12. A 2004 study estimated that Wal-Mart's low wages forced its California employees to depend on $32 million a year in state-provided health-related services and $54 million per year in other government assistance. Arindrajit Dube & Ken Jacobs, *Hidden Costs of Wal-Mart Jobs: Use of Safety Net Programs by Wal-Mart Workers in California*, UC Berkeley Labor Center Briefing Paper Series (Aug. 2, 2004), http://laborcenter.berkeley.edu/lowwage/walmart.pdf.

13. *Jones & Laughlin Steel*, 301 U.S. at 43–44.

14. *Id.* at 29 (1937).

15. Robert S. Vance, *A View from the Circuit: A Federal Circuit Judge Views the NLRA Appellate Scene*, 1 Lab. Law. 39, 40 (1985).

16. 313 U.S. 177 (1941).

17. *Id.* at 182–83.

18. George Feldman, *Workplace Power and Collective Activity: The Supervisory and Managerial Exclusions in Labor Law*, 37 Ariz. L. Rev. 525, 526 (1995).

19. A secondary boycott occurs when a union exerts pressure on an employer indirectly by targeting a "secondary" employer who is not involved in the dispute. Secondary boycotts were made illegal when Section 8(b)(4)(B) was added to the NLRA in 1947.

20. 502 U.S. 527 (1992).

21. 324 U.S. 793 (1945).

22. *Id.* at 798.

23. *Id.* at 802 n.8 (quoting from the NLRB decision below).

24. NLRB v. Jones & Laughlin Steel Corp., 301 U.S. 1, 34 (1937); *see also id.* at 43–44.

25. Civil rights boycotts have been treated more favorably by judges. Gary Minda dissects cases to help explain what has led judges to treat them differently. One of his findings is the types of analogies judges use to describe each type of boycott. Gary Minda, *Boycott in America: How Imagination and Ideology Shape the Legal Mind* (1999).

26. Alan Story, *Employer Speech, Union Representation Elections, and the First Amendment*, 16 Berkeley J. Emp. & Lab. L. 356 (1995).

27. UAW–Labor Employment & Training Corp. v. Chao, 325 F.3d 360 (D.C. Cir. 2003), *cert. denied*, 124 S. Ct. 2014 (2004).

28. Cf. Marshall v. Barlow, 436 U.S. 307 (1978). Only a system in which workers are empowered can assure that workplace laws are actually enforced. Gottesman, *Wither Goest Labor Law*, 2794–96.

29. 91 N.L.R.B. 333 (1950).

30. A wage-effort bargain is an implicit agreement of a certain amount of work for a specific level of pay.

31. 306 U.S. 240 (1939), *see also* James Gray Pope, *How American Workers Lost the Right to Strike, and Other Tales*, 103 Mich. L. Rev. 518, 520–24 (2004).

32. H. K. Porter Co. v. NLRB, 397 U.S. 99, 103–04 (1970).

33. Karl Klare, *Critical Theory and Labor Relations Law,* in *The Politics of Law* 61, 78–79 (David Karirys ed., rev. ed. 1990).

34. Dan M. Kahan, *The Logic of Reciprocity: Trust, Collective Action, and Law,* 102 Mich. L. Rev. 71, 84 (2003).

35. William R. Corbett, *Waiting for the Labor Law of the Twenty-First Century: Everything Old Is New Again,* 23 Berkeley J. Emp. & Lab. L. 259, 262 (2002). This is a global phenomenon. *See, e.g.,* Ellen Dannin, *Working Free: The Origins and Impact of New Zealand's Employment Contracts Act* (1997); Ellen Dannin, *Hail, Market, Full of Grace: Buying and Selling Labor Law Reform,* 2001 L.Rev. Mich. St. U.–Det. Coll. L. 1090.

36. Christopher Lee, *Bush Seeks Federal Workforce Overhaul: Nation's Security at Stake, Bush Administration Says,* Washington Post, June 8, 2003, at A01.

6. NLRA Rights within Other Laws

1. James A. Gross, *Incorporating Human Rights Principles into U.S. Labor Arbitration: A Proposal for Fundamental Change,* 8 Empl. Rts & Empl. Pol'y J. 1 (2004).

2. *See* Nina Totenberg, *Supreme Court Increasing Use of References to Foreign Law in Decisions,* Morning Edition, National Public Radio (July 13, 2004), http://www.npr.org/templates/story/story.php?storyId=3351007.

3. Caryn L. Beck-Dudley & Steven H. Hanks, *On Virtue and Peace: Creating a Workplace Where People Can Flourish,* 36 Vand. J. Transnat'l L. 427 (2003).

4. Thomas C. Kohler, *Propter Honoris Respectum: The Disintegration of Labor Law: Some Notes for a Comparative Study of Legal Transformation,* 73 Notre Dame L. Rev. 1311, 1326 (1998).

5. David Brody, *Labor vs. the Law: How the Wagner Act Became a Management Tool,* 13 New Lab. Forum 9, 13 (Spring 2004).

6. 15 U.S.C. § 17.

7. 29 U.S.C. § 102.

8. *Id.* § 113(a), (c). *See also* Richard Michael Fischl, *Self, Others, and Section 7: Mutualism and Protected Protest Activities under the National Labor Relations Act,* 89 Colum. L. Rev. 789, 843–58 (1989).

9. Staughton Lynd, *Communal Rights,* 62 Tex. L. Rev. 1417, 1430–35 (1984). Lynd also says that First Amendment rights are of "the people" and not of the individual. *Id.* at 1432.

10. A secondary boycott means that a union exerts pressure on an employer indirectly by targeting a "secondary" employer who is not involved in the dispute. Secondary boycotts were made illegal when Section 8(b)(4)(B) was added to the NLRA in 1947.

11. Unions are allowed to picket for recognition, but Section 8(b)(7) limits the time to under 30 days. After that time, the picketing may be enjoined if no petition for recognition has been filed.

12. For an example of how the issue has been tried and then treated by the courts of appeals see *Soft Drink Workers Union Local 812, International Brotherhood of Teamsters, Chauffeurs, Warehousemen & Helpers of America, AFL-CIO v. NLRB,* 937 F.2d 684, 687–88 (D.C. Cir. 1991):

> The Union appeals also to a higher authority: "It is hornbook law," we are told, "that if § 8(b)(7)(B) is so construed, then the section has to be deemed to abridge freedom of speech in violation of the First Amendment." The Union fails to cite even a hornbook, however, and the law to be found in the law reports leads us to conclude that § 8(b)(7)(B), as construed, is within constitutional bounds. Cf. Building Service Employees Int'l Union, Local 262 v. Gazzam, 339 U.S. 532, 540, 94 L.

Ed. 1045, 70 S. Ct. 784 (1950) (state injunction barring post-election picketing seeking recognition of a defeated union does not violate First Amendment); Miller v. United Food and Commercial Workers Union, Local 498, 708 F.2d 467, 471 (9th Cir. 1983) ("Courts of Appeals have uniformly upheld [against first amendment challenge] the section 8(b)(7)[C] restriction against picketing for recognitional purposes as a legitimate exercise of that authority to promote labor democracy and the orderly settlement of representational controversies") (citing, inter alia, Dayton Typographical, 326 F.2d at 649).

13. 441 U.S. 463 (1979); *see also* William B. Gould, *Labor Law and Its Limits: Some Proposals for Reform,* 49 Wayne L. Rev. 667, 673–74 (2003).

14. *Id.* at 466–67 (internal citations omitted).

15. To name just a few of the key cases, *Hudgens v. NLRB,* 424 U.S. 507 (1976); *Central Hardware Co. v. NLRB,* 407 U.S. 539 (1972); *Amalgmated Food Employees Union, Local 590 v Logan Valley Plaza, Inc.,* 391 US 308 (1968); *NLRB v. Babcock & Wilcox Co.,* 351 U.S. 105 (1956).

16. James Gray Pope, *The Thirteenth Amendment versus the Commerce Clause: Labor and the Shaping of American Constitutional Law, 1921–1957,* 102 Colum. L. Rev. 1 (2002).

17. Linda M. Keller, *The American Rejection of Economic Rights as Human Rights and the Declaration of Independence: Does the Pursuit of Happiness Require Basic Economic Rights?* 19 N.Y.L. Sch. J. Hum. Rts. 557 (2003).

18. Franklin D. Roosevelt, *The Economic Bill of Rights,* excerpt from January 11, 1944, message to Congress on the State of the Union.

19. Ruth Bader Ginsburg, *Looking Beyond Our Borders: The Value of a Comparative Perspective in Constitutional Adjudication,* 22 Yale L. & Pol'y Rev. 329 (2004).

20. *Id.* at 330.

21. For a discussion of ILO operations in a recent case involving a North Carolina law, see Paul Germanotta, *Forced Labor of Public Employees in the United States: A Note from the 2002 International Labor Conference,* 7 Working USA 81 (Summer 2003).

22. 86th Sess. (June 1998).

23. ILO Convention No.87, Freedom of Association and Protection of the Right to Organise Convention, 31st Sess., art. 11 (1948); Janice R. Bellace, *The Future of Employee Representation in America: Enabling Freedom of Association in the Workplace in Changing Times Through Statutory Reform,* 5 U. Pa. J. Lab. & Emp. L. 1, 29–31 (2002).

24. ILO Convention 98, Right to Organise and Collective Bargaining Convention, 32d Sess., art.1 (1949).

25. G.A. Res. 2200A(XXI), U.N. GAOR, Supp. No. 16, at 52, U.N. Doc. A/6316 (1966) art.22 (1966).

26. International Labour Organisation, Declaration of Philadelphia, 26th Sess., art. 1 (1944).

27. G.A. Res. 217A, U.N. GAOR, 3d Sess., pt. 1, Supp. No. 23(4), at 71, U.N. Doc. A/810 (1948). *See also* James A. Gross, *Incorporating Human Rights Principles into U.S. Labor Arbitration: A Proposal for Fundamental Change,* 8 Empl. Rts & Empl. Pol'y J. 1, 29–30 (2004).

28. Preamble, art. 23–25, G.A. Res. 217A, U.N. GAOR, 3d Sess., pt. 1, at 71, U.N. Doc. A/1810 (1948).

29. State Sector Act 1988 (New Zealand), Long Title (e).

30. State Sector Act 1988 (New Zealand), § 56(1).

7. Trying Cases

1. New York Univ., 332 N.L.R.B. 1205 (2000).

2. Brown Univ., 342 N.L.R.B. No. 42 (2004).

3. Graduate students were recently held to be employees in Title VII cases in *Cuddeback v. Florida Board of Education*, 381 F.3d 1230 (2004).

4. NLRB v. Yeshiva Univ., 444 U.S. 672 (1980).

5. David Wolcott Kendall Memorial School v. N.L.R.B., 866 F.2d 157 (6th Cir. 1989).

6. 502 U.S. 527 (1992).

7. Gena Stinnett, *Comment: Why California Shopping Centers Can't Protect Mickey Mouse from Union Handbilling*, 37 Loy. L.A. L. Rev. 1799 (2004).

8. 516 U.S. 85 (1995).

9. Truth in Employment Act, S. 1981, 105th Cong. (1998).

10. Jane S. Schacter, *Metademocracy: The Changing Structure of Legitimacy in Statutory Interpretation*, 108 Harv. L. Rev. 593, 594–95 (1996).

11. For a concise overview of different views see Cass Sunstein, *After the Rights Revolution: Reconceiving the Regulatory State* (1990); Allan Hutchinson & Derek Morgan, *Book Review: Calabresian Sunset: Statutes in the Shade*, 82 Colum L. Rev. 1752, 1754–55 (1982).

12. Phelps Dodge Corp. v. NLRB, 313 U.S. 177, 185 (1941).

13. Beth Israel Hosp. v. NLRB, 437 U.S. 483, 500–01 (1978). Judicial deference was hotly debated by the majority and dissent in *Lechmere, Inc. v. NLRB*, 502 U.S. 527 (1992); *see also* Section 10 (e); Administrative Procedure Act, 5 U.S.C. § 706 (2)(E); Universal Camera Corp. v. NLRB, 340 U.S. 474 (1951).

14. Catherine R. Fayette, *Judicial Decisions on an Employer's Duty to Bargain: Balanced Analyses or Personal Bias?* 51 Wayne L. Rev. 1221 (2004).

15. Judge Robert Vance provides helpful advice on trying cases before federal courts of appeals, including information on scope of review. Robert S. Vance, *A View from the Circuit: A Federal Circuit Judge Views the NLRA Appellate Scene*, 1 Lab. Law. 39 (1985).

16. 303 N.L.R.B. 386 (1991), *enforced*, United Food & Commercial Workers Int'l Union, AFL-CIO, Local 150–A v. NLRB, 1 F.3d 24 (D.C. Cir. 1993).

17. NLRB rules and regulations, case handling manuals, decisions, and other official materials may be found through its Web site, www.nlrb.gov.

18. *NLRB Casehandling Manual, Part One—Unfair Labor Practice Proceedings* §§ 10264.1, 10062.5 (2003).

19. *Id.* § 10407.4.

20. National Labor Relations Board, *Rules and Regulations and Statements of Procedure* § 102.15 (2002).

21. *Id.* § 101.8.
"The Agency has a responsibility to periodically reexamine and update its remedial strategies. Accordingly, the Regional Office should be alert to any remedial initiatives which the General Counsel has decided to pursue. Under most circumstances, before seeking a nontraditional remedy the Regional Office must first seek authorization from the Division of Advice. *See* GC Memo 00–03 and OM 99–79." *NLRB Casehandling Manual, Part One* § 10130.12.

22. *NLRB Casehandling Manual, Part One* § 10264.2.

23. *See, e.g.*, Unbelievable, Inc. v. NLRB, 118 F.3d 795, 810 (D.C. Cir. 1997); Avondale Indus., Inc., 15–CA-12639 (July 6, 2001).

24. *NLRB Casehandling Manual, Part One* § 10266.1.

25. *Id.* § 10388.1.

26. National Labor Relations Board, *Rules and Regulations* § 102.29; see also Section 102.24 for general requirements for filing motions.

27. The NLRB's Rules and Regulations do not require that requested remedies be included in the complaint. *Id.* § 102.15. Not all regions include a prayer for relief in the complaint, but the regions are instructed: "Where appropriate the complaint should contain a prayer for relief. Indeed, the complaint should set forth the requested remedy

whenever any other than a routine remedy is sought." *NLRB Casehandling Manual, Part One* § 10268.1.

28. Int. Bus. Machs., 339 N.L.R.B. No.120 (Aug. 13, 2003). "When the remedy sought is novel or unique, in order to provide respondent adequate notice, the complaint should contain a separate request for specific remedial relief. *See* § 10407.1. Such a request should specifically reserve the General Counsel's right to subsequently seek, and the Board's right to ultimately provide, any other appropriate remedy." *NLRB Casehandling Manual, Part One* § 10266.1. "Indeed, the complaint should set forth the requested remedy whenever any other than a routine remedy is sought. Where the Regional Office's determination of the need for a special remedy arises only after issuance of complaint, the respondent should receive prompt notification and the complaint should be amended." *Id.* § 10268.1.

29. While the complaint should set forth any special remedies requested, the Board's *Casehandling Manual* advises the Board attorney to "reiterate and expand upon the reasons for such remedies at hearing, in addition to arguing for such remedies in the brief." *NLRB Casehandling Manual, Part One* § 10407.1.

30. National Labor Relations Board, *Rules and Regulations* §§ 101.10(a), 102.38.

31. *Id.* § 101.10(b)(2).

32. *NLRB Casehandling Manual, Part One* § 10407.3.

33. National Labor Relations Board, *Rules and Regulations* §§ 110.10(a), 102.39.

34. Fed. R. Evid. 402.

35. *Id.* 401.

36. "A party offering an exhibit may request its inclusion in the "Rejected Exhibits" if the exhibit has been refused admission." *NLRB Casehandling Manual, Part One* § 10398.3.

37. "Any objection with respect to the conduct of the hearing, including any objection to the introduction of evidence, may be stated orally or in writing, accompanied by a short statement of the grounds of such objection, and included in the record. No such objection shall be deemed waived by further participation in the hearing." National Labor Relations Board, *Rules and Regulations* § 102.41.

38. In *Vincent Industrial Plastics v. NLRB*, 209 F.3d 727 (D.C. Cir. 2000), the court stated that an affirmative bargaining order had to be justified by an analysis based on "a reasoned analysis that includes an explicit balancing of three considerations: (1) the employees' Section 7 rights; (2) whether other purposes of the Act override the rights of employees to choose their bargaining representatives; and (3) whether alternative remedies are adequate to remedy the violations of the Act." *Id.* at 738.

39. Community Health Servs., Inc., 342 N.L.R.B. No.33 (June 30, 2004). The Board agreed with the administrative law judge that an affirmative bargaining order was warranted as a remedy for the employer's unlawful refusal to bargain. Members Liebman and Meisburg stated that an affirmative bargaining order is "the traditional, appropriate remedy for an 8(a)(5) refusal to bargain with the lawful collective-bargaining representative of an appropriate unit of employees." Member Schaumber disagreed and argued that the Board should follow the D.C. Circuit's position that a case-by-case analysis is required to determine whether the remedy is appropriate.

8. Using the NLRB as a Resource

1. One such incident is discussed in Ellen Dannin, *Finding the Workers Law*, 8 Green Bag 19 (2004).

2. *NLRB Casehandling Manual, Part One—Unfair Labor Practice Proceedings* §§ 10012, 10012.3 (2003).

3. *Id.* § 10012.2.

4. The Agency can investigate unfair labor practice allegations only upon the filing of an appropriate charge. *Id.* § 10010; National Labor Relations Board, *Rules and Regulations and Statements of Procedure* § 101.2 (2002).

5. *NLRB Casehandling Manual, Part One* § 10052.7.

6. Office of the General Counsel, Memorandum GC 05-01: Summary of Operations Fiscal Year 2004, 6 (Dec. 10, 2004), http://www.nlrb.gov/nlrb/shared_files/gcmemo/gcmemo/gc05-01.pdf.

7. *NLRB Casehandling Manual, Part One* § 10012.3. The merit rate for such charges filed though information officers was 29.9 percent in FY2004, consistent with historic levels. Memorandum GC 05-01, at 5.

8. The most recent period for which there are statistics is FY 2004. These statistics come from Memorandum GC 05-01, at 5.

For an overview of election statistics through FY 2004, see *Performance and Accountability Report—FY 2004* 69–71, http://www.nlrb.gov/nlrb/shared_files/reports/NLRB.pdf; *Outline of Representation Procedures under Section 9(c), Performance and Accountability Report—FY 2004*, Appendix D 76, http://www.nlrb.gov/nlrb/shared_files/reports/NLRB.pdf

9. Memorandum GC 05-01, at 6.

10. Ellen Dannin, *Collective Bargaining, Impasse and the Implementation of Final Offers: Have We Created a Right Unaccompanied by Fulfillment*, 19 U. Tol. L. Rev. 41 (1987).

11. *Gissel* bargaining orders are remedies for significant employer unfair labor practices that would tend to undermine a union's majority and taint an election. They are ordered when the Board finds that the unfair labor practices are so serious they make it unlikely their effects can be erased and a fair election can be held. The union must show it had the support of a majority of employees. Usually this is done by showing that the union had signed representation cards from a majority of the employees in a bargaining unit. The doctrine was first announced in *NLRB v. Gissel Packing Co.*, 395 U.S. 575 (1969).

12. All evidence—documents and testimony—must be proved to be authentic before it can be admitted into evidence. To prove that evidence is authentic requires proving that the document or testimony is what it is claimed to be. Cards can be proved to be authentic by testimony from the person who signed the card, an eye witness about the circumstances under which they were solicited and signed, or a handwriting expert who as compared the signature on the card with another signature known to be authentic and by that same person. Calling each signer or hiring a handwriting expert to examine signatures and testify about them are the most complex and time consuming of these three methods of authentication.

13. Section 10(j) of the National Labor Relations Act allows the NLRB to seek an injunction in cases involving serious unfair labor practices. The injunction can order an employer to reinstate discharged workers and bargain with the union while the NLRB tries the case before an administrative law judge.

14. *NLRB Casehandling Manual, Part One* § 10054.4.

15. NLRA § 11(1), 29 U.S.C. § 161(1).

16. Ellen Dannin, *Labor Law Reform: Is There a Baby in the Bathwater?* 44 Lab. L. J. 626 (1993).

17. Office of the General Counsel, Memorandum GC 00-02: Investigative Subpoenas (May 1, 2000); *NLRB Casehandling Manual, Part One* § 10054.5.

18. *NLRB Casehandling Manual, Part One* § 11770.

19. *Id.* § 11770.2.

20. *Id.* § 11770.4.

21. *NLRB Casehandling Manual, Part Three—Compliance Proceedings* § 10592.3 (1993).

22. *Id.* § 10592.3.

23. Examples may be found in these cases: *Dunkin' Donuts Mid-Atlantic Distribution*

Center, Inc. v. NLRB, 363 F.3d 437 (D.C. Cir. 2004); *Pioneer Electric of Monroe, Inc. & Pioneer Electrical & Mechanical Contractor, Inc.*, 333 N.L.R.B. 1192 (2001); *Southland Manufacturing Co.*, 94 N.L.R.B. 813 (1951); *Avondale Industries, Inc.*, 15-CA-12639 (July 6, 2001); *Ronn English*, Cases No. 36-CA-8501–2, 36-CA-8597 (Apr. 26, 2000).

24. *NLRB Casehandling Manual, Part Three* § 10596.

25. See *NLRB Casehandling Manual, Part Three* §§ 10592.8, 10594.3. The *Golden State* letter may be found at *id.*, app. 5.

26. *NLRB Casehandling Manual, Part Three* § 10596.3 (2002).

27. Memorandum GC 05-01, at 7.

28. *Id.* at 4–5. (Dec. 10, 2004).

29. Fawn Johnson, *Should Consider Card-Check Bill Before Adopting New Organizing Rule, Specter Says*, Daily Lab. Rep. (BNA) DLR AA-1 (Sept. 24, 2004).

30. Fawn Johnson, *Norwood Says He Would Back More Funds for NLRB to Conduct Secret Ballot Elections*, Daily Lab. Rep. (BNA) AA-1 (Oct. 1, 2004).

31. American Hosp. Ass'n v. NLRB, 499 U.S. 606 (1991).

32. A Unit Clarification (UC) petition is used to clarify whether particular employees should be included in or excluded from an existing unit. It is often filed when there have been changes in the employer's operation and the employer and union cannot agree whether to include or exclude the employees. In some cases, the existence of the UC process makes it possible for an employer and union to agree to a representation election, even though they are uncertain about the status of certain employees. The UC petition process can be used after the union wins the election to decide the status of those individuals. Their status may also be decided after the election through agreement on their status or through a hearing if they are challenged and if the number of challenged ballots is sufficient to affect the outcome of the election. A UC process could be used if the employees whose status is in question did not vote so there were no ballots to challenge or if the challenged ballots were not determinative of the election's outcome. *NLRB Casehandling Manual, Part Two—Representation Proceedings* § 11490.1 (1999).

33. *See, e.g.*, Verizon Info. Sys., 335 N.L.R.B. 558 (2001).

34. There have been no studies on the length of card check/neutrality campaigns or on the number of failed campaigns, so it is impossible to compare the time to representation rights with NLRB elections. We do know that at least some of the visible campaigns have taken years.David Montgomery gave an example of a four-year campaign to get a card check and neutrality agreement as "remarkably successful." David Montgomery, *Turning to the States*, 13 New Lab. Forum 17, 19 (2004). Usually the times given are only for time to organize after a neutrality/card-check agreement is reached. Stewart Acuff, *Fifty Ways to Get to Yes*, 13 New Lab. Forum 23, 23–24 (2004).

35. Lisa Jordan & Robert Bruno, Do the Organizing Means Determine the Bargaining Ends? (2005) (unpublished paper presented at the Labor & Employment Relations Association Conference, Philadelphia).

36. Office of the General Counsel, Memorandum OM 05-40 (rev.): New "Full" Consent Election Agreement Procedure (Mar. 21, 2005), http://www.nlrb.gov/nlrb/shared_files/ommemo/ommemo/om05-40rev.pdf.

37. Int. Paper Co. v. NLRB, 115 F.3d 1045 (D.C. Cir 1997).

38. Pacific Beach Hotel, 342 N.L.R.B. No. 30 (June 30, 2004).

9. An Invitation

1. Pauline T. Kim, *Norms, Learning, and Law: Exploring the Influences on Workers' Legal Knowledge*, 1999 U. Ill. L. Rev. 447; Pauline Kim, *Bargaining With Imperfect Information: A Study of Worker Perceptions of Legal Protection in an At-Will World*, 83 Cornell L. Rev. 105 (1997).

2. Lydia Saad, *Labor Unions Broadly Supported,* Gallup Organization (Aug. 29, 2003), http://gallup.com/poll/releases/pr030829.asp.

3. Reinhold Fahlbeck, *The Demise of Collective Bargaining in the USA: Reflections on the Un-American Character of American Labor Law,* 15 Berkeley J. Emp. & Lab. L. 307, 314 (1994).

4. Saad, *Labor Unions Broadly Supported.*

5. Richard B. Freeman & Joel Rogers, *What Workers Want* (1999); Richard B. Freeman & Joel Rogers, *Introduction: Worker Representation . . . Again!* 3 U. Pa. J. Lab. & Emp. L. 375 (2001); Kate Bronfenbrenner, *What Do Workers Want: Reflections on the Implications of the Freeman and Rogers Study,* 3 U. Pa. J. Lab. & Emp. L. 385 (2001).

GENERAL INDEX

access to employer property, 12–13, 27, 46–
   47, 89–90, 105–7, 131
Advice, NLRB Division of, 140, 141
anti-union discrimination, 84–86. *See also*
   NLRA statutory sections: 8(a)(3)
at-will employment, 15, 21–25, 166

bargaining impasse, 114, 150–51, 155. *See
   also* implementation of employer offers
   at impasse
bargaining units, 135, 158–59
burdens of proof, 135–38

card-check/neutrality agreements, 159–60,
   166
Clark, Kenneth B. and Mamie, 40
Clayton Antitrust Act, 97, 118
Cohen, Larry, 4
collective bargaining
   under international law, 123–26
   nature of, 67–69
common law, 18
   and unions, 5, 15
   defined, 171n3
   influence on judges, 25–35, 38
contempt citations, 155
Convention on Freedom of Association, 124
Convention on the Right to Organise and
   Collective Bargaining, 124
corporation law, 24–25, 56, 69–70, 100
corporations, 64–65, 103

Declaration of Independence, 121, 123
Declaration of Philadelphia, 125

Declaration on Fundamental Principles and
   Rights at Work, 124
democracy
   NLRA role in, 51–52, 62–67
   union role in, vii–ix, 9–10, 51–52, 65–66
Department of Homeland Security, 8, 116
doll experiments, 40
dues, union, 19, 44–45, 72

economic bill of rights, 121–23
economic experiments, 72, 74, 77
elections. *See* NLRB elections
employee, defined, 171n23
employee investment in job, 26–28
employee rights. *See also* NLRA policies
   clash with employer rights, 80–98
   in job, 101–5
   judicially created, 18
employer, good, 126
employer property
   access to, 27, 46–47, 105–6
employer rights, 80
   clash with employee rights, 80–98
   influence on judges, 80–81
   managerial rights, 81–83, 87, 106, 110–
      11
   property rights, 82, 87, 99–106, 111
   to go out of business, 81–83
employers as parties, 140–41
Equal Access to Justice Act (EAJA), 149
evidence, rules of, 29, 142–43

faculty union rights, 131
freedom of assembly, 108–9

freedom of association, 69–71, 109–110, 119–20, 123–26. *See also under* NLRA policies
freedom of speech, 71, 105–7, 109–10, 119–20, 131. *See also under* NLRA policies
free riders, 72

gaps in legislation ,33–35, 87, 133
Gissel bargaining orders, 152–53, 187n11
globalization, 56–57, 75
Golden State successors, 156
graduate students, 130–31

Human Rights Watch, 10

implementation of employer offers at impasse, 7–8, 17, 19, 31–32, 34–35, 91–96, 114–15, 150–52, 155
individualism, 71–72, 74
information requests, 150–51
injunctions
    labor, 15, 97
    10(j), 8, 153, 187n13
interest arbitration, 54–55, 143
International Covenant on Civil and Political Rights, 124–25
International Labour Organisation, 123–26
international law, 7, 10, 71, 117, 123–26
interpreting statutes, 33–35, 87, 129–34
investigative subpoenas, 153–54

Johnson & Johnson, 103
judges
    appellate, 29–31
    biases, 20–21, 29, 30
    credibility determinations, 29–30
    deference to NLRB, 30, 43, 52–53, 134
    incrementalist decision making, 17, 29–33, 39
    influences on, 20–33
    knowledge of labor law, 30, 37–47
    and NLRA policies, 60–61
    studies of, 20, 30
    understanding of worklife, 29, 41–43

Kim, Pauline, 22
Kirkland, Lane, 4–5

labor peace, 42, 60–62, 110, 121–22
law clerk knowledge of labor law, 41–42
litigation strategy
    examples of, 19, 40, 41, 43–50, 72, 79–98, 105–7, 139–43
    obstacles to, 45–46, 49
    expert evidence and, 40, 47–48, 142, 151
lockouts, 8, 31–32, 161
Lynd, Staughton, 11, 58, 74

Mackay Radio & Telegraph Co. *See* striker replacement
master and servant law, 28–29, 34–35, 42, 60, 66, 80–81

National Association for the Advancement of Colored People Legal Defense Fund (NAACP-LDF), 3, 39–40
National Labor Relations Act. *See* NLRA, attacks on; NLRA, constitutionality of; NLRA policies; NLRA remedies; NLRA statutory sections
National Labor Relations Board. *See* NLRB, attacks on; NLRB, criticisms of; NLRB attorneys; NLRB budget; NLRB charges and complaints; NLRB elections; NLRB employees; NLRB General Counsel; NLRB trials
National Right to Work Legal Defense Foundation (NRTW LDF), 3
New Zealand, 71
    law, 126–27
    unions, 71–72
NLRA, attacks on
    by Republicans, 8, 12
    by unions, 4–5, 10–11, 14, 146
NLRA, constitutionality of, 101–2
NLRA policies
    choosing representatives, 60–61, 70, 104–5
    collective bargaining, 7–8, 67–69, 84, 95, 114–15, 150–51, 155
    commerce, 60–62, 82
    equality of bargaining power, 61, 87
    freedom of association, 69–73, 105–7
    freedom of speech, 105–7, 109–10
    friendly adjustment of disputes, 60, 67–69
    in general, 7, 58–62
    industrial peace, 42, 60–62, 110, 121–22
    joining unions, 81–82, 84
    mutual aid or protection, 13, 58, 73–74, 89–90,105, 106
    public acceptance of, 38, 42–43, 51–52, 56–58, 60–67, 79–81, 166–67
    wages, improving, 42–43, 75–77, 82, 84–86, 87, 105–7, 121–23
NLRA remedies
    backpay, 7, 13–14, 30, 53–54, 144–45, 149
    bargaining orders, 54–55, 143, 152–53, 155
    cease and desist orders, 155
    contempt orders, 155
    interest arbitration, 54–55, 143
    notice posting, 154–55
    novel, 139–40, 141–42
    to promote NLRA policies, 5, 7, 35, 44, 48, 52–55, 60, 83, 142–43
    strengthening, 19, 53–55, 139–40

undervalued, 13–14, 144–45
visitatorial clauses, 46–47, 154–56
weak, 5, 8, 13–14, 144
NLRA statutory sections
  1, 3–4, 25, 42–43, 56, 87, 100–101. *See also*
    NLRA policies
  2(3), 13, 58 , 106–7, 110, 132, 177n23
  2(9), 179n54
  7, 42–43, 58, 71, 87. *See also* NLRA policies
  8(a)(1), 81, 87
  8(a)(3), 5, 81, 84–86, 87, 152
  8(a)(5), 95. *See also* NLRA policies:
    collective bargaining
  8(b)(4), 119. *See also* secondary boycotts
  8(b)(7), 119
  8(c), 109–10. *See also* NLRA policies:
    freedom of speech
  8(d), 95
  9(b), 131
  10(c), 5, 7, 8, 52–55, 143. *See also* NLRA
    remedies: to promote NLRA policies
  10(j), 8, 153, 187n13
  11(1), 153–54
  13, 5, 7, 58, 87
NLRB, attacks on
  by Republicans, 8, 12
  by unions, 4–5, 10–11, 14, 144–46
NLRB, criticisms of, 3–5, 13–15, 144–45,
  162–63
NLRB attorneys, 8, 22 , 37–50, 141–42, 145–
  46, 148–49
NLRB budget, 8, 11, 146–47, 150
NLRB charges and complaints, 11, 139–42,
  150–54
  assistance in drafting, 147–48
  dismissal of, 162
  information requests related to, 150–51
  investigation of, 147–49
  investigative subpoenas, 153–54
  knowledge of employee activity, 152–53
  merit factor, 148–49, 162
  naming parties, 140–41
  notice to parties, 139–41
  novel issues, 139–41
  and organizing, 161–62
  response to, 153–54
  settlements, 149, 161, 162
  strategies around filing, 11,14, 150–53,
    160–62
NLRB elections, 15, 53, 130–31, 135, 152–53,
  156–60
  bargaining units, 135, 158–59
NLRB employees
  assistance to public, 146–47
  staffing, 8, 14, 145–47, 157
  as union members, 10–11,14
NLRB General Counsel, 145–46

NLRB trials
  burdens of proof, 135–38
  intervention as party, 140–41
  novel issues, 142
  parties to case, 140–41
  party liability, 155–56
  procedure before hearing, 139–41
  procedure during hearing, 141–43
Norris LaGuardia Act, 118–19

Page, Leonard, 154
PATCO, 8
picketing, 119
property rights, 46–47, 80
  in job, 26–28, 100–105
poverty, 1–2, 8–9, 65, 76–77, 121–23, 125
pursuit of happiness, 121

radio talk show, 38
Rathke, Wade, 4
Republican politicians, 8, 12
Roosevelt, Franklin D., 121–23

salts, 8, 11–12, 132, 177n25
secondary boycotts, 105, 119, 182n19
Sherman Act, 97
society's investment in jobs, 27–28, 101–5
solidarity, 13, 58, 73–74, 89–90, 105, 119. *See
  also* NLRA policies: mutual aid or
  protection
speech rights, 105–7, 109–10. *See also* NLRA
  policies: freedom of speech; NLRA
  statutory sections: 8(c); U.S.
  Constitution: 1st Amendment
statutes
  ambiguous, 133
  interpreting, 129–34
  new laws, 17
strike
  right to, 5, 7, 58, 87
  unfair labor practice, 155
striker replacement, 5, 7–8, 17, 19, 86–89, 115
sweat equity in job, 26–27

Taft-Hartley Act, 15, 59, 71–72
thin unionism, 71
toothpaste tube theory of law, 132
trials. *See* NLRB trials
Trumka, Richard 5, 169–70

unemployment, 9, 56–57, 122, 125
unions
  and democracy, viii–x, 9–10, 51–52, 62–67
  as illegal conspiracy, 8, 15
  and organizing, 12–13, 19, 44–45, 53,
    161–62. *See also* NLRA policies:
    mutual aid or protection; salts

:ation, 188n32

.titution

.nendment, 71, 109–10, 119–20

. Amendment, 23, 120

.nterpret NLRA, 119–23

Preamble, 120–21

Universal Declaration of Human Rights, 125–26

unorganized employees, 15, 90, 118–19, 165–66

visitatorial clause, 46–47

wage-effort bargain, 113, 182n30

wages, 56–58, 73, 75–77

competition based on, 76, 84–86

Wagner, Robert, 60, 61, 64, 68, 75

Wagner Act, 169n9, 179n54

work and citizenship, 62–67. *See also* unions: and democracy

workplace

balance of power, 24–25, 56–57, 100–101

Yager, Daniel, 70

INDEX OF CASES DISCUSSED

Adkins Transfer Company, NLRB v., 30, 84–86

Brown v. Board of Education, 39–40, 47
Brown University, 130–31

Cherokee Marine Terminal, 46–47
Consolidated Edison Co. v. NLRB, 53–54
Curtin Matheson Scientific, NLRB v., 55

Darlington, Textile Workers Union v., 30, 81–83
Dorsey Trailers v. NLRB, 95–97
Dubuque Packing Co., 135–38

Eastex v. NLRB, 73
Elk Lumber Co., 112–13

Fansteel Metallurgical, NLRB v., 113–14
First National Maintenance Corp. v. NLRB, 93–94

Gissel Packing Co., NLRB v., 395 U.S. 575 (1969), 152–53

H.K. Porter Co. v. NLRB, 91, 101, 114

International Paper Co. v. NLRB, 31–32, 94

Jones & Laughlin Steel Corp., NLRB v., 61, 70, 104, 107

Lechmere v. NLRB, 12–13, 89–90, 105–6, 110–11, 131, 132

New York University, 130–31

Pearson v. Murray, 39
Phelps Dodge Corp. v. NLRB, 62, 104–5

Republic Aviation Corp. v. NLRB, 106–7

Smith v. Arkansas Highway Employees, Local 1315, 120

Town & Country Electric, NLRB v., 132, 177n25
Trans World Airlines v. Independent Federation of Flight Attendants, 55, 88

United Food and Commercial Workers Union, Local 1036 v. NLRB, 44–45

Yeshiva University, NLRB v., 131